MAINTAINING AND REPAIRING OLD HOUSES

A Guide to Conservation, Sustainability and Economy

MAINTAINING AND REPAIRING OLD HOUSES

A Guide to Conservation, Sustainability and Economy

BEVIS CLAXTON

THE CROWOOD PRESS

First published in 2008 by
The Crowood Press Ltd
Ramsbury, Marlborough
Wiltshire SN8 2HR

www.crowood.com

British Library Cataloguing-in-Publication Data
A catalogue record for this book is available from the British Library.

ISBN 978 1 84797 035 0

Disclaimer
The author and the publisher do not accept any responsibility in any manner whatsoever for any error or omission, nor any loss, damage, injury, adverse outcome, or liability of any kind incurred as a result of the use of any of the information contained in this book, or reliance upon it. Readers are advised to seek specific professional advice relating to their particular house, project and circumstances before embarking on any repair, restoration or building work.

Drawings and photographs all copyright Bevis Claxton/Old House Info Ltd.

Frontispiece: However unkempt an old house has become it would usually respond to repairs using simple old fashioned technology but, as this book explains, some repairs using modern technology have not always proved beneficial to old houses: Some modern methods are simply good at masking existing problems while creating new ones.

Designed and typeset by Focus Publishing, Sevenoaks, Kent

Printed and bound in Singapore by Craft Print International

Contents

Dedication

To Janet, for sharing architecture, conservation and a special building at risk. We raise a glass of IPA to Bill whose van was first on the scene. Thanks also to Bob and Vera for trips north of the border.

Acknowledgements

The material for this book has been gathered over several decades of practical experience repairing old buildings and designing new ones, from countless textbooks and articles, chance meetings, lectures and from wise old practitioners and tradespeople, young and old. It is impossible to credit every piece of information accurately, and the author is grateful to the many people who have shared their knowledge and enthusiasm, particularly when helping to solve live problems on buildings. Parts of the book are based upon information previously presented by the author in talks, articles and from the author's work published on the website www.oldhouse.info. Some of the author's drawings have been published previously in *Old House Care and Repair*, by Janet Collings (Donhead, 2002) or on the website www.oldhouse.info. Photographs include the author's projects and also photographs of unconnected but interesting buildings noticed over the years, so, if one of these happens to have been yours, thank you for keeping it so photogenic.

Introduction

OLD HOUSES ARE DIFFERENT

Old houses work very differently to modern constructions, even though some of the building materials may look similar. The experience of the twentieth century has shown that many modern building products and methods, while fine for modern buildings, can disrupt the original survival mechanisms of old houses and accelerate decay.

Owners of old houses, built from the medieval period up to the early decades of the twentieth century, who want to protect their investment will need to know how to avoid repeating the mistakes of the last century when repairing and redecorating.

The knowledge exists in the practical experiences of professional conservationists and is promoted by government and conservation organizations, but their voice is small in a vast commercial market. There are, unfortunately, still many people wasting their money on ill-advised modern repairs that could reduce the life, and value, of their old house.

Maintaining and Repairing Old Houses

For Conservation ...
This book aims to bring to the owner of an old house some of the knowledge with which a conservationist would approach various routine maintenance, repair and redecoration tasks.

An understanding of the methods employed on old houses to cope with damp and movement, an awareness that there are alternative attitudes to insect pests and rot and examples of how some modern materials can harm old houses – can all help the owner to make informed choices about repair and redecoration.

Unnecessary, harmful or inappropriate work on old houses is often carried out innocently by those who want to do a good job but are suddenly faced with an apparently awful problem outside their experience. They may panic and throw money at the problem, creating future pitfalls in the process. This book aims to put repair problems into perspective.

For Sustainability ...
Before the Industrial Revolution house building involved the consumption of little or no fossil fuel. Houses were built with manual labour, renewable energy and mainly locally-sourced materials. Their builders worked without mechanized transport or tools, and for many years afterwards these buildings were heated with 'carbon-neutral' wood fires. The 'embodied energy' in the fabric of old houses has served for up to several hundred years. Translated into modern terms, old houses have been the absolute ultimate in sustainable dwellings.

Those houses that have survived may have been altered in unsustainable ways or they may currently be forced into unsustainable functions, but they still have longevity to their environmental credit. While they survive, they reduce the need for new, environmentally-damaging, building operations to replace them. And they will always have the potential to be retuned to fully sustainable operation.

Many of the traditional craft-based processes that have survived, or been revived, to repair old houses are inherently low-technology and use the original sustainable materials. These can often be substituted for modern, environmentally-wasteful processes and products.

A wide variety of traditional techniques and styles have proved themselves capable of coexisting happily, while modern construction methods can follow a different road.

... and Economy

The philosophy behind building conservation is to retain as much original fabric as possible and to favour repairs that are 'like-for-like' with the original materials. Conservation, like sustainability and like economy, is about conserving more and consuming less. This sparing approach has the potential to be cheaper than the complete, new reconstruction of damaged parts. It tends to avoid the high-technology materials that are associated with higher environmental, as well as financial, costs.

A repair that is incompatible with the fabric of an old house can be running up some serious financial trouble for the future even though it may look good. A repair that looks unsympathetic has the potential to put buyers off the property in the future, even if it is functional. Incompatible and unsympathetic repairs are not always the cheapest option, so there is every reason to learn more about conservative repair.

WHAT THIS BOOK SETS OUT TO DO

The book introduces some of the thinking behind the repair decisions that building conservationists make. Because old houses are still so tragically misunderstood, it concentrates on helping owners and occupants to understand enough of a very extensive subject to be able to step back and square up to a few important questions before they reach for the key to the tool shed or pick up the telephone for a builder or architect:

- Do all old houses do this?
- Can modern repair methods harm traditional construction?
- Are there kinder, or less expensive, alternative solutions?
- What lessons have conservationists learnt from experience?

- How can that experience and those answers be accessed?
- Is there a real opportunity to help the environment?
- How can an old house look and perform more as it was intended to?

An old house can be more distinctively individual than a machine or a human body. The components are only *similar*, not standard, and a house is strongly influenced by its immediate environment. So no one book can be a universal 'workshop manual' and specific, professional advice may always be necessary, like a visit to a doctor. But there is enough generic information to create a user's guide that should help a house's owner to make informed choices as a client and consumer.

How This Book Is Organized

Beginning at the top of the house, with the chimneys, and working down through the fabric element by element, there are, along with the text, photographs and drawings of generic examples of construction. Between chapters coloured pages introduce general topics that are relevant to the whole house.

Towards the end are, arguably, the most feared topics: dampness and rot. But by then the reader should have learnt enough about conservation attitudes to take a broader view and understand that drastic modern solutions are not the only possible options.

Finally, for those wanting to engage professional support, there are summaries of the roles of some of the main participants in the building industry connected with domestic house repairs and an introduction to the several official processes that exist in this country.

Some Words of Caution

The techniques and materials referred to here are part of a continually developing understanding of practical conservation in the United Kingdom. The demands of sustainable living and climate change may develop in ways that cannot reasonably be anticipated within the scope of the book. Regulations and laws can differ across the country and may also be subject to change over time. The information in this book is generic, it cannot relate to every building or every circumstance and is not a substitute for professional or technical advice. It is not possible to refer to every relevant organization or website, there may be others of equal merit, and those mentioned are referred to in good faith but with no responsibility for their conduct or content.

CHAPTER 1

Chimneys

HISTORICAL PERSPECTIVE

Chimneys were originally simple tubes of non-flammable construction designed to direct smoke quickly out of a house rather than let it gather inconveniently and blacken the interior. Chimneys were expensive but more efficient and less dangerous than the alternative of timber flaps and louvres, so masonry stacks were 'retro-fitted' to earlier houses during the later Middle Ages and in time became a standard feature of new houses. A single, large chimney might have heated and cooked for a whole household and made a big contribution to holding up the house. Chimneys enabled the upper areas of the house to become usable, so allowing first floors to be inserted into earlier medieval 'hall houses'. Extra rooms meant extra fireplaces in the chimney, which meant that the insides of chimneys had to be subdivided into a number of flues.

Changing from the burning of wood to the burning of 'hotter' coal allowed grates and fireplaces to be smaller, so the late Georgian and the Victorian period probably saw much alteration of medieval chimneys. Old houses can have all sorts of unexpected flue configurations. It can be awkward to rework them now, but we do have video (and maybe remote-controlled repair soon), so we can do more than light our fires and hope. In mid-twentieth-century Britain the expectation of cheap nuclear electricity, plus the reality of even cheaper North Sea gas, saw many open-fire chimneys blocked up or taken down. Seen as draughty, dirty and space-consuming, the chimney's days were thought to be over. Sustainability may now turn that around.

THE VERY TOP

Out of Sight, out of Mind

The tops of chimneys are a long way up, problems are out of sight and might be ignored for many years. Much of the fire's heat, along with soot and the products of combustion, take their toll on the masonry and mortar of the chimney walls, leading

Chimneys in stone and brick, with and without pots.

to distortion and weakening. Worse, the tops of the chimney not only have an aggressive chemical environment internally but an aggressive climatic environment externally.

Pots and Flaunching

Pots have been used as decoration even when not technically necessary. The bed of mortar that tidies up the top of the masonry flue and provides a seating for the pot is called flaunching. Following twentieth-century maintenance, these have often been changed from original lime mortar to cement mortar on old houses and, because this is an exposed location and because cement is brittle, the flaunching is nearly always cracked.

Past Failures at High Level

Medieval chimneys were put together with lime mortar since it was just about all there was to use, apart from mud and dung. Generally lime (*see* Info pages: Lime) makes an excellent sympathetic mortar for old buildings because it does not trap dampness within bricks and walls (as cement tends to) and because it can allow bricks and stones to 'shuffle about' with less chance of cracking than with cement. But along with these benign qualities, lime is not highly durable in extremes of exposure. In most areas of domestic building this is not a problem, but it is quite understandable that, once cement had been invented, builders sent up to repair eroded lime on

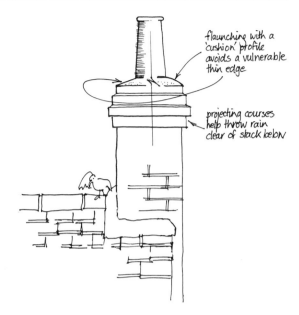

Features of a typical stack.

chimneys opted instead for cement. And no one really noticed that the cement might have cracked, damaged the bricks and let in water for some time.

Re-flaunching and Re-bedding Pots

Exposure and maintenance problems have in the past persuaded even conservationists to use a cement/ non-hydraulic lime/sand mortar mix for re-flaunching. As confidence in the rediscovered technology, and the experience of tradespeople, in lime has grown, hydraulic lime (*see* Info pages: Lime) might now be used. Whatever the mix, the profile of the flaunching can help it to survive – laying it in a 'cushion' profile avoids a thin and vulnerable edge. The purpose of flaunching is to provide a weathered top to the masonry of the stack and to help to secure the pot. Pots are heavy and modern practice is to build the pot securely into the top of the stack, but the old practice was often to prop the pot on slivers of brick, tile or slate across the stack's corners and hope the flaunching did the rest. When the flaunching disintegrates, the pot may be vulnerable to being dislodged by wind or sweeping brushes. Modern concerns with safety at high level mean that it is worth making a thorough job of chimney repairs

Typical cracking and breakdown of flaunching.

11

while all the scaffolding and equipment are in place: every chimney will be different but some intelligent rethinking of how existing pots are re-bedded safely, and compatibly, with an old building fabric can prove a long-term investment.

OTHER PROPERTIES AND PROBLEMS OF CHIMNEYS

Chimneys reach from the top to the bottom of a house. Many are only occasionally used for open fires, many contain gas or oil appliances and some are sealed up. The principal fires in a house in the past may have been more or less constantly burning for cooking and household purposes. In current, winter-only usage, an empty fireplace might smell of soot during the summer, but, if covering the fireplace for the season, remember to leave a reasonable ventilation path to keep the flue dry and the house aired.

Gas and Oil Flues in Old Houses

Old house chimneys acquired gas and oil appliances as they became available. Now there are strict regulations about the suitability of flue construction: The traditional masonry flue will almost certainly be considered inadequate to deal safely with the exhaust gases produced; owners can find out more from the gas and oil industries' guidelines and the Building Regulations and Standards (*see* the organizations and websites in chapter 7: Building Services – Mainly about heating). Older flue liners may now not be up to standard or be made of materials that have corroded, so they should be checked – especially flexible metal liners. There is a requirement to renew metal liners when an appliance is renewed. Gas and oil combustion also need special chimney-top terminals designed to assist the proper dispersal of gases and to prevent birds and debris getting in to block the flue.

Ventilation

There are requirements under the Building Regulations (and their sister regulations in Britain) for adequate ventilation to provide oxygen for fuel combustion and to ensure that there is also oxygen for the occupants to breathe. The dangers that combustion gases, such as carbon monoxide, may build up from faulty appliances or blocked chimneys

are increased where occupants deliberately block ordinary room vents to stop draughts. As a result, many types of appliance might be provided with dedicated ventilation, such as a vent in front of an open fireplace or a grille in the same room as a gas boiler – these should not be blocked. Gas boilers have been available for many years with 'balanced flues', no chimney is necessary as they draw air in through a sealed wall vent from outside and emit fumes direct outside through a separate pipe in the same vent. Balanced flue boilers have become more sophisticated, and some now allow for a boiler to be installed some distance from an outside wall. They have spread from natural gas appliances to some other fuels.

Old houses, designed for open fires, happened to have many tiny draughts (through floorboards from cellars, around window frames and under doors) which usefully fed oxygen to the fireplaces and, on the way, dried out the fabric they passed through. These draughts cannot easily be quantified and so cannot always be assumed to feed modern fossil-fuel appliances adequately, as well as overcoming the risk of combustion gasses. Many householders have tried to seal them up with draught-stripping, carpets and fillers.

In the summer, if the fires are out, traditional open chimneys create a 'stack' ventilation which moves air through the property and can reduce summer overheating. This form of 'passive' (non-mechanical) ventilation has recently been reinvented in new building as a 'green' alternative to mechanical ventilation and energy-hungry air conditioning. Old houses knew of these benefits centuries ago.

Wood-burning Stoves

A good, hot blaze is effective at warming, and drying, old properties that have kept their draughts (*see* chapter 8: Damp, Breathability and Ventilation). Burning wood is environmentally preferable to the use of fossil fuels. Cast-iron wood-burners and other types of sealed stove have been popular with owners of house owners as a pile of neatly cut logs fits the image of an old property. But the heat that these stoves can generate in the flues far exceeds that of a 'traditional' open wood fire. Our forefathers were fairly easygoing about building techniques and it is not unknown for old chimneys to have joist ends or

Unused flues can be kept dry with vented caps or plugs; two clay types are shown here, lighter metal versions may better suit tall pots or those with unknown fixings; caps and plugs have to be removed if ever the flue is to be used.

other timbers embedded in them; these may have been lucky enough to have survived open-fire temperatures, but they may not survive really hot gases. The heat can even transfer through the bricks to timbers or thatch and ignite them. Some local authorities actively discourage the combination of wood-burning stoves and thatch. It is now a condition of the installation of most of these appliances that a new flue liner and register plate are also installed, they are not intended to issue into an old unlined flue. Many new solid-fuel stoves will require an insulated flue liner to prevent tar from condensing on cold surfaces. Within the room, the stoves need to be properly separated from furnishings and those rustic woodpiles. It should not be assumed that an old chimney can automatically cope, and owners considering such installations should ensure that their chimneys are checked and are fit for any new use.

Chimneys and Thatch

The particular hazards of mixing wood-burning stoves with thatch are that the high flue temperatures can transfer through the flue to the thatch and ignite it. The risk is greater where the thatch is very thick, not only because the insulation retains the heat but because the chimney will effectively have been 'shortened' over the centuries if the thatch has built up ever higher. Any type of fire or boiler is going to present a

risk with thatch, and the twentieth century devised the spark-arrestor, a grid or gauze of metal, intended to trap any sparks or glowing embers that floated up the chimney. The theory was good but the idea can fail in practice since, once the grid is caked with soot and tar, it becomes a torch waiting to be lit – a danger not a safeguard, so regular cleaning is essential.

It should not be assumed that modern gas or oil flues designed for concrete tiles on modern houses will technically suit thatched roofs. Do not rely just on the standard guidelines in positioning these flues but seek specialist advice from reputable heating and thatching organizations (*see* also chapter 2: Roofs), the local authority and enlist the experience of the local fire-prevention officer.

Sealed or Removed Chimneys

Many fireplaces were simply blocked up in a room. If the chimney pot itself was still open this meant that rain and birds' nests could get down and cold, moist air condense inside the flue, causing dampness on surrounding walls. A compromise was to put a ventilator in the middle of the old fire opening. A better compromise was a room ventilator plus a vented plug for the chimney pot – letting air in and out but keeping out rain and birds.

Some older houses have had the chimney breast removed from one or two rooms, leaving the chimney stack on the roof inadequately supported.

Chimney breasts may also have buttressed walls, so their removal can weaken a house. Terraces of houses have been put at risk where several houses have had chimney breasts (perhaps also internal dividing walls) removed.

Today's interest in sustainability, the realization that wood as a fuel is a relatively green option (*see* chapter 7: Building Services and Info pages: Sustainability) and the rediscovery of the 'passive stack' ventilation of homes for health and comfort, all mean that chimneys could become popular again. If reopening a disused chimney have it surveyed, preferably by video, since. while a flue was disused, it may have been adopted for cable and pipe runs or ventilator extracts.

CLEANING, MAINTENANCE AND IMPROVEMENTS

Cleaning

The cleaning of chimneys is a dark art in more ways than one. Old houses' chimneys were often tortuous in the first place, but old conversions from large, wood-burning fireplaces into narrow coal grates has left voids and ledges where soot can accumulate, risking a chimney fire. This hidden soot can escape ordinary sweeping unless care has been taken to understand the flue. Seeking references and recommendations is useful when looking for a sweep (*see* chapters 9: The Professionals – Finding people and 7: Building Services – Mainly about heating). Sweeps are listed by the National Association of Chimney Sweeps – www.chimneyworks.co.uk and the Guild of Master Sweeps – www.guild-of-master-sweeps.co.uk

Old chimneys may have been lined with a 'parging' of cow-dung render; surprisingly, this was sometimes still practised well into the twentieth century. Pieces fall off after some time and are difficult to repair, worrying pieces of brick and slate are also likely to fall into the fireplace when sweeping and it can be difficult to identify where they came from. After sweeping, it is wise to inspect the stack walls from the roof space, looking for gaps. If the chimney appears otherwise sound, it still pays to be vigilant for leaks and smoke everywhere in the house and attic. A smoke alarm in the attic linked to other sounders in the house could be installed for added security and thatched properties should certainly have a reliable method of automatic fire detection in the roof spaces. There are recognized air-tightness and smoke tests for chimneys that can be adapted for old buildings.

Clay pots give an extra push skywards and designs have evolved aiming to improve draw; pots may still be found in a variety of shapes and colours, but an exact match might be difficult.

How Traditional Chimneys Work

Hot air rises, so the dangerous or unpleasant combustion gases should tend to be buoyed upwards from an open fireplace. A warm (regularly used or well-insulated) flue will help this process by keeping the gases warm. By being as smooth as possible, a flue offers less resistance to passing gases. A tall chimney takes advantage of the slight potential for differences in air pressure between the fireplace and the chimney pot to give air an extra push up the chimney, and an old house traditionally had plenty of draughts to back up this circulation and feed the fire with oxygen.

Why Chimneys May Smoke

Some chimneys are inherently too cold to draw properly, perhaps being on an outside wall, or are too short, or there are external eddies due to surrounding buildings, or internal eddies due to damage or deposits in the flue. These all can inhibit a good flow to take the smoke away. Few old houses now maintain a working fire that keeps the chimney always at peak operating temperature, so the warm chimney effect will take a time to become effective. Another cause of smoking is that many old houses have had the useful oxygen-supplying draughts sealed up in the name of comfort. The chimney might be in good drawing condition but there may not be enough air to suck in. Sometimes smoking is simply down to the weather, so take a look at the wind direction and a barometer. Having an open fire can mean reconnecting with nature.

Some Solutions to Smoky Chimneys

Time, use and the weather can alter a chimney's dynamics permanently or temporarily. No chimney will be at peak performance at all times. As old houses became fashionable in the later twentieth century, many owners wanted a romantic open fire, but on their own terms. Perhaps without realizing that smoking may have been due to sealed-up draughts or the use of a cold chimney, various fixes became common: fire hoods, register plates (a horizontal plate above a large fireplace to restrict the chimney entry), ducted air supplies and the raising and lowering of fire baskets were regularly experimented with. For large, old, open fireplaces and

A stone chimney during repair and lining.

inglenooks these are still routine methods for managing the rate at which air enters the flue and 'retuning' the chimney. Because each chimney is unique, the actual solution may lie in trial and error. For convenience, efficiency or to deal with smoking, some have opted for a new manufactured fireplace, such as an enclosed fire, a convection fireplace or a wood-burning, cast-iron stove (*see above*). These can be much more efficient at heating the room, though the 'wasted' heat from a traditional open fire used actually to contribute to gently warming the thermal mass of the chimney stack, which could benefit the whole house.

Modern Flue-liners

Part of a new fire or boiler installation is a flue-liner. Special liners are available in a variety of forms and materials to fit into existing flues, but the geometry of an old chimney can sometimes be so contorted that these are difficult to fit properly all the way up without much disturbance.

Stainless Steel

Flexible, stainless steel liners are mainly used with gas and oil boilers and these do not technically suit all fuels, conditions or appliances, nor are they considered permanent, but, where they are suitable, are relatively easy to install. Specially insulated versions of stainless steel liners are specified for use with solid-fuel stoves. Though very resistant, stainless steel is not invulnerable as the chimney is a highly corrosive environment so these liners need to be renewed periodically. Stainless steel liners also come in rigid, insulated, sections for some applications.

Solid Liners

If the old chimney is fairly straight, generously-sized and needs lining, then pre-cast, solid liner sections (clay or cement-based) that look similar to drain pipes and fit together by being lowered down the chimney can be a sturdy solution. They could be largely independent of the old structure and they tend to be backfilled around the outside with loose, non-combustible insulation.

In situ Linings

A twentieth-century solution to 'leaking' chimneys was the lining of old chimneys with an insulating concrete mix pumped around an inflated former, the intention was to provide a smooth and insulated, continuous flue. To the conservationist, this can seem an aggressive and perhaps over-optimistic solution as it involves a heavy mass of relatively inflexible concrete inside a crumbly tube that before was able to move slightly and 'breathe'. Sealing with concrete implies a risk of cracking and of damp retention. The practical problems of inserting the former into an

unseen space mean that weak spots might occur at corners. The many houses with these liners already installed should have them periodically checked rather than assume that the problem has been dealt with forever.

Another recent idea is a new, thin surface coating applied to the inside of an existing flue. The same practical cautions as above would apply to the use of any non-breathable and movement-intolerant coatings within traditional fabric, and, as ever with chimneys, access and inspection may be difficult. Should it ever become available, a system that reinstates the breathable, movement-tolerant qualities of traditional cow-dung parging would seem promising for old houses.

Technological Longstops

Modern regulations work with known modern building methods and are less able to predict performance and safety with the unknowns of an old building. In practice, assumptions may not always be correct and householders should consider back-up from devices such as carbon monoxide detectors, as well as the familiar smoke detectors. Smoke and heat detection could also be usefully extended to roof spaces in old properties (a must for thatch), linked to sound alarms in the main house.

BACK OUTSIDE

Deformed Chimneys

Some brick chimney stacks have become bowed or twisted; this is thought to be caused by sulphur chemicals from combustion attacking mortar in the chimney walls at different rates according to their exposure to wind and rain. A chimney that is so badly deformed or so loose that it is at risk will need repair or to be rebuilt in accordance with good conservation practice, usually meaning a like-for-like repair and reusing any sound, original masonry.

Stay Bars

Some tall or exposed chimneys may warrant a stay bar to prevent their rocking in high wind, the prelude to collapse. There is little tensile strength in brickwork (a giant hand could snap a stack like a damp biscuit, but not bend it nor extract it whole from the

Stay bars are a traditional way to help to stabilize a stack, though they may not pass modern calculation.

house), so it makes sense to restrain vulnerable chimneys. If a modern-day engineer is asked to design a new support by calculation then quite a substantial brace may result, to take all anticipated forces. Untroubled by calculation, our forbears often made do with slender rods that might buckle if pushed against but which evidently have succeeded in resisting pulling forces, thus preventing a destructive rhythm from being set up. Existing stay bars should be checked for rust and for the security of fixings.

Aerials, et cetera

Television and radio aerials and satellite dishes have traditionally been attached to a chimney, the highest point of a house. Telephone and power cables also find chimneys convenient to give height over adjacent obstacles. Though convenient for installers, the additional tensile and wind forces on the chimney do no particular good to the stack, added to which the rust-staining from brackets and bolts can disfigure masonry and the roof finish beneath. There are (*see* chapter 7: Building Services) often other places in which to site these services, avoiding damage and clutter (and perhaps making receiving equipment less vulnerable to lightning). With a listed building or in regulated areas such as Conservation Areas or National Parks there are likely to be recommendations and limitations on the siting of aerials and dishes.

Decorative Items

Decorative, mass-produced, fired clay pots were available from catalogues via the rail network in the late nineteenth century. It can now be quite difficult to match a broken or missing pot for shape and colour with a new one. Size tends not to be such a problem as the building industry in Britain still works on a legacy of imperial brick dimensions. Firms exist that produce a range of pots and it is possible to get a reasonable match for single pots second-hand (but *see* Info pages: Conservation Terminology – Salvage). If replacing one of a row of identical pots the search may be harder, but it is generally better, and cheaper, to have a replacement that is slightly odd than to sacrifice all the other originals just for the sake of a match. It is also worth looking into repair if the pot is not too badly damaged (*see* chapter 2: Roofs – Fancy ridge tiles), or at least keep the pieces in the attic for future generations who may have access to superior repair or copying technology.

Lime

HISTORICAL PERSPECTIVE

Traditionally, lime has been made by heating naturally occurring chalky substances (chalk, limestone, sea-shells, even bird droppings allegedly) in a rudimentary kiln to produce a substance that, when remixed with water, produces – after a rather violent reaction – a caustic but useful, putty-like substance. This can be mixed with other materials, such as sand for strength and bulk, and moulded, poured, diluted and painted, and will adhere to things and eventually dry to a substance similar to the chalk or limestone that it came from. It is like having liquid stone and must have greatly pleased its discoverers. When used as a render (or 'plaster') the lime/sand mix can be reinforced with animal hair (a technique that anticipated modern, glass-reinforced plastics) to improve tensile strength. Lime has been useful for thousands of years, not only in building but also in agriculture and elsewhere in industry.

Newly-invented Cement Began to Displace Lime

Until the nineteenth century lime was the mortar of choice worldwide, wherever civilization had sought something superior to mud. The Romans had tinkered with the recipe to produce something remarkably hard, which survives in their buildings and civil engineering to this day. But it was not until the nineteenth-century engineers wanted a truly waterproof and quick-curing mortar for their great engineering projects that lime was eclipsed. Lighthouses, bridges and drainage works were creating a demand for a mortar that would set hard quickly and in the absence of air. Traditional lime was vulnerable to being dissolved by water and would not set if kept unventilated. A lime variant called 'hydraulic' lime was already known, incorporating clay with the source limestone; it sets more reliably by reaction rather than by just 'drying'.

Because of the Industrial Revolution's familiarity with furnaces, it was a short step to applying higher temperatures to burning limestone, with clay and occasionally other additives, producing a different product from lime. First popularly introduced as Portland cement, this proved to cure quickly in the absence of air, be relatively waterproof, was able to resist frost much better than lime and was comparatively harder when used in mortars and renders. Cement made for reliable concrete foundations was usable for more of the year than highly frost-sensitive lime. Cement was still prone to burn the skin and eyes but less so than lime, cement set to a working strength more reliably than lime, it was usefully waterproof in many applications, cement products were easier to mix mechanically and required less skill to use. It is not surprising that cement gained ground during the nineteenth century and traditional lime, though still used for ordinary brickwork until the early years of the twentieth century, fell into disuse for most of the rest of that century, surviving in builders' merchants as an admixture to make cement mortars more pliable in use and it was also used in agriculture.

There were drawbacks with cement, however: a glance at construction textbooks dealing with old buildings shows that they were anticipated, but unfortunately the enthusiasm for cement was too strong.

The Cracks Begin to Show in Cement

From Victorian times onwards cement made inroads into the building of houses, where it was substituted direct for lime and for most of the rest of the twentieth century old buildings were repaired with cement, which was perceived to be better because it was harder, more resistant, more waterproof and apparently almost indestructible; but it was too indestructible for old buildings. Old masonry and timber shifts with the seasons and on rudimentary foundations. Cement does not 'give' like lime but remains resolutely hard and, where inserted into joints and cracks, acts to grind away at the softer, original fabric, or, where applied as a thin render, cement itself cracks under the strain of movement, allowing water to penetrate into the heart of the softer, underlying, old walls.

Not only was cement too good at being hard (or brittle), it was too good at being waterproof. Old building materials were rarely waterproof, instead they tended to soak up dampness but were permeable enough to let it dry out later – which is how they defended themselves against frost attack and rot. Cement was eagerly waterproof, but, when it cracked, it let water in – but not out – and, where it was applied as pointing around old soft bricks, it trapped water in them so they became saturated and began to shatter in the first frost.

Renaissance of Lime for Old and Sustainable Buildings

By the end of the twentieth century the lessons had been learnt and nearly all building conservationists had realized that cement was inappropriate for most old buildings – even in small quantities in a mix. But by then many old houses had been repaired with cement and the skills for using the traditional lime alternatives had been largely forgotten by mainstream builders. Suddenly to specify lime when few knew how to use it could produce unsatisfactory results and risk failures, and a great deal of effort has gone into relearning what once every bricklayer and plasterer knew as second nature.

There is now a better public understanding of the need for old buildings to 'breathe' and to be able to move unencumbered; that message has taken a lot of perseverance by conservationists to get across. Meanwhile, the building design and construction industry has become much more specialized and so, while mainstream building may never return to lime, there is a growing confidence in the use of lime among conservation-oriented architects, surveyors, engineers and contractors. It can also be a more environmentally-friendly material both in manufacturing and long-term use so it is favoured by those building sustainably. Lime may once again become the product of choice, but it requires care, skill and experience to use, even though it may be a 'low-technology' material.

THE SCIENCE OF LIME

Limestone chunks (calcium carbonate) burned at around 900°C produce quicklime (calcium oxide). When this is added to water ('slaked') – very carefully because there is a violent and hot reaction – a thick, creamy substance known as 'lime putty' results (calcium hydroxide).

Lime has a long history, its manufacture does not have to be by men in white coats in complex factories.

The satisfying, creamy texture of lime putty.

Once lime putty is exposed to the air, having been used in mortar, render or limewash mixes, it will 'carbonate' as it dries and reverts to its original form of calcium carbonate by reabsorbing carbon dioxide driven off when the limestone was burnt. Once set, it is therefore chemically close to the limestone that it started from. The absorption of carbon dioxide (a greenhouse gas; *see* Info pages: Sustainability etc.) by lime from the air as it sets is thought to at least equal the amount released during the heating of limestone in the first place, which suggests that lime qualifies as a 'green', carbon-neutral product – although in modern usage heating fuel and transportation skew the equation. Traditionally-produced lime, made locally using wood or charcoal as fuel, is thought likely to have brought about a net reduction in atmospheric carbon dioxide. The potential exists for low-carbon projects to exploit this in the future.

THE MAIN TYPES OF LIME FOR BUILDING

Some General Hazards and Limitations

Lime is caustic, it burns until it sets, so eye and skin protection are vital. This property is useful if handled correctly since limewash could automatically sterilize mould on walls as it is applied. Lime is frost-sensitive, and as 'ordinary' lime putty limewash, mortar or render mixes might take between days and months to dry, they should be used strictly in the spring and summer months in Britain. This can present problems as building contract dates are legendarily flexible, but there is absolutely no point in trying to bully lime into being used in the cold. Chemical anti-freezes have been tried but were felt to compromise unsatisfactorily the final quality; there have been suggestions that traditional vegetable additives may have solved this once, but this, if workable, has not yet entered the mainstream and there is no option but to programme lime into warmer conditions. While a long setting period may be inconvenient, this is a small price to pay for the way that lime can protect old buildings in the long-term by 'resetting' itself after minor movement, and by its breathability.

Home Use in DIY

As we have indicated, lime is caustic and can react violently in being mixed so properly protective gear is essential, particularly for the skin and eyes. But, having said that, it dries to docile calcium carbonate, is extremely satisfying to use and arguably less messy and frustrating than some expensive, modern products, once its principles are understood. Because a different set of precautions is necessary from those most of us are familiar with in DIY products, it is essential that some form of training is given to introduce newcomers to the material. Courses are run by a number of bodies, some commercial, some educational, including the Society for the Protection of Ancient Buildings (the SPAB, www.spab.org.uk), the Scottish Lime Centre Trust (www.charlestownworkshops.org) and some local authorities, such as Essex County Council (www.essexcc.gov.uk).

Ordinary 'Non-hydraulic' Lime: Hydrated Lime and Lime Putty

Non-hydraulic lime putty can be acquired in two forms. It can be made relatively cheaply from a (minimally slaked) hydrated lime powder ('bag lime') stocked by most builders' merchants. This is combined with just enough water to make a thick, creamy lime putty and, as with 'slaking' above, the reaction may be lively and the result is certainly caustic: in addition to gloves and goggles, a mask is necessary when using the powdered forms. However,

20

bag lime powder that has been stored too long or not been kept dry and airtight would be likely to have already have turned to chalk and so be useless. Once mixed, lime putty from bag lime can be allowed to 'mature' in airtight plastic tubs. Alternatively, lime putty can be bought in plastic tubs in its fully slaked form; the containers must be kept airtight. Many believe that this form is superior as it can have had the opportunity to mature in the tubs and is less likely to contain the pockets of un-mixed or prematurely-carbonated lime that may occur with mixing bag lime. This 'tub lime' was initially supplied for conservation work by smaller lime-making concerns, while 'bag lime' has long been available from cement manufacturers. Both should nowadays be readily available through builders' merchants.

Hydraulic Lime

Its name comes from its ability to be used and to cure in wet applications and for its setting being stimulated chemically by water rather than air. This was the material that was supplanted in engineering works when cement was invented. Whether made from naturally occurring, clay-containing limestone deposits or controlled mixes of the two substances, hydraulic lime is available in bagged powders in three recognized 'strengths', known by the old school as feebly hydraulic, moderately hydraulic and eminently hydraulic, they are now graded NHL2, 3.5 and 5 in ascending order of initial setting strength after twenty-eight days. It is quicker setting than non-hydraulic lime, potentially more durable and can be more adaptable to mechanized processes created for cement. In terms of breathability and mobility, hydraulic lime possesses these qualities to a useful degree, but may not always be as 'gentle' as ordinary, non-hydraulic lime, and though the quicker setting of hydraulic lime means that it can face the elements sooner, that does not necessarily mean that it is a tougher product in all conditions. Some conservationists feel that it may set too hard to be a satisfactory universal substitute for lime putty. It has, however, found favour as an alternative to, or admixture with, lime putty mixes for localized, highly exposed applications (such as pointing-up chimneys and ridge tiles), where the less acceptable alternative has previously been to add some cement.

PRINCIPAL LIME PRODUCTS USED IN CONSERVATION

Lime Mortar
At its simplest, this is a mixture of lime putty (non-hydraulic lime) and sand (fine, coarse or a mix of sands, depending on the application). This can be kept almost indefinitely in airtight containers once mixed, setting on exposure to air. Some believe that it improves with age the longer it is kept unused. Hydraulic lime mortars cannot be kept mixed as they set despite being kept airtight.

Lime Render (or Lime 'Plaster')
A similar mix to mortar but often containing animal hair for the base coats, this helps to reinforce over cracks and to grip between the timber laths in traditional lath and plaster ceiling construction. The finishing coats may be richer in lime and use extra fine sand to give a smoother surface. Since limepits were once used to destroy animal carcases, it makes no sense to leave a mortar mix containing reinforcing hair unused for any length of time.

Limewash
This a a slurry of lime putty and water used as a painted-on finish to lime render or masonry, sometimes with very fine sand or powdered stone added to bind and colour it. Pigments may be added, ideally 'natural earth' pigments or vegetable dyes; generally, those additives should not exceed 10 per cent of the mix. Industrial pigments, anti-freezes and bonding agents are not generally compatible with the chemistry or the desirable breathable qualities of limewash and may destroy the mix. Traditionally, limewash was given extra water-shedding properties by adding tallow to the mix, but this also served to decrease its useful breathability. (*see* Info pages: Paints, etc.)

Lime-ash Floors
A stiff mix of lime, wood ash and maybe other fillers, such as sand. Perhaps simply used, historically, to finish a beaten-earth floor. It was also used in the past to create structural floors 'vaulted' between timber beams or with wattles or timber as tensile reinforcement, or boards or mats of reed as permanent 'shuttering'. It may look at first sight like a concrete floor.

The mix varied greatly (and, for substantial repair, might need to be analysed) and is thought to have been a way of recycling residual lime and fuel from lime-burning.

Lime Concrete

Now that greener alternatives for cement-based concrete are being sought for floors and foundations, lime (usually hydraulic lime) is being paired with aggregates and pozzolans (*see below*) aimed at providing a breathable, firm substrate for floors in old and new buildings. The name is loosely applied to a number of differing mixes, while various additives and processes are being experimented with; for example, the use of light aerated rocks similar to pumice as an aggregate can reduce transport costs and potentially increase breathability and insulation. Although the Romans evidently perfected similar substances, some of which have lasted 2,000 years, modern builders and manufacturers will be refining and evaluating their promising new versions for a few years yet.

With quite accessible skill and care, limewash can provide a workable, modern-day solution for old house decoration.

Pozzolanic Additives for Lime

Named after volcanic rock used for centuries in Italy, pozzolans are additives, specifically containing silica and alumina, that can be mixed with lime to speed its setting or add strength in certain applications. They may include crushed (well-burnt) brick or pulverized fuel ash (an industrial by-product). Since modern cement falls into this category but has been felt to alter the lime mix unfavourably, not all pozzolans are totally benign. They are thought to replicate the action of the naturally entrained clays present in natural hydraulic lime. Some believe that modern lime production and mixing are too sterile and that there would, historically, have been intrusions into the mix of earth and clay from the sides of the limepits, acting as 'accidental pozzolans'. The very durable 'cement' surviving in Roman buildings has been thought to be lime mortar with deliberate pozzolanic additives, thus making it a close relation to modern cement.

THE BENEFICIAL QUALITIES OF LIME IN OLD BUILDINGS

Breathability

Lime products, those without additives, are inherently vapour-permeable, permitting some soaking of rainwater and damp but equally allowing that and any other moisture ('rising' damp, condensation, leaks) to dry out rather than remain trapped in the fabric.

The degree of breathability is reasonably compatible with that of traditional, soft brickwork and even timber such as oak, meaning that lime is less likely than cement to trap pockets of damp in those materials. When used as a mortar for brick or stone, lime tends to be 'sacrificial', that is, it will suffer degradation first, thereby preserving the masonry (which is, of course, the more difficult of the two to replace *in situ*). This sacrificial quality was thought a weakness by the twentieth-century mainstream and, as a result, many walls with perfectly viable, but apparently 'soft', lime mortar were needlessly repointed in cement that was much harder than the bricks or stones. The relative hardness of cement caused the softer bricks and stones to become the sacrificial element, taking up water and decaying. So the bricks or stones can wear away, leaving mortar. It is far better to have to replace lime pointing every hundred years than replace all or some of the bricks or stones every few decades.

Mobility

Lime, once set, can often tolerate slow, low-grade movement without cracking, accommodating seasonal shifts and settlement by appearing to 'reset' itself in the new position. If chemistry is involved in this process it ought to be interestingly complex and bordering on magic; however, the practical result can be seen in countless old brick and stone walls. Cement, on the other hand, being unbending and quite brittle, stubbornly attempts to hold its shape until finally it cracks: used as mortar, cement often cracks the bricks to which it is attached, and, used as render, cement cracks where it does not have the flexibility to move, admitting water which cannot easily evaporate out again.

Repairability: Limewash, Lime Mortars and Renders

Limewash and lime renders are relatively easy to recoat if they become physically damaged, provided that they retain their key to the background. Limewash is good at visually 'healing' small surface cracks and blemishes in previously limewashed surfaces and lime renders. Limewash is examined in more detail in Info pages: Paints etc. and lime mortars are looked at in the context of brickwork and stonework repairs (chapter 4: External Walls). Because lime render has applications for a variety of wall situations, it is examined in this section, below. All existing lime-based mixes can be scientifically analysed to determine their original composition when being repaired, which can be valuable knowledge, but the original composition may not necessarily have been ideal. An experienced craftsman will often have a feeling for the appropriate mix.

Performance of Lime Products

Local climate and the degree of physical exposure will determine the suitability and life of lime mortars, renders and limewashes. Limewash can survive reasonably well for a number of years in even a marine environment in the south of England, but it is likely to be less durable on the north coast of

Cement has proved too hard to mix with softer, more porous fabric such as traditionally-made bricks, it traps water in them and causes their decay.

Scotland. Local traditions in each case should have selected the best solution hundreds of years ago by trial and error and it can be worth a little local research to get the mix right, perhaps beginning with the local council's conservation officer.

Because an old house, traditionally built, could be expected to provide a compatible surface for its original limewash, then the finish could be expected to last. The all-round performance from an all-traditional system on an old house ought to be more satisfactory than where there is an incompatible mix of old and new techniques. Hacking-off cement and stripping off 'plastic' paint to restore lime finishes can be expensive and require a leap of faith – and professional guidance – but it could help to ensure the long-term survival of an old house, as well as make it look more attractive in the meantime (*see* chapter 4: External walls and Info pages: Paints and paint removal).

Repair Considerations for Lime Renders

Mixes

A basic mortar or render is made from lime putty (a strongly caustic substance, requiring safety precautions in its handling) and sand: typically about 1 volume of lime to 3 of sand; but experience is necessary to judge, for example, the wetness of the sand

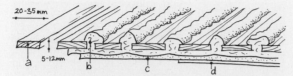

a rough timber laths, spacing as thickness of laths
b hair reinforced lime/sand plaster keys into slots
c second coat, without hair, to level – or with hair to take...
d optional third coat, finer sand, worked to a smooth finish

The second (the 'floating') coat (c) could be one volume of lime to about three of sharp sand (1:3), while the first (the 'scratch') coat with hair (b) might have a little less sand and the top coat (d) may have much more lime for smoothness (as much as 3:1); none of the coats is much over 12mm, while the top coat could be half that. Plaster direct to masonry would usually omit the hair from the 'scratch' coat and the mix adjusted to suit the background.

and the cohesiveness of the mix. The mix would be adjusted to suit different surfaces – porous brick, hard stone, soft earth walls and daub. A finer top coat can be had by making it lime-rich. The proportions for each coat will be gauged by experience or trial and error. Internal and external lime renders intended to 'hang' from timber laths were most often reinforced in their base coats with chopped animal hair (this has

to be not too short and needs to be microscopically 'barbed' for grip, so it may come from exotic species such as the yak; some hair, including human, is too smooth). There is no cement of any kind added to any of these mixes as, should that happen, the mix takes on some of the characteristics of cement, which are unhelpful to old buildings.

Lime putty can be bought ready mixed, with several grades of sand for use as mortars or top-coat renders, or bought 'neat' and mixed with sand and hair as necessary for each coat. Depending on the balance of available time and skills in a project, it may be more economical for building contractors to buy and mix the several ingredients when carrying out extensive works, in which case the quantities for mixing need careful control and skill, particularly when incorporating hair. Unlike cement, which begins to set once mixed, lime putty can be kept, in airtight containers, for several months by itself or as a wet mix, setting only on exposure to air (it is unwise to leave hair ready-mixed for a long time as it might decompose).

Properties
Render might be applied direct to masonry or on timber laths over a timber-framed building (*see* chapter 4: External walls, and chapter 6: Internal walls, etc.). Limewash gave external render extra defence against the weather; however, similar render

Lime is versatile and slow-setting, there is time for it to be moulded to match old surfaces; here a repair is built up in coats.

LIME

Lime render commonly survives on internal walls and ceilings; here the render had lost its key and fallen away, but the laths were still sound and well fixed so new lime render is about to be applied; the render hangs on to the timber laths by the blobs of hair-reinforced lime pushed through the gaps.

mixes and techniques were used for both external render and internal 'plastering' with lime. Sometimes internal renders were made from lime mixed with chalk instead of the usual sand, and sometimes the thin finish coat might contain gypsum for internal work. These variations would need careful consideration when repairing now.

Like lime mortar, finished lime render is soft and may appear superficially crumbly when compared with a hard, modern, cement coating. Like lime mortar, a lime render is able to cope with the requirements of an old house to breathe and to be able to accommodate slight movement or flexing. Cement render, on the other hand, is just as hard, impervious and unforgivingly inflexible as cement mortar. During the twentieth century, exterior lime render was frequently replaced, or over-coated, with cement and that would have had a dramatic effect on the viability of the structure beneath as its breathability is likely to have been compromised. Internally, lime render was also repaired with cement, but also with the many gypsum plasters, some of which behave unhelpfully in combination with lime by holding dampness, for example.

Lime render was sometimes wrongly diagnosed as failed because of its intrinsic softness, or because it did not provide a stable enough background for modern plastic paint (which should not really have been applied to it in the first place). Lime render, that

had lasted for maybe hundreds of years, quickly suffered under inappropriate maintenance and paints in the twentieth century, particularly external render.

Repairs
Subject to there being no other structural or underlying problems, superficial cracks in render that is adhering well on either side can simply be wetted and filled with a compatible mix or, for larger areas, a succession of mixes can be built up, according to the depth and the width of the repair in layers, as if for new work. Each layer, and the finished product, will need 'tending' until set. Tending can be as simple as providing a cover against sun, wind and rain (just as with modern cement) or may involve the pressing together of surface cracks or the gentle reworking of the unset surface. An area of failed render that has lost its 'key' to the background might be mechanically resecured rather than stripped and reapplied, but these techniques require expertise – they have to be learnt and practised to avoid making matters worse. In all repairs, the underlying cause of failure must be addressed first.

Lime render takes a long time to set, each coat may have to be left for weeks before it can be coatable again and it carries on setting long after it is complete. Because of the long setting time, it is inadvisable to use lime products at any time other than spring or summer (early summer in Scotland).

Safety and Buildings

THE HAZARDS

The building industry is acknowledged as one of the most accident-prone. In an attempt to deal with this, recent legislation has required more attention to be paid to the organization of building sites and to the design of buildings to minimize the risk in building and subsequent maintenance.

Old buildings were constructed when there were no safe scaffolds, when few in authority gave much thought to the dangers of access, of lifting, of toxic materials and it probably never occurred to anyone at all that future maintenance might have to be carried out by a risk-averse culture. Despite modern legislation, dangers are still lying in wait for the owner of an old house and DIY-practitioner who, along with one-man-band builders, is less well protected by mandatory safety procedures.

DIY repairs may prove difficult to outlaw entirely, though the law now puts much work to domestic gas, electricity and plumbing installations outside the scope of DIY. It is important to work only within the regulations, and then also to know one's own limitations, to plan work properly, to use appropriate safety equipment, to be aware of hazards to third parties and to understand and use tools appropriate to the job, but not so complex nor over-powered that they themselves put the operator at risk. Old houses were built with hand tools, so it might be appropriate to use some of those and write off the extra effort as healthy exercise, saving a trip to the gym.

Unfamiliarity
DIY repairs are, by definition, amateur. People unfamiliar with how buildings are put together can make wrong assumptions about the load-bearing capacity of parts of their building. Feet can be put through ceilings, ladders can be rested on fragile tiles or rotten window cills, apparently solid decorative features used as handholds can come away … the list is endless, and that is just while carrying out repairs. When it comes to alterations it is astounding how many people have made openings in walls without the faintest notion that it is necessary to put in a properly-sized beam to hold the remainder of the wall up.

It is not just unfamiliarity with buildings that is a hazard. Working off a ladder (now voluntarily banned by a few contractors on some sites) is an art involving balance, logistics, nerve and self-control. To people more used to, say, sitting behind a desk or driving a van, shinning up a ladder might look easy and liberating. But they may be tempted to overreach and fall off and, even if they are reasonably athletic, may not even think of tying the ladder to stop it moving or of protecting people who may pass underneath. A falling object or a falling person can be just as lethal at 6m as at twenty storeys.

For people who do not know the risks there are plenty to blunder into innocently; for example, stripping old lead paint is a serious potential health hazard and so not only should this be restricted to certain kinds of wet process, and while wearing a suitable mask, but it should not be allowed to endanger others downwind. To disturb asbestos could be potentially fatal, but how many DIY enthusiasts know what it looks like, where it might have been used and where to go for help on its safe disposal?

Although electrical, gas and some plumbing fittings are, legally at least, now outside most amateur dabbling, they are easily disturbed by clumsy building operations and can accidentally and instantly become dangerous.

Some Potential Special Hazards of Old Buildings

Asbestos

This was withdrawn from use in buildings in Britain during the last decades of the twentieth century following the linking of the inhalation of its fibres to fatal respiratory disease. Asbestos was derived from natural mineral sources, familiar as white, blue and brown asbestos, and processed into several extremely useful materials. It was used to insulate against heat and cold, it is virtually fireproof, its fibrous structure makes for useful reinforcement and it had many other industrial applications in such as gaskets, brake pads and filters (ironically, it was also used in wartime gas masks). It would be surprising if any house built before it was banned is entirely free from it, and even later ones may have acquired asbestos in old heaters or ironing boards, for example. Be wary of all old building products, including pipe and boiler lagging, ceiling and wall boards, fibrous mortar pointing, plastic floor tiles, textured ceiling and wall finishes, fire doors, electricity fuse boards, cookers, ironing boards, pipes, flues, rainwater gutters and downpipes, caulking, old wall fixings, storage heater insulation, oven door seals, cooker insulation, under-sink sound-deadening pads, any old heating appliances, fire-surrounds, hearths and chimneys. Asbestos boards were not just used for special fireproofing or insulating purposes, there were asbestos-cement boards for ordinary ceilings and walls, corrugated roofing sheets and 'artificial' slates. There are too many applications to present a complete list here. Current regulations address, for example, the hazards of asbestos, its handling and disposal, with penalties for its abuse. These and the associated advice are liable to develop over time so see the Health and Safety Executive website (www.hse.gov.uk) for directions to further information about the different forms of the material, whom to contact for testing and to find out about options for sealing up or disposal as appro-

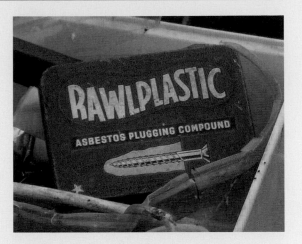

Asbestos is now classed as highly dangerous, but it was so versatile that its legacy of use in buildings will continue to appear for very many years more, though not always so well labelled as this.

priate. Under existing legislation certain categories of building owner already have a legal obligation to identify, record and manage all asbestos on their property.

Lead

Still used for roofing work and flashings, lead has been banned from all but very special paint applications (it has been able to be used under licence in paint on certain Grade I and II* listed buildings in Britain). Care is required if working with the metal and the ingestion of dissolved lead and the inhalation of dust or fumes are also concerns, so the collection of drinking water from a lead roof is clearly a bad idea. It is perhaps best not to disturb lead paint more than necessary when preparing for a new coat of paint. The rubbing down of any suspect paint should be done when wearing an appropriate mask and with the work kept dust-free by thorough wetting. Burning off produces fumes that are harder to deal with safely and is usually inadvisable for other reasons.

Lead has long been banned from use in pipes for domestic water and it is also banned from use in the solder used to hold copper pipe joints together. Lead water supply pipes still serve many old houses and it would represent a significant problem to locate and

Lead paint was withdrawn because of the toxic dangers of accidental ingestion.

replace all these at once, but there is a programme in many areas to achieve this over time. The presence of lime scale or regular, continual flushing have been suggested by some to reduce exposure to lead in drinking water, but the truth of this is ought to be assessable through testing. Look for current advice on the government H&SE websites regarding all forms of contact with lead and how to manage them (for lead paint *see also* www.defra.gov.uk).

Anthrax and Bio-hazards

It has been proposed that anthrax spores could be surviving on the animal hair present in old plaster-work. However, to panic and demolish a wall for that reason would almost certainly release any such spores, if there were any. There is official guidance on this subject online (www.hse.gov.uk).

Common sense should alert us to avoid animal faeces, carcases or biting and stinging creatures, but these can unexpectedly get very close when one is clearing gutters or drains or accessing corners of roofs; suitable gloves are a sensible minimum precaution along with scrupulous hygiene. Once again, the H&SE is the first stop for information.

Chemicals

These may range from insecticides and fungicides to the content of adhesives used in particle boards and insulation materials. From time to time chemicals are banned from specific uses, as their side-effects become apparent. Unfortunately, many of these are already locked up in existing properties due to the twentieth century's unquestioning acceptance of industry's exploitation of science. The control of dust from work on previously treated roof timbers would be one sensible precaution, and to avoid those timbers from coming into contact with people. Some perceived fume hazards might be expected to dissipate over time as solvents evaporate, but the existence of long-term guarantees for timber treatment implies that they were expected to remain toxic for some time. Toxic fumes can be generated by burning or heating a variety of building materials with blowlamps or hot air guns. It may be of some comfort to those living in old houses to know that materials such as plastics, man-made fibres and composite boards made from glued timber particles have raised concerns about their continuing release of fumes or gases; these would more likely be associated with modern houses where these materials are used in quantity and ventilation tends to be sealed up. (*See also* COSHH, below.)

Glass

Glass is potentially physically dangerous when broken, and for centuries this risk has been tolerated because of the benefits the material brings. In the windows of old houses a grid of timber glazing bars supports the glass and might help limit injury, but, nevertheless, surviving old glass is sometimes fragile and thin. Modern regulations have introduced requirements for glass in certain locations to be 'safety glass' that either resists breaking or breaks in a controlled way (there are further regulations requiring the use of glass treated to conserve energy).

These may appear to conflict with the preservation of characterful old glass, but there are various ways (*see* chapter 5: Doors and windows) to do this and meet the regulations. One of them is to apply special self-adhesive film to the glass.

COSHH

The Health & Safety Executive has details of the regulations on the Control of Substances Harmful to Health, with guidance applicable to various situations: www.hse.gov.uk/coshh

HEALTH AND SAFETY IN PRACTICE

Regulations

To view the industry's standards see the Health & Safety Executive website (www.hse.gov.uk): Construction Design and Management Regulations 2007. The CDM regulations first came into force in the 1990s, were revised in 2007, extending their scope, and will no doubt continue to be strengthened. They are designed to reduce the risk of death and injury to those on building sites during building operations and also to those who use and will maintain the buildings afterwards. They do this by requiring, not only safer practices on building sites, but by requiring designers and builders to consider the implications of the tasks they are setting and the situations they may be creating, even into the future. The regulations are not a substitute for common sense and anyone coming within range of any building operations should still be extra vigilant since building operations are inherently risky.

The regulations were, in their early years, applied in a less administratively onerous way to domestic work and they are, of course, difficult to apply retrospectively to old buildings in terms of their past design. But the regulations' scope is likely to increase as the rules are revised, and their effect on working practices will be likely to spread through the industry into domestic work. In the future, more and more tradesmen may refuse to carry out tasks at height from ladders, or perhaps be restricted by their insurance from doing so. Already some large building contractors forbid the use of ladders in some circumstances, whereas a one-man-band builder will still be reliant on a ladder to carry out much of his work. Fortunately, temporary scaffolds, hoists and hydraulic platforms are becoming more available.

Risks of Unregulated Working

The many health and safety regulations are sometimes accused of being over-protective, but they are that way for a reason: we do not all go around with our common sense switched on all the time. The fact that certain types of work may not fall within the regulations is not a reason for celebration but to be extra careful since, effectively, no one is looking out for you. If considering repairs and minor DIY that may not actually require the formal adoption of current precautionary regulations, be aware of what regulations would apply to professionals doing the same job. Understanding the risks and, where possible and reasonable to do, replicating the necessary precautions would be a step towards safer working. The DIY enthusiast and the lone builder may not face the complex dangers of a busy, large commercial building site but they are often at extra risk because they may be working alone or be less familiar with certain tasks, so getting someone to check on them regularly and taking advantage of the slower pace of work by thinking though any actions in advance would be sensible steps towards fostering safety.

Understanding Our Limitations

This book is aimed at providing an understanding of some of the options available for repairing an old house rather than offering step-by-step instructions. Some of these options might be appropriate for suitably prepared and equipped DIY-ers, others would be suitable only for experienced professionals. It is not possible to anticipate every circumstance so no categorization has been attempted regarding which repairs might be suitable or unsuitable for DIY. Building jobs are easy to underestimate, particularly when investigating the unknown source of a problem and even more so when one has no particular building experience. If in any doubt, get professional help, a good builder can do jobs faster than a DIY-er, has experience to help to anticipate where a problem might lead and either has, or should know where to get, the proper equipment

29

A light aluminium tower can feel more comfortable than a ladder, but even these require a head for heights and need to be secured properly to avoid accidents.

needed for a task. Building work can be dangerous enough, but misplaced, amateur optimism, machismo with power tools and innocent ignorance can make it lethal.

The Hazards of Fire

Fire can totally destroy a building and so owners and occupants owe it to themselves to make full precautionary use of smoke- and heat-detectors (and better still, automatic fire alarms), to keep appropriate fire extinguishers to hand and install a fire blanket in the kitchen. Risk might be further reduced by reasonable physical protection and vigilance, such as in turning appliances off and shutting doors at night (and considering how constructional fire barriers might be discreetly created; see Info pages: Sustainability – Insulation). Thatch plus wood-burning stoves, and wiring plus mice or squirrels can each be an incendiary combination. Candles are increasingly implicated in home fires and smoking has been associated with this, more immediate, route to fatalities for long enough to generate special regulations about the flammability of furnishings. In a fire, it is not just heat and flames but smoke that is deadly, and, as with carbon monoxide emissions from faulty boilers and heaters, people can be suffocated without ever having been aware of a fire. Burning buildings, particularly with plastic contents, can give off toxic fumes or cause a rain of molten material that hinders escape, rescue and fire-fighting.

The guidance of experienced, serving fire personnel would seem a sensible route to practical fire precautions, and such advice was for a long time available to commercial buildings. At the time of writing (2007) many fire services are able to inspect homes free of charge: occupiers of older houses ought to particularly benefit as their homes are less likely to have ever had the basic detection and alarm measures required by the building regulations for new buildings (*see also* www.firekills.gov.uk and www.communities.gov.uk/fire). Having building works carried out can create additional risks with flammable materials and tools such as blow lamps on site; old buildings are particularly at risk from this (some conservation organizations ban 'hot works' from their buildings altogether).

Electrical Safety

There has been a requirement for some time for new houses to have any sockets likely to be used for external equipment (such as lawn mowers) protected by devices that can help to reduce the severity of electric shock. These are known as RCDs (residual current devices, or formerly ELCBs (earth-leakage circuit breakers). Put simply, they turn off the power on detecting a leak to earth. They have to be properly installed and correctly rated and they offer different performance from the circuit-breaker switches (MCBs) or the rewireable or cartridge fuses found in ordinary old consumer units (fuse boxes) and plugtops which simply respond to an overload. Old houses will have RCD protection only if they have been recently rewired to modern regulations or if someone has bothered to provide it, and protection may not be complete.

RCDs have often been installed to control a number of circuits together but can also control individual circuits. Have all this checked by a qualified electrician and consider installing these devices if they are not in place. RCDs are a worthwhile protection to have for circuits in kitchens and bathrooms as well; new installations to these areas will have to be protected by them (pending regulation changes expected soon after this book is published). They need to be installed in such a way that a fault on one circuit does not plunge the whole house into darkness. Some overhead-supplied houses have ELCBs or RCDs as part of the electricity supplier's equipment, but these may not be suitable to protect against electric shock. The current at which an RCD shuts off is measured in milliamps (mA), and 30mA is the rating that appears on safety devices: a higher number means that the equipment is probably there for a different purpose. Portable plug-in RCDs are available and individual socket outlets can be simply converted to serve this function.

Another device, an RCBO (a combination of RCD and MCB) can be installed one per circuit in place of the existing fuse-box switches. This has the advantage of limiting isolation to that circuit in the event of a fault, and it has been suggested that RCBOs may give some extra protection against any fire resulting from rodent damage to cables. Installing permanent RCDs or RCBOs may require fundamental, though relatively simple, alterations to the wiring and earthing regime in a house that has not been rewired for some time.

The British system of a cartridge fuse in every plug has its merits, but, as people have been slowly weaned off understanding electrical DIY, there is probably still confusion about which rating of fuse to use for which appliance, resulting in many appliances having plugs with unnecessarily highly-rated 13 amp (A) fuses when a lower rating (3, 5 or 10A) might suffice for the electrical load of the appliance and offer slightly better protection. Those who are not familiar with amps and watts should consult an electrician and increase their electrical safety. Properly qualified electricians are now required to be engaged for all but very small repairs to domestic installations. Before January 2005 such work was less regulated and anyone could install new wiring (there were post-installation checks on extensive or officially-notified work). Information is available in a download via www.communities.gov.uk. Existing homes may therefore have had parts of their mains or appliance wiring installed by amateurs. Modern-looking switch-plates and socket outlets are no guarantee of the age or quality of the wiring behind. Many old houses still have significant amounts of old rubber-sheathed wiring, or even the earliest lead-encased type, which may now be past its ability to perform adequately and safely. This needs to be tested with care since some test procedures themselves might turn old, but safe, wiring into faulty wiring (*see also* chapter 7: Building Services).

CHAPTER 2

Roofs

HISTORICAL PERSPECTIVE

The British Isles have a very broad range of geology and this is the reason for the great variety in roofing materials. Some rocks (slates, limestones and sandstones) that were laid down millions of years ago in beds will conveniently split along their bed lines into workable thicknesses that can be squared-up into roofing slates and hung on a nail or oak peg.

Areas without suitable rock but which grew cereal crops could use the straw stems to make thatch. Or, if they had a clay soil, they could bake it into tiles. Areas with poor soils and unsuitable rock may have had to resort to using layers of heather or whatever vegetation was abundant until transport was established from other areas. That was probably how most roofs began since it takes quite a settled society to quarry stone and manage crops. We get to see only

what has survived, and often that is a few steps up the ladder from the first efforts: the location and age of an old house will therefore determine what its original roof covering might have been. Transport – sea, canals and railways – brought non-local materials, first to the richer houses and then more universally. The wealthiest favoured lead, as did the Church, for durability and architectural effect. After the railways slate dominated until concrete copies of clay tiles took over in the factory age of the twentieth century. Historically the natural logic of supply could be distorted by taxes, which could favour one material over another.

The shape of vernacular buildings is strongly determined by the original roofing material. Many old houses have steeply pitched roofs, intended to help the rain to run off their original thatch quicker. The roofs are still steeply pitched but perhaps have

East coast pantiles.

been covered in clay tiles for hundreds of years since. In towns thatch is difficult to abut to other roofs, and there is the risk of fire, so tiles would have been preferred as soon as these towns felt the pressure of space. Slate and pantiles can accommodate much lower pitches, making for cheaper roof construction, and so a steep roof in those materials was either a design extravagance or is evidence of former thatch. Stone roofs tend to splay at the eaves, once that shape was established it might remain despite any replacement roofing material.

Roofs are the dominant areas of any house, thus any replacements should be considered with great care: old roof materials tend to be multi-coloured, natural expressions of the weathered material, the roof surface may undulate and has interesting texture. Modern 'non-natural' roofing tiles and slates can be relentlessly uniform, perfectly regular, with the colour tending to weather ungraciously like concrete.

CHARACTERISTICS OF COMMON ROOFING MATERIALS

The lifespan of tile and slate roofing materials is influenced by the life of their fixings, which have proved shorter than the life of clay and stone in many cases. Oak pegs can still be found holding clay peg-tiles in place on old buildings, whereas iron nails have rusted, even later galvanized ones. Modern practice is to use alloy or copper nails, depending on the roof material, to get round this problem. But it is not

It is likely that many old houses that are presently all tiled were once thatched.

uncommon to find tile and slate roofs still serviceable after a century: if they need to be relayed many of the individual units may be capable of reuse.

Thatch

Thatch needs a pitch of at least 45 degrees in order to shed rainwater faster than it can soak through the stems. The three most common types of thatch in Britain are long-straw, combed wheat reed (actually straw, the 'reed' being an old term for a straw) and water reed. Long straw has dominated in the southern counties of England eastwards from Dorset and was once perhaps the most widespread nationally. Combed wheat reed was prominent west of Dorset. Water reed grows in Norfolk and is extensively used in East Anglia; it has a long history in other areas

A sharp-edged profile without visible edge-binding is associated with water-reed thatch [above], while its cousin, combed wheat reed, is laid in a similar manner with a bristly, ends-only, look – like carpet pile, seen here in close up [right].

Long straw, perhaps once the most common thatching material in England, is laid in shaggy layers then trimmed and its edges 'sewn' into place with 'liggers'.

with reed beds (including Dorset again). Heather and turf variants have been traditional in the mountainous northern and western areas of the country and several grasses and brush-like plants have been used elsewhere in the past, with occasional examples surviving. Straw and reed thatches are reckoned to be sound for a generation, but that is entirely dependent on the quality of the thatch and the roof's exposure.

Plain and Peg-tiles

Clay tiles developed alongside British thatching traditions so their size and overlap has been geared to cope with the same pitch and roof shapes. In the

Exposed coastal areas took extra precautions to keep thatch in place, and where local agriculture did not produce grain then heather, grass and even turf were used.

An old roof with a large number of more modern, more regular tile replacements that are altering the character.

A roof recently re-laid in modern, 'handmade', clay plain tiles with repaired, reused Victorian ridge tiles.

fifteenth century there were attempts to standardize the size of clay tiles by royal decrees and these, after a patchy uptake, have generally held true to the present time. An old house with a plain or peg-tile roof now might last have been re-roofed up to a hundred years ago, and then a number of the tiles might have been reused from a hundred years before that. The Victorians devised machines to speed up the production of tiles, but those tiles could be very smooth and flat compared with the earlier, handmade variety and so have a different character. Modern 'handmade' clay tiles look more like pre-industrial ones but, because production is centralized, local clay variations are absent and colours are achieved by applied minerals that can weather differently to historical versions. It is common to adopt a 'ready-weathered' colour to blend new tiles, but in the past new tiles would have stood out as bright yellow, orange or red and it is reasonable to do this today on complete, newly relaid roofs.

Not every course of tiles is actually nailed into the roofing battens through the holes formed in the tiles – just enough to restrain the vulnerable areas (official codes of practice, building construction books and often manufacturers' technical literature provide details for a variety of situations). Some plain tiles have hanging nibs at the head, plus holes for occasional nailing. With peg-tiles (no nib, just holes) oak pegs were used, later replaced by nails, to hang over the battens. Some areas have a tradition of mortaring tiles on to the battens instead of hanging them on pegs, this allowed for the reuse of damaged tiles and has proved surprisingly durable, but is alarming to repair as a whole area of roof might be dislodged at once.

Pantiles

Pantiles were traded between Britain and the Low Countries from medieval times, as well as being locally-made; they appear all the way down the east coast from Scotland to East Anglia and around ports elsewhere. Their interlocking design means that there is less overlap than with plain clay tiles, so just one

The underside of a traditional, oak-pegged roof.

The adaptability of pantiles for shallow pitches make the traditional 'Norfolk' dormer feasible on roofs originally pitched steeply for thatch.

thickness of tile in most places, but, despite that, they were considered capable of being laid to pitches as low as 30 degrees, hence their ability to form the characteristic Norfolk dormer window, which would be impossible in plain tiles. Pantiles have a long life, similar to that of plain tiles, though reuse may be made difficult by the existence of different profiles (or different widths for old tiles). As with plain tiles, machine manufacture resulted in a smoother, more uniform tile, but this is less obvious since pantiles are heavily profiled. Similar to plain tiles, any one pantile may either be hung on its nib or nailed in place, depending on its vulnerability on the roof. In housing, pantiles may have been laid over a roughly woven straw mat, a practice that continued until at least the 1930s in Norfolk.

Slates and Stone Slates

Slates
Cornwall, the north-west of England and many parts of Scotland and Wales once produced vast quantities of the thin, relatively smooth roofing slates that can be accurately shaped and tightly overlapped. Welsh slates, which tend to cleave the thinnest and reveal a very smooth surface, have been in steady commercial production to the present, yet are now in competition with imported slates of varying quality. Both the Cornish and the distinctive green Lake District slate (known to the industry as Westmoreland slate) are still sourceable, though production is reduced from former times. There are hopes to revive some of the many former Scottish quarries. Welsh slates happen to cleave very thinly and very smoothly, and can be reliably dressed into regular and quite large sizes. Many other British slates split less evenly, so to use the resulting assortment of sizes, roofs are laid in 'diminishing' courses with larger sizes reserved for the critical, lower part of the slope (*see also* chapter 4: External walls).

Generally slate sizes are linked to pitch, larger sizes (610mm long × 355mm) might have been used on pitches as low as 22½ degrees, with a sliding scale of suitability up to 45 degrees for 305mm × 205mm slates traditionally. With Welsh slates, at any point on a slate roof there are two thicknesses of slate and the nail holes can also be covered by two thicknesses (head-nailed slates). The procession of sizes, originally in inches, have excellent traditional names echoing

Glass pantiles were for daylight in outbuildings and attics.

Westmoreland slates, prized for their green colour, were popular nationwide with Edwardian builders.

Welsh slates were valued for their ability to cleave thin and smooth; the colours vary from grey to purple and can age without fading.

precedence: empresses, small duchesses, wide countesses, small ladies and so on, much more interesting than millimetres. Slates are fixed by holes near their top, head-nailed, or are 'centre-nailed', more usual for larger sizes and helping to prevent wind lift.

Stone Slates

Stone slates (also known as stone tiles), the large, heavy, sometimes rough sandstone and limestone varieties (*see* chapter 4: External walls – Stone) do not fit closely together so their water-shedding ability is based on a balance of tile size and pitch. Shallower courses at the eaves help to prop up the higher courses as well as slowing down and projecting run-off rainwater (important in the days before gutters). Bigger tiles at the bottom reduce the number of vulnerable joints where more water is flowing than at the top. Stone tiles are individually hung on oak pegs or, latterly, corrosion-proof, metal nails. For extra stability they are often found 'torched' underneath, that is coated with lime mortar.

All types of stone slate are, naturally enough, relatively heavy and the battens and roof timbers will have had to be sized and fixed to cope with this. It is advisable to have structural checks if considering switching back to these materials where a house has had a modern replacement roof at some time.

Lead and Other Metal and Flat Roofs

Lead has been used for centuries to create almost flat roofs. Its cost traditionally limited it to houses that

The look of traditional Scottish slate [right] may now be difficult to replicate, so it is hoped that some Scottish slate quarries might be reopened.

A new Cotswold stone roof complete with traditional-style lime mortar 'torching' covering the underside of the tiles.

Different varieties of stone roofing seen from inside and out.

tended to be large, but it will be found trimming more humble roofs as flashings and valley gutters or for small areas of roof, such as porches or dormers. Sometimes copper and, in more recent times, zinc was used as an alternative to lead for both pitched and flat roofs. As world commodity prices rise, the more valuable metals may be at risk from theft so owners need to contact their insurers and crime prevention officer for guidance. The materials most likely to appear on twentieth-century, flat-roofed extensions to old houses are built-up 'felt' roofing ('three-layer felt') or asphalt. Felt roofing was self-finished with green grit or topped with loose white chippings to protect it from the sun; asphalt eventually came to be painted with solar reflective paint

Lightweight and attractive, timber shingles may have once been more commonplace; the timber has to be selected and cut to minimize curling and splitting.

Lead is very durable if properly laid and looked after, but degenerates more quickly in acid conditions such as those generated by moss and lichen.

Corrugated iron started as a utilitarian roofing option but has acquired dignity and admirers over time, due perhaps to nostalgia rather than its beauty.

(grey, white or silver) for the same reason. Asphalt has a better reputation in terms of life-expectancy and can be specified in grades that can be walked on. Both can be temporarily repaired with liquid compounds and there are newer roofing products too, but, as flat roofs are essentially modern constructions, that is another subject. If the roof is old, was once lead and has been replaced by felt, asphalt or some other material then the performance of the fabric underneath may be affected by that change so it should be examined if possible and consideration given to reinstating lead. If a flat-roofed extension is recent then it might be possible to re-roof it with a pitched roof, provided that this would not obstruct or dominate the rest of the house. The usual permissions would be necessary (*see* Info pages – Red tape).

SPOT-REPAIRS TO ROOFS

Because of possible access problems, roofs are best left to professionals. The repairs examined here are based on experience and are for information on what might be possible by appropriately-equipped people. Roof leaks can be difficult to pin down, a great deal of water can get in through an almost invisible crack or hole. If safe access is possible, playing a hose across the suspect area can narrow down the source of a leak. As materials put into a roof at the same time are likely to wear out at the same time, be prepared for a

damp patch inside being the result of not one but two simultaneous leaks from different sources. The first step is to decide what it is about the roof that actually needs repair: if that fault can be tackled without disturbing the bulk of the roof and the remainder of the roof is still sound, then repair what is broken or weak and leave the rest.

The Ridge
The topmost capping, the ridge, has to form an angle bridging the two slopes, so, with the exception of clay tiles, it is often in a different material from most of the roof (for instance, tile or lead for slate, sedge for reed thatch). Ridge tiles are often blown off in gales and, though modern tile manufacturers have devised clever ways of securing them, the owner of an old house usually has to simply replace what was there and hope for the best. It may seem counter-intuitive but the use of a 'weaker' lime mortar at least has the benefit of allowing ridge (and any other mortared)

tiles to be reused, whereas concrete grips so hard (at least to the tile) that the tiles are usually unfit for cleaning and reuse and may crack in use. A lime-mortared ridge will probably need to be repointed during the life of the roof so the mortar should be carefully selected and competently applied (*see* Info pages – Lime).

Fancy Ridge Tiles

Crested Victorian terra cotta (clay) ridge tiles were available in many patterns and some of these are still replicated by specialist manufacturers. But, if the pattern or colour is not available, then it might be possible to try a do-or-die repair using stainless-steel armatures and modern adhesives. With a rare or valuable piece, or with a roof to which access is particularly difficult, the economics may favour a complete copy being made from the pieces. There is nothing to be lost by storing the pieces of a presently un-repairable decorative ridge tile in the loft space in the hope that these will be repairable or copyable in some more cost-effective way in the future.

Thatch Ridges

As with tile and stone roof coverings, the thatch ridge covers the join between two slopes and requires a material that can be formed into a right angle. Straw might be used on straw, but water reed is too brittle to fold and so sedge tends to be used on those roofs. It is usual to replace the ridge several times during the lifetime of a thatch in order to prolong the life of the whole roof; a thatcher may need to be consulted to help decide when.

Decorative clay ridge tile.

Missing Tiles and Slates

An experienced roofer can remove and replace a single broken tile or slate effectively from the outside. An inexperienced person can break a lot of surrounding tiles and risk their own life and the lives of those who may walk underneath. With most roofs this is not a job for amateurs. Fortunately, many traditional clay tiles (plain tiles and some pantiles) and slates have been made in standard sizes for hundreds of years and so finding a matching replacement is considerably easier than with the many modern patented 'interlocking' designs, even so, slates and tiles sometimes have to be trimmed to fit an existing location.

Ridge and patch repairs to long straw thatch.

Temporary replacement of a missing peg tile with a small sheet of lead; adjacent slipped tiles have been gently secured with wire to avoid an avalanche.

Plain Tile Repair from Inside

If there is access and no underlay, inspecting a plain or peg-tiled roof from the inside can reveal whether there are any slipped or slipping tiles that need attention. It is not difficult in most situations for a roofer to slot new tiles in from outside to replace those that have slipped. If faced with a sudden missing plain clay tile in an otherwise sound roof and the undersides of all the tiles are visible (that is, the roof has not been 'underdrawn' with felt, mortar or timber boarding), then it may be possible from inside the roof to negotiate a tile-sized sheet of lead into the space once occupied by the missing tile, secured by turning down the top over the timber tiling-batten. Though only a temporary repair, this can save potentially damaging, or difficult, access from outside. It needs as much care as any regular, professional repair since there is the potential for dislodging tiles on to people below or for the repairer to fall through a ceiling.

It may be extremely difficult and dangerous to try to patch-repair roofs where clay tiles are held in place only by a layer of mortar (*see above*) rather than with pegs, nibs or nails.

Pantiles

Like clay plain and peg-tiles, it may be possible to slot in a replacement traditional pantile from the outside, though there are many variant profiles to such pantiles and sourcing replacements can require determination.

Slate Tingles

Slates (the thin variety, like Welsh slates) are larger and sit closer and more tightly overlapped than clay plain tiles, but a traditional repair with metal 'tingles' (such as zinc) from the outside can restore continuity where a slate has slipped. There are proprietary versions of slate repair devices.

Stone Slates

The thick, sandstone and limestone types range from pieces the size of paving slabs to those smaller than a dinner plate. Being irregular and often very heavy, a repair will depend on circumstances and the ingenuity of the roofer.

Patches

The twentieth century devised methods of patching failing roofs either by applying a reinforcing fabric/compound to the outside or by spraying an adhesive foam to the inside. Either could make the slates or tiles ultimately unreusable, and meanwhile harmfully inhibit ventilation of the roof space. The external covering would usually be subject to planning, listed building and conservation area controls, and probably for this reason it seems to have been used very little in recent years. Conservationists are concerned that the internal foam versions tend to seal up the timbers they touch, so preventing them from breathing and potentially accelerating their decay. Short-term fixes that alter things too much may not be best for longer-term repair.

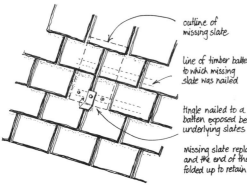

outline of
missing slate

Line of timber batten
to which missing
slate was nailed

tingle nailed to a
batten exposed between
underlying slates

missing slate replaced
and the end of the tingle
folded up to retain it

Tingles have been seen as an effective temporary repair in the past to broken, slipped or unnailed slates; a rash of them might indicate a widespread problem with corroded nails, or possibly the repairs following a fallen branch; tingles that are 'unfolding' can mean that the slates are still moving.

Damaged Thatch

Thatch does wear locally, due, for example, to water concentrating into run-off courses, or due to the attention of birds and animals. Long-straw thatch can be patched because of the way the straw was laid in the first place – more or less in layers. Combed wheat reed and water-reed thatch tends to rely on a 'full-thickness' lapping, with only the ends of the stems showing and so patch repairs are more difficult, though loosened areas can be knocked back up.

Moss on thatch is not automatically bad, and may even provide a beneficial coating in some cases, unless, of course it is blocking run-off and causing a localized build-up of water in the thatch. All types of thatch can be resecured according to the tradition of the material, while ridges can, and should, be replaced at regular intervals. All repairs are work for expert thatchers, the same people or the same firm who laid the thatch in the first place should be aware of the original working methods.

Lead

Lead is repairable, the Lead Sheet Association has for a long time published standard details for its proper use when installing the metal and this can guide repairs too. Lead expands and contracts and so needs

to be joined in a way that allows for this; laps and steps (in near horizontal work) accommodate lead to lead joints and sheets must be divided into sizes in which movement is containable. Lead flashings may wriggle free from mortar or wedge fixings over time.

Welding lead repairs *in situ* can present a fire risk, which conservation organisations get round by either banning it totally and favouring alternatives, or by putting stringent monitoring in place. Gluing patches is an alternative, or, for pinholes or temporary repairs to lead that has reached the end of its repairable life, a liquid repair as in the next heading may suit. In conservation work additional ventilation is often incorporated into repairs of old lead roofs to reduce harmful condensation that can form on the underside of the sheets and begin to attack the metal.

Gullies and Valleys

These features occur where, instead of a simple pitched roof falling to gutters either side of the house, the roof consists of several pitches that may meet and intersect other than at the edges of the building, necessitating some kind of joint between two roofs.

Traditionally these 'valley gutters' would have been made in lead. Unfortunately, they were not all designed in such a way that they lasted or were readily accessible for maintenance and many were replaced during the 1950s and 1960s with optimistic repairs in the sort of roofing felt more suited to sheds. Where this has failed the proper answer is to revert to lead, but that can mean stripping back much of the surrounding roof and, where the roof is old and fragile, bring forward an expensive total re-roofing project. Even with the will, and money, to revert to lead it will sometimes be difficult to comply with today's codes of practice for laying lead in a way that ensures sufficient fall: lead should be divided up into lengths that can cope with thermal expansion without puckering or cracking, it was not always so.

Not surprisingly, many houses have struggled through to the present with ad hoc bitumen repairs to the failed felt valleys and gutters, or even bitumen repairs over old, stretched and cracked lead. But bituminous roofing is highly susceptible to cracking – especially if it is exposed to sunlight. Relatively recent remedial products combine glass-fibre reinforcement entrained in a thick acrylic compound. This product, when applied, emits a heady solvent vapour so, while its formulation might be improved in that respect, it can nevertheless provide a quick and effective temporary solution to cracked, split and blistered bituminous felt in some situations. Although the manufacturers do not seem to suggest this, the compound appears to be adaptable to application over glass-fibre plasterer's scrim tape for reinforcing local spot repairs.

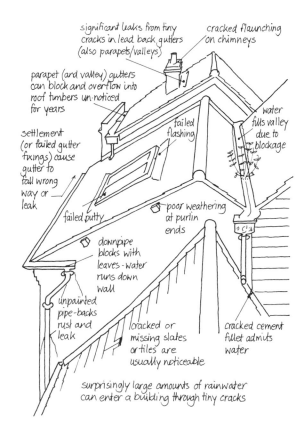

Some common causes of roof leaks.

In the past, a former lead finish must have failed in this valley gutter, presumably because it was inadequately stepped. It had already been replaced in bitumen felt and, to make a lasting repair in lead now, a better step would need to be introduced, changing the line of the tiles, and so it has made sense to resurface the bitumen with a glass-fibre reinforced compound to help the valley to last until re-roofing is appropriate.

RE-ROOFING

Terraces of old houses can be seen with individual roofs up to a hundred years apart in age, indicating that, at some point, a re-roofing may have been done when only a repair was necessary. But re-roofing, when that is the only way to ensure that the house beneath stays dry and properly ventilated, is money well spent. Roof repairs have to be taken seriously or the character of an old house can be lost. Firms engaged in re-roofing may not always consider what makes an old building look special when they are called to provide a new roof, and even if an old house is neither listed nor in a protected area, re-roofing ought to be discussed with the local authorities. Most traditional materials can be sourced new without resorting to salvage (*see* Info pages: Conservation terminology, etc.). Modern substitute versions of tiles and slates made from non-traditional materials may be really too precise, bland, flat and sharp-edged to suit an old building. It is not always easy to source the original, matching materials locally, but the householder should make thorough enquiries and establish all the options for themselves before accepting compromises.

To Re-roof or Not – Slates and Tiles

Unless the roof has actually failed significantly, the decision to re-roof is always a difficult one. An old roof on an old house is probably not going to meet the rigorous standards of today in terms of its security of fixings and detailing, but can it be improved? Old roofs whose slates or tiles are hung on ordinary iron nails can last a hundred years. The tiles or slates may suffer from frost at varying rates, and one or two may crack and fall. The nails may rust away to nothing and whole tiles or slates slide away in a strong wind. Until the time of writing, it has been possible to patch repair these defects and take a view on the life of the roof. It has not been uncommon for roofs, that the inexperienced or over-zealous would have condemned outright, to last a further ten or twenty years. Professional roofers have a good feel for the condition of a roof and, though one would expect them to want to drum up trade, firms with a reputation to uphold might be quite reassuring about a roof that looks borderline to the layman. An old rule of thumb used to be that if the number of dislodged (that is, out of line rather than missing) tiles or slates exceeds 25 per cent of the total then a re-roof was more economical than spot repairs. However, that equation may have been distorted since the advent of hydraulic platforms ('cherry-pickers') for spot repairs and also the present, more stringent, requirements for scaffolding for static access.

There are certainly things that can be done to extend the life of a roof and, for all roofing types, attention to the weaker areas – eaves, ridge, valleys,

Previous tile replacements identify a suspect area at which to begin investigations into whether a re-roof is necessary and into the condition of the battens and roof timbers; only a few of these old tiles were reusable and were relaid on a lower outbuilding, backed up by a breathable underlay.

verges and hips – can pay dividends in extending the life of the whole roof. If partial relaying of these areas can be shown to be cost-effective, then that may be worth considering. In the near future it is likely that more stringent health and safety legislation will increasingly influence such decisions, for the provision of safe access is becoming a major part of the cost of any high-level project. Similarly, society is likely to become less and less tolerant of the real, if rare, risks of injury from falling slates and tiles; nevertheless, even a brand new roof is capable of shedding tiles or slates at times.

To Re-roof or Not – Timbers

If the underlying timbers are rotten, the roof covering may have to be removed, regardless of its condition. There may be circumstances where a broken rafter can be repaired from the inside without sacrificing too much of the roof. But, if significant parts of the roof structure, or all the tiling battens (the thin strips of wood on which the tiles or slates are hung or nailed) are rotten, or their nails have failed, then there is little satisfactory option but to strip and re-roof. (*see* chapter 4: External walls for some repair options for structural timber).

Modern softwood tiling battens have usually been treated against decay (chemical preservative treatments have recently had to be modified), whereas much older ones were simply riven timber, usually hardwood. If well ventilated and not subject to wetting, old battens can survive well, but might perhaps succumb to insect attack and may be weak, and this itself can be a cause for re-roofing because entire groups of tiles may slip. In conservation work sometimes new riven native hardwoods are used again for re-roofs; hardwoods generally have not been so easy to treat against decay and so should be chosen for their innate durability. Traditional riven battens would normally be used now only where the inside of the roof was on display.

Temporary Roofs

A full re-roof or extensive repairs are likely to involve a full complement of scaffolding around a house (*see* Info pages: Safety and buildings). It is possible to strip a reasonable (smallish, cottage-size) area of roof and cover it over with roofing underlay in a single, dry summer's day. But it is not possible to guarantee the

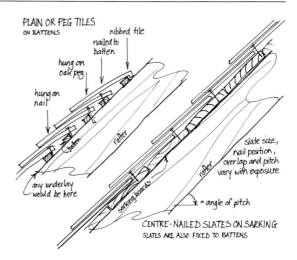

Some typical tile and slate constructions shown in cross-section.

weather and it is not possible to guarantee that there will not be hold ups due to the discovery of unforeseen problems with the roof timbers. A temporary roof over the whole house, supported on scaffolding, has become relatively affordable and could offset the labour costs of weatherproofing again at the end of each day's work.

Stripping

It is possible to sort and grade old tiles and slates for reuse without holding up the stripping process; this requires organization. Sound reusable tiles and slates are still seen being thrown into skips, but this is a sad waste of a resource, even if it may make economic sense to the contractor at the time. Even if the old roofing materials are not appropriate for reuse on the original house (maybe they were recent, not-traditional replacements) they can be of use elsewhere (*see* reuse below). For the implications of some resident bats *see* Info pages: Gardens and trees, vermin and other animals – Bats.

Underlay

Traditional Underlays

Old houses were built without roofing underlays. Before it was invented, mats of rush and straw may

Roof failing due to a mixture of broken tiles and failed tiling battens; clay peg-tiles are stripped and sorted and relaid on new battens which have been fixed over a breathable underlay.

have been used to insulate and to dissipate any incidental leaks due to wind or snow. In Scotland particularly the practice of 'sarking' a roof with loosely-butted timber boards was a precursor of underlay (the modern sheet material is sometimes called sarking felt). Slates might be fixed direct to sarking boarding, whereas clay tiles would more likely be fixed to battens over any boarding. Crucially, rush, straw and timber sarking did not interfere with the all-important 'breathing', so important to old buildings (*see* chapter 8: Damp, breathability and ventilation).

Conventional 'Black Felt'

By the 1950s it was standard practice in much of Britain to lay new roofs on a black bitumen, fabric-reinforced underlay that has been around ever since. It is a close relative to the felt used to waterproof shed roofs, and to what many in North America seem to regard as a perfectly adequate final roof finish on ordinary houses. In post-war Britain it was seen as a belt-and-braces approach that allowed houses to use lower-pitched roofs – and therefore less timber. This, also known as 'untearable felt' (though it is not that tough when compared with some modern underlays), is good at dealing with leaks from broken or missing tiles or wind-blown snow. It was adopted unquestioningly when old houses were re-roofed. It is bad at allowing air to circulate through the tiles/slates and around the roof timbers, and, by the 1980s, it was found that these roofs, if otherwise unventilated, had often suffered from dampness, condensation, mould and even decay.

If re-roofing, but leaving sound battens and existing black felt in place, then ensure full ventilation of the roof timbers and roof-space in accordance with the Building Regulations/Building Standards. This may have to be by unblocking some over-packed insulation at the eaves or by introducing discreet proprietary or purpose-designed vents, preferably in the tiles. It is possible to hold open the overlaps in black underlay by using simple pegs with the hope of increasing natural ventilation.

New 'Breathable' Underlays

Regulations were introduced to make ventilation mandatory in new roofs, and, in time, new breathable underlays were marketed, often made of 'spun' or non-woven, man-made textiles. These do not all breathe (that is, allow the passage of air and water vapour) at the same rate and it is worth pressing professional advisers and roofers to get the manufacturers to be specific on this. Other points to watch with the new underlays are: being less stiff than the old black roofing felt, the newer materials can flap audibly in the wind and some people do not find this restful – manufacturers' fixing recommendations may address this. Long-term performance when exposed to sunlight or abrasion may be implied by manufacturers' tests, but this is no comfort if experience proves otherwise: black felt used to rot in sunlight so, having these new felts overlaid by something tougher and ultra-violet resistant at the eaves to keep the sun off the crucial strip that dresses into the gutter is a cheap and worthwhile precaution. It is also worth considering belt-and-braces reinforcement immediately under ridges and valleys, where, with a professional adviser's input, it may be safe to trade breathability for waterproofness very locally.

Re-use of Slates and Tiles

An old roof that needs to be replaced now and which contains a high proportion of genuine old slates or tiles in good condition (the roof may need to be replaced because of failed nails or battens, for example) should ideally have its tiles or slates carefully sorted for reuse. Clay tiles are of standard sizes so the principal concerns are condition and colour; slates can be resized or perhaps turned over (as slate

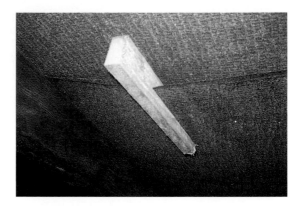

Old, 'non-breathable' felt underlay can inhibit ventilation; here timber pegs try to hold open a vent gap in an old installation; some new underlays are more breathable.

size relates to pitch, they may be reusable on a different roof if they have to be cut down). It has to be decided whether to mix the old and the replacement units all together, or assign them to separate areas out of sight of each other. Alternatively, old tiles and slates can be reapplied to lower buildings or outbuildings where any early failure would be less troublesome.

For clay tiles, modern factory-made, 'handmade' replacements have long been accepted as a satisfactory match for conservation purposes, although the standard ranges may not always approximate to the required local colours without some determined enquiries. Small local manufacturers may exist in some areas, or larger manufacturers may have leftovers of special orders. Originally, new tiles would have been brightly coloured, so, if replacing a whole roof and not matching-in, it is not strictly correct to buy tiles that are coated with a pre-weathered colour finish – they will weather naturally soon enough.

Slates are a similar story. The native British quarries that supplied the original nineteenth-century building boom have dwindled to a handful which have faced increasing competition from overseas suppliers and from substitute materials, such as concrete, asbestos cement and other fibre-reinforced cement and even recycled tyres. Original British slates are identifiable through colour and most real slate is subtly varied in colour when dry, with a recognizable not-quite-perfectly-flat surface and delicately rough-dressed edges; real slate will wear predictably and gracefully.

It used to be common practice to turn slates when re-roofing (sometimes the old staining from the overlap gives this away and turning can depend on the original nail-hole position), and slates in cities used to suffer more extreme degradation due to the type of air pollution they experienced and the proximity of particular polluters such as gas works. Slates may have suffered from condensation on their undersides, so turning them over needs to be assessed by a professional.

All roofing tiles and slates may seem surprisingly fragile for the job they do and roofing requires skill to provide just enough restraint to keep them in place, while not enough to snap them under stress. Though people do it, one should no more walk on slates and tiles than on crockery.

Salvage

Salvage is a contentious issue in conservation (*see under* Info pages: Conservation terminology, etc.) since the availability of reclaimed old building materials for sale means that an old building has been demolished or stripped, and who knows whether it could have been saved whole instead? For this reason the 'official' conservation attitude has been to nurture the regrowth of traditional crafts by specifying newly made but authentic traditional materials.

However, this is not always achievable and the pressures of planners and others to match-in seamlessly can sometimes lead even conservationists to the salvage yard.

Insulation of Awkward Sloping Ceilings

Insulating hard up against roof tiles or slates often works counter to the provision of the all-important ventilation and breathability, so the traditional insulation of ceilings (the 'floor' of the loft) is generally sensible, this also avoids heating the unused loft space. However, attic rooms of old houses are sometimes built into the roof space (like a modern chalet-bungalow). These also need to be insulated and it is sensible to look at the possibilities when re-roofing.

Sadly, insulation to modern levels often will not fit into the available space between the ceiling and the tiles or slates, so some compromise may be necessary in the amount of insulation that is possible while maintaining ventilation and breathability around it. At the time of writing, old, or at least listed, buildings can claim some exemption from the more extreme forms of alteration it would take to comply with current insulation requirements. The diagram of an attic room and text in Info pages: Sustainability – Insulation explains some of the considerations when insulating.

Re-roofing and Mess

Re-roofing makes a lot of mess. The old, broken tiles and battens may end up on the skip, but mortar dust, birds' and wasps' nests and broken bits and pieces will come to rest all over the roof insulation and ceilings and percolate down through roof hatches. Loft insulation works by having its spaces filled with air, not dust, so it pays to sheet over the roof space before repairs begin. Be sure to have the sheeting removed as part of the clean up after the work as it could impair breathability and possibly contribute to the overheating of electrical wires.

Re-thatching

Re-thatching is expensive, but, when the time comes, there is no real alternative to it. In the later part of the twentieth century thatching skills and materials were more difficult to source than in the past, and it was often permissible, even necessary, to re-thatch by using non-local materials and traditions, just for the sake of keeping some kind of thatched roof. Earlier in the century many thatched roofs had been lost as part of a continuing move to convert to slates and tiles. But now thatch is seen as an attractive asset, and is replaceable in materials approximating closely to local traditions; this is likely to be enforced by local planning laws.

As mentioned above, the three most common types of thatch in Britain are long-straw, combed wheat reed and water reed, along with heather and a few other regional specialities. During the twentieth century water reed made inroads into the geographical areas previously dominated by the straw thatches. This was because mechanized harvesters and new,

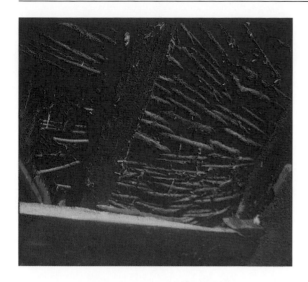

Surviving underlayers associated with original medieval thatch can display smoke blackening from pre-chimney and pre-first-floor days, an archaeological reason not to completely strip when re-thatching.

sturdy, short-stemmed, cereal crops no longer left an abundance of long straw stems in good condition and fertilizers reduced the stems' resistance to decay. Water reed was perceived to have a longer lifespan than straw. Water reed has been gathered in areas such as the Norfolk Broads specifically for thatching and so supplies remained accessible.

Unfortunately, due to different fixing techniques from those used with straw, the use of water reed in the old straw areas is potentially damaging to the archaeology of old houses: when a water reed roof is laid, all the old thatch might be stripped back to the roof timbers to secure a fixing. Straw, on the other hand, being a little lighter, was traditionally allowed to build up over time and could reach thicknesses of around a metre, while sometimes retaining, at the bottom, the very first medieval layer. That first layer might be blackened with soot which could date from the fifteenth or the sixteenth century when the house was a single internal space with no chimney, just a hole in the roof – reason enough to preserve it as a rare survival. Thatching straw is available again, specially grown, although this can sometimes mean importing it, making it less sustainable in environmental terms than if it were a by-product of the field next door. Water reed is also available from a number of sources, including traditional Norfolk and other reed beds.

Underlays or interlayers intended to act as a fire-break or provide additional insulation have come into use, but have not been around long enough in sufficient numbers to evaluate fully. There have been issues where these trap condensation and generate

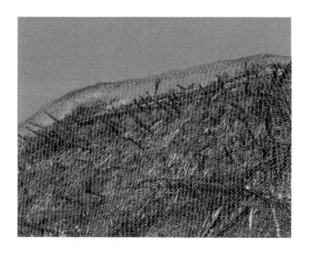

Eventually thatch loses volume, as may be seen where it parts company with any protective wire mesh.

A stack of water reed bundles, a single bundle and the bundles being placed.

decay, so their installation should consider ventilation and not just be a matter of adding a layer for good luck. Thatch owners should consider professional advice: all types of roofing need an expert in the material but thatch does especially. There is a National Council of Master Thatchers for each region and a National Society of Master Thatchers, and, as thatched houses are likely to be listed or in a conservation area, their owners should first contact their local conservation officer; the SPAB (*see* UK organizations, at end) may also offer general advice.

Old House Style and Lifestyle

From the second half of the twentieth century old houses in British towns and countryside became desirable where, only decades before, they might have been thought little better than slums (see Info pages: Conservation terminology, etc.). In recent years, a modern house for the same money could often offer more space, more convenience and promise less maintenance than a period property, nevertheless, old houses have stayed popular. For some the attraction was individuality, for others an old house was a badge of status or taste, while to many an old house conjured up an imagined idyllic past, perhaps a fitting backdrop for period-style furnishings and antiques. Owning an old house may still be a lifestyle choice but current requirements (such as sustainable living or compliance with listed building and conservation area controls) mean that the idea of 'custodianship' is gaining ground. That is, looking after the properties more as they were intended to be and preserving their interest for the future instead of dominating and altering them. Not everyone is suited to an old house and, if they are not, then it can be better for them, their pocket and old houses if they are honest about their needs and consider buying a modern house instead.

IS AN OLD HOUSE THE RIGHT CHOICE?

Probably Not if …

We are not all the same. Living in an old house can be frustrating for those who expect ancient doors to shut with airlock precision and who want everything to be straight and new. If these concerns lead to

unnecessary rebuilding, straightening, throwing away viable old components and introducing modern materials – then not only can an old house's looks and originality be lost, but its vital, inbuilt defence mechanisms against damp and movement can suffer. As well as having the potential to reduce the property's value, such work could also generate genuine defects in the future, which can easily result in a spiral of ever more inappropriate and ever more expensive, environmentally-damaging, modern remedies. And, even having done all that, there is still the potential to lie awake listening to mice, wondering if they are about to assault the wiring.

New owners of an old house will often say that

If the thought 'redecoration' comes to mind before the thought 'interesting', then an old house may not be good for you, and vice versa.

they want to 'restore it to its former glory'. The truth about many old houses is that formerly they did not have much glory. It is easy to be seduced into imagining lifestyles promoted by advertising or glimpsed in period dramas, but they are often little to do with actuality. The greater proportion of old houses were originally simple backdrops for an equally simple, often hard, way of life: they were certainly not all fitted out like stately homes, and even stately homes were a bit short on bathrooms and other luxuries. But what old houses did genuinely have was an uncomplicated, and, in most cases, accidental, 'good taste' that derived from handcrafted solutions to practical building and aesthetic problems, developed over centuries. What they never had were kitchens and multiple bathrooms full of energy-hungry appliances, nor were such utility rooms lined with materials transported from half way round the world.

Much Better if …

Old houses constitute a handmade world. Owners who make allowances for an old house's age and the standards of its period, and who actively love the slight imperfections that give character, should make a happy match with old houses. Many of the gadgets and status symbols we are pressed into incorporating in our homes are transient and will soon be superseded: owners who understand this are less likely to compromise an old house by continually readapting

it for passing fashion. There are enough enthusiasts among us with a passion for old things – cars, antiques – who ought to be able to understand that old houses need similar respect: putting PVC windows in a listed building is like putting alloy wheels on a 1920s roadster; installing halogen downlighters in a lath and plaster ceiling is like cutting a hole for computer cables in an eighteenth-century, Sheraton-style desk – upgrades maybe, but at what cost. If it is second nature not to do these things, then old house and owner should get on well. Owners also need to recognize that the general care of an old property will be different from ordinary modern maintenance: just like the need to find out what grade of oil is right for the 1920s' roadster and what type of polish is best for the desk. Vintage cars and antiques may seem exclusive items, but in terms of monetary, even historical, worth they are often way behind old houses – so why not care for old houses with the same respect?

Making Allowances

Many old houses are currently not able to provide the same level of physical performance as modern ones do, at least not without being harmfully rebuilt. This can be particularly true of thermal insulation. After carrying out all the sensible measures to reduce heat loss (*see* Info pages: Sustainability and insulation) many old houses will still require a degree of hands-

 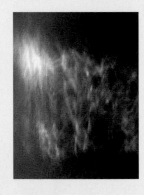

Transient effects may take months to show themselves, so take time to see what an unfamiliar house has to offer so that it may be enjoyed rather than be accidentally swept away.

on husbandry to manage the heating controls and, to police the closing of shutters and doors for warmth. And, to keep fuel use on a par with that of more modern houses, the occupants of old houses may need to accept lower temperatures and wear more clothes indoors. Why do people bother when there are modern houses that perform much better in calculations of efficiency? The answer is that the mathematics has not yet addressed the value of experiences like sunrise over an old-established garden seen through a casement of ripply old glass. If that seems to you like a reasonable trade for a few degrees off the temperature of the bedroom and a 6m hike to the bathroom, then an old house it has to be.

Make the Right Choice

If you are considering moving into an old house, does it offer adequate accommodation and facilities as it stands? If not, then it might be better to keep looking for one that does, since extensions and alterations are expensive and erode the originality – and therefore the historic value – of an old house. Most people initially want to make some modifications or carry out redecorations to suit their own circumstances and taste. It can be tempting to do this immediately and make a clean sweep of things; but it is advisable instead to live with the house (and this applies also to any garden) through all the seasons before making any irreversible changes. Like becoming accustomed to a different car, a house will have its own characteristics. There will be surprises, some of them very pleasant, some less so, and these ought to be what informs the brief for any work to be done to the house, rather than prejudices imported from another house or wish-lists generated by advertising. The way the light is scattered by uneven old window panes on an equally uneven old wall, or the patina of old polish on timber floors seen in firelight are the sorts of charming and unsuspected feature that can so easily get swept away for ever, if there is no time allowed to get to know them. And it is those sorts of thing that many owners find compensate them for any physical inconveniences.

The Romantic View

The photographs that visitors take of old houses, pretty villages or stately homes reveal a lot about

Like people, old houses may be desperately attractive; care needs to be taken that this attractiveness is not lost in pursuit of 'perfection'.

what they find attractive. Unlike media pictures of people, who are now required to look freshly-minted to be considered beautiful, old buildings can look better if they show signs of having been around a bit. Even formal, classical buildings can appear more defiantly noble where their perfection is challenged by discolouring and erosion. An old building that is too perfect can look to the modern eye like a restoration, a fake, just too sugary. This is something that the architects who care for the nation's most prized protected buildings are keenly aware of when repairing and redecorating. There is no reason why ordinary old houses should not benefit from the same type of care.

BRIEF GUIDES TO MAINTAINING OLD HOUSE STYLE

Paint for Presentation and Preservation

Old, traditional paints looked and weathered differently from the paints that have become commonplace in modern housing (*see* Info pages: Paints). Where a modern house might have a slick, 'plastic' masonry paint on its walls, an old house would have been painted with chalky limewash. Modern paint tends to have a uniform colour and uniform sheen, which may be fitting on a modern building, but limewash varies pleasantly across its soft surface, kindly disguising the lumps and cracks that an old

Limewash has a matt, gently varied surface, which can be additionally textured with fine sand and brushing; it can be good at disguising irregularities.

breathable regime and increasingly traditional, breathable paints are being marketed for use on old buildings; they can be expensive but, as they are generally quite simple products, they need not be, so shop around. Conventional modern paints are marketed in historical or period colour ranges; but it does not matter how historical the colour, if the paint is not usefully breathable then it does not belong on the walls of an old house if it will prevent them from breathing; these paints may better suit those who live in a modern house and who want some old-house style. Traditional colours reflect not only the state of development of dyes in the past, but also the qualities of the paint: limewash and distemper are based on white chalk, so most colours that are not overloading the paint with pigments naturally tend to be pastels.

house will have been built with or acquired through time. If an old house is fortunate enough to retain its original limewash it makes sense to do everything possible to preserve its benefits because, not only can lime look better, it can be allowing the old walls underneath to 'breathe', helping to preserve them against rot. Limewash, though simple enough to make, had virtually disappeared from the building trade until the recent interest in conservation revived its popularity. It can now be ordered ready-made and coloured to choice (*see* Info pages: Lime, also paints).

Internal paints too can be part of a traditional

Distressing

Applying modern finishes to old houses often went hand-in-glove with an unfortunate desire to straighten them up and smooth them over, but, at the other extreme, there was once a tendency to 'rough up' repairs to old houses to emphasize their age. Remember pubs whose stick-on beams had heavy-handed adze marks? Now that genuine traditional materials have returned along with new generations of craftsmen to use them, there is no reason to resort to distressing because the real thing usually blends in naturally and automatically.

Modern masonry paint tends to appear as a slightly glossy 'shell', now so many old houses are painted in this way.

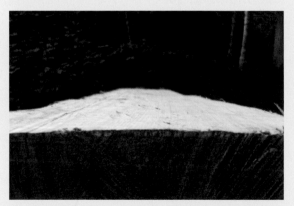

This traditionally axe-finished oak it is not dead straight, but it is a pleasing 'off-perfect' finish and is not cheesy fakery.

Knowing What to Leave

New owners of old houses are sometimes gripped with a desire to make their mark on the property and to 'sort things out'. This can range from simple redecoration to acts approaching vandalism, such as unnecessarily replacing windows and chopping down harmless trees. Even over-zealous redecoration can take away the history of a house: a Victorian front door prepared and painted to a mirror-like finish might look fine in a paint manufacturer's catalogue, but it says little about the history of the house. That door need not be left undecorated and shabby, but if, after being repainted, it still bears some evidence of a century of passing hands, baggage, keys and boots then it will continue to be history and more than just a door. As more old houses become over-restored, those that retain signs of their past life – in things such as doors, windows and floorboards – become ever more interesting.

Interiors

There is no shortage of interior design ideas from retailers and television, but that is usually a one-way process generated from afar by people who have never seen the homes they seek to influence. Rather than importing someone else's ideas, try analysing from within the home to see what, if anything, is needed. Not everyone can do this, and often an architect or designer can help, but they will need to start from within the home. Owners of old houses should remember that the physical make-up of the paints, fabrics, papers and floor finishes have the potential to help to preserve, or destroy, the house. As ever with old buildings, a key issue is understanding breathability, which, when an old house was functioning as originally intended, meant that rain, damp and condensation would not be trapped inside walls and other areas. Traditional materials worked well in this way, but some modern materials tend not to be compatible. Getting advice from professional designers who are fully attuned to the building science of conservation should help in avoiding expensive mistakes.

Houses get new roofs and windows at different times, even though they may have been built together; some manage to retain their original identity while others adopt newer fashions and materials.

Simple interiors can benefit from simple accessories.

Odds and Ends

There is an abundance of 'period-style' fixtures and fittings for the home; many are mass-produced for a worldwide market and may not suit any recognizable British period. The range of available accessories does not end at the DIY superstore and there are also specialist and one-off suppliers. Georgians and most Victorians had no electricity and so would be unlikely to recognize the square, brassy, switch plates with knobbly edges that are named after them. Very often simple is best when introducing more modern features into an old house; being honest about them saves dressing them up as fake antiques. But, if they are not to overwhelm the period feel of the house, then modern accessories do need to be discreet.

Help

We do not all consciously realize exactly what it is about old buildings that appeals to us, that is clear enough from the way people have already destroyed their home's appearance by well-meant but misguided 'improvements'. Without careful analysis, it is easy to inadvertently destroy what is best preserved and enjoyed. Technical and aesthetic guidance can be obtained from conservation professionals (*see* chapter 9: The Professionals). Britain is fortunate in having a reasonably robust system to protect its heritage of old buildings through listed buildings legislation and protected areas such as the National Parks and Conservation Areas. These recognize that appropriately preserved old buildings make a positive contribution to our quality of life, and, as so many of them have already been lost or altered beyond recognition, those that remain deserve protection. It can be useful to get the local planning department, and particularly the conservation officer, involved from an early stage in any proposals that may require official consents. It might just save the wasting of time developing an unacceptable solution, and it might even generate new design options that could produce a more satisfying result. Whether or not an old house is officially protected, an increasing awareness of conservation issues among housebuyers means that its financial value may ultimately be related to the appropriateness of the maintenance and decoration it has been given.

Two neighbouring houses, one retains its original look, the other disguises it.

CHAPTER 3

Rainwater Disposal

Rain, in Britain at least, has been the most wide-spread force for decay in old houses. By its nature, water can enter a building very easily, but, as it has to obey physical laws, it is also usually easy to predict its performance and conduct it safely away from a building. Buildings ancient and modern benefit from centuries of trial and error experience in the management of rain. Conserving rainwater for its reuse is not new, but the idea fell out of fashion in the last century as mains water was cheap and easy to tap into.

HISTORICAL PERSPECTIVE

The Route to Ground

Gutters and downpipes, now on virtually every old building, were once a luxury for the rich. The elaborate lead hoppers and pipes seen on stately homes would probably not have been present on nearby estate cottages. Thatched roofs were, in any case, difficult to provide with gutters since water drips from a wide area. In times when roads were unpaved the addition of more water cascading down from roofs was simply another reason to stay indoors. Georgian facades tamed the water flowing from roofs by collecting it behind parapets and sending it down lead pipes. Pre-gutter buildings would have had a generous overhang at the roof's eaves to throw water clear of the walls. This is why many Victorian buildings do not have overhangs, they had gutters from the start and overhangs cost money. The availability of relatively cheap, cast-iron gutters and pipes in the latter part of the nineteenth century meant that rainwater could be managed once it left tiled and slated

roofs and conducted to single points. The arrival of town drains and paved roads meant that there was some reason to conduct the water to a particular point as it could be removed from there. Iron rainwater goods were retrospectively applied to older buildings, and gutters and downpipes have been considered essential ever since.

Thatch does not deliver all the run-off water in one plane since some seeps into the thickness of the thatch; some owners of thatched buildings have tried very broad timber gutters, but few bothered.

Cast Iron Is, Often, King

Because cast iron was the first material exploited to make rainwater goods widely affordable, it quickly became associated with most old buildings. It eventually rusts unless it is thoroughly painted and it is heavy, which are big disadvantages in comparison with later materials such as plastics and aluminium. Nevertheless, cast iron is often cited as the 'correct' material for old buildings so its advantages need to be understood.

Part of the visual appeal of cast iron comes through familiarity and association – it looks right. That is probably because it is a modular system designed when engineering was still combined with art and the components were cast from sculptured moulds. There was a limited set of components and rules about how to assemble them, the discipline required to assemble something that works also produces a certain grace. Plastic and aluminium components might be manufactured to copy iron, and some have, but generally manufacturers have designed components to suit the material and so installations differ visually from iron.

Aluminium and plastic have their critics, environmentally, in that the one consumes vast amounts of energy in its manufacture while the other uses potentially harmful chemicals. Properly maintained, cast iron can outlive even plastic. Iron, having solidity, also acts to deaden the noise of running water and dripping, which can be significant in older layouts with external hoppers. Cast iron undoubtedly has acquired a visual 'rightness' on old houses, but in some situations issues of weight and any limitations on access for regular inspection and redecoration may call for some, very sensitive, localized use of modern alternatives.

MAINTENANCE

Falls

Gutters are level or have a slight fall towards the downpipe positions. Shallow, 'half-round' profile gutters tend to fall, while deeper, 'ogee' and other fancy moulded profiles tend to be level as they are usually part of the architecture. As the preferences changed over time and as old fixings can be difficult to alter, first look at putting the system that is in place in good order before tinkering with falls.

Defective rainwater goods are often the first step on the road to ruin, but preventive measures can be simple.

Joints

Gutters and downpipes are sectional and rely on sound joints to keep them watertight. The twentieth century introduced rubber-type gaskets to join gutters, but early, cast-iron ones relied upon caulks and putties that, over time, become brittle and crack. Alternatively, sections can weld themselves together with rust. Modern refurbishments of cast iron have to choose whether to leave sound (or stubborn) old joints in place and paint over them or carefully dismantle each and, having thoroughly repainted all surfaces, rejoin them with a modern silicone mastic; special formulas are designed for guttering, while downpipes, generally, rely on interlocking and gravity rather than a mastic.

Gutter Brackets and Pipe Fixings

Gutter brackets are there to stop the gutter from toppling off the building and to support its weight, not always to clamp the gutter rigidly. This applies to cast-iron, aluminium and plastic, since all move thermally. Gutters can twist and joints can fracture if thermal expansion is not allowed for. Many early iron gutter brackets simply held the gutter like a cupped hand and the gutter can sometimes, alarmingly, be lifted free with little effort. Old gutter brackets might be found screwed or nailed to real or fake rafter ends, or to fascias, or spiked direct into mortar joints in masonry walls. If brackets are made of wrought iron then they would have been malleable enough to bend once in place to fine tune the installation. Modern steel brackets are available in similar patterns to traditional iron ones (but should be galvanized or of stainless steel for durability) as well as 'rise and fall' versions that have a threaded bar to permit more subtle adjustment than bending. Rather than removing failed or redundant existing brackets it can be kinder to history to leave them in place where this is feasible and supplement them as necessary with new ones of a matching style. Gutter brackets will almost certainly have to support snow loads – perhaps a whole roof-slope's worth – as well as the inadvisable, but often unpreventable, casual use as a ladder-rest, so it is worth being generous with brackets.

Cast-iron pipes and hoppers were traditionally fixed through 'ears', either cast on to the component

Spacing rainwater goods from the wall needs a little ingenuity, but makes repainting easier and more effective.

or strapped around it. This is more elegant than some modern hangers but has two disadvantages, which can be overcome. The first is that old fixings tended to be made by driving an iron spike into the wall. These are difficult to remove and precarious to replace. It is sometimes advisable to replace them with a stainless steel screw, bolt or an expanding anchor (depending on the wall). While doing so, the other disadvantage can often be tackled: that of pipes being fixed too close to the wall for them to be repainted; introducing a spacer around the fixing bolt can solve this, but it can have a knock-on effect on any hoppers and 'swan-neck' pipes above that may need to be addressed.

Checking Cast-iron Gutters and Downpipes

If it is safe to do so, gently check whether fittings feel soundly attached (obviously not if on a ladder, nor so as to risk dislodging a heavy section of iron). If possible, check for rust between gutter-bellies and brackets. Feel behind downpipes for any tell-tale roughness indicating rust. Check inside hoppers for rust and perforations. Confirm that the caulking or mastic sealing the gutter joints appears to be water-tight. A hose or watering can provides localized and controllable simulated rain for pinpointing leaks and checking falls.

Local foundries gave their products individuality.

Further Checks for All Rainwater Goods Materials

Ensure that leaves and debris do not clog the system – blocked downpipes can be difficult to clear. A leaf-guard, a wire cage over the downpipe outlet at the gutter, might be considered if leaves are a proven problem, but the guards themselves can cause a dam in the gutter and lead to that overflowing. It depends which is going to be more of a nuisance – a blocked gutter or a blocked downpipe. Keep any gullies and traps at the foot of each downpipe flowing freely. Leaves, mud, live toads or dead rats can block these, and, if no one bothers to clear them, the water flows instead around the house's footings for years and leads to expensive repair work.

When rainwater goods first appeared the rainwater soakaway pit was born, as described for many years in detail in the Building Regulations. The very early ones, before the regulations, could be little more than a remarkably optimistic, small, clay pot. If an old house has downpipes that simply disappear into the ground, with no hint of where the water ends up, it can be worthwhile gently digging around to see whether underground pipes are involved and where they go.

Repairing Cast Iron

Although there were individual manufacturers' variations, cast iron settled down into a generally cross-compatible series of components, aided by a British Standard. Builders became adept at 'fudging' joints between any different cross-sections they found, and the owner of an old house needs to be prepared to find that wood may form some critical elements of their guttering – stop-ends are a favourite. Obviously each situation needs to be assessed on its merits but, with a little ingenuity, worn out botches can often be replaced with more intelligently designed repairs that we might call 'pragmatic adaptations'. Where a long-discontinued, decorative gutter section has broken above the waterline it might be reinstated with a glass-fibre-reinforced epoxy filler, perhaps assisted by a bolted metal strap. More serious repairs to irreplaceable components that have to carry water need to be referred to a specialist metalworker, who might be able to bolt, braise or even weld a repair. Such repairs might be made watertight but cannot always be load-bearing and so might need additional support; they cannot take the weight of ladders. One of the weaknesses of cast iron in good condition is that it appears strong enough to lean a ladder against, and so generations of decorators, roofers, aerial installers and window cleaners have done just that. Apart from the fact that this is dangerous because the gutter brackets were probably designed only to support the weight of a gutter, cast iron is relatively brittle and sections can snap off.

Repainting Cast Iron

Preparation

It is not always possible to take down a complete run of cast-iron guttering successfully. This is because the mastic, or rust, securing old joints may be very thoroughly seized and rusted bolts securing each joint invariably have to be cut off. Cast iron can be quite brittle and requires careful handling. Sometimes gutters and downpipes have become inadvertently built in to the house, perhaps becoming embedded into render. Leaving cast iron attached to walls and brackets will mean that it will not be possible to paint those surfaces in contact with the house and that they will eventually rust through – joints and bracket-to-gutter contact points being weak areas. A view has to be taken on whether it is better to risk destroying part of the installation, or the building, by its removal or whether it can sensibly be left until another round of decorations becomes necessary before dismantling it. The answer depends upon such factors as the consequences of failure and the difficulties of access, and so they have to be assessed on a case by case basis.

Ideally, every component should be dismantled and laid out for stripping and repainting; this includes all iron-to-iron contacts and the insides of gutters and hoppers (it is not practicable to paint inside downpipes). There are many opinions on the best specification for repainting cast-iron rainwater goods and many traditional specifications have fixed

themselves into habit. The following is a summary of just one system that has worked well, but decisions have to be made on what is found at any particular building.

Since iron does not have to breathe, it is one of the few aspects of old houses where conventional, modern, non-permeable paints can be used to advantage. Added to which modern metal primers offer some chemical protection against rust. It is preferable to strip an entire component back to bare metal to expose any corrosion under the paint, but this may not be feasible because the old paint may be toxic (lead) or historically interesting (evidence of past colours). Therefore stripping the component to bare metal may have to be limited to where the paint is already damaged and not adhering well. Appropriate precautions should be taken against lead inhalation and contact (*see* Info pages: Paint, etc.).

Any sound paint that remains needs to be adequately keyed by sanding (roughened, so that the

Building iron downpipes into walls may sometimes seem unavoidable but it risks trouble.

new paint sticks) and confirmed as compatible with new coats – ask the manufacturer of the new paint. It used to be normal to coat the insides of gutters with bituminous paint and any remains of this need to be thoroughly removed as it can peel and trap damp if it was badly applied. It is also important to ensure that the backs of hoppers are well prepared for repainting. Rust can be chemically neutralized with special gels or liquids, used in accordance with their manufacturers' directions. Bare metal is primed with a specialist protective metal primer (zinc-based) in at least two coats, followed by two coats of micaceous iron oxide (MIO) paint on all painted surfaces. MIO is a thickening intermediate coat that is available as a smooth top weathering coat or in a rougher finish that may be used under further coats of decorative gloss, as MIO comes in only a limited range of colours. Several coats of glossy MIO can be used as a finish inside gutters and hoppers for smooth-running, as well as on the backs of hoppers.

All cleaned and repaired inner and outer surfaces of guttering and hoppers, and outer surfaces of downpipes, should now be completely covered in two coats of MIO paint over sound, well-primed and rust-free metal. This ought to be a reasonable standard of protection against the elements in normal domestic exposures, so, depending on the circumstances of the installation, the visible areas can receive a top coat or two of the decorative colour either before or after any re-fixing to the building. It is important to make good accidental damage to the paint film after re-fixing. If this work has been done thoroughly then, at the next redecoration cycle, it may be necessary only to freshen up the top gloss coat to revitalize the colour, having repaired any chips or rust locally according to the original system above. Too thick a build up of paint may suffer from thermal movement of the iron: it is more important to keep any bare metal protected than to keep repainting over sound paint.

The chemical make-up of paints is being changed by regulation to move away from 'volatile organic compounds' (VOCs) linked with human irritation and environmental damage. This might come to affect the availability or performance of the paint system described above. Selecting paint from a manufacturer offering technical back-up enables the user to ask questions about the compatibility of coats with each other, with the background and with the environment in which the paint is to function.

If a building has for some time had only the visible areas of cast-iron guttering painted then it is likely that the edges of the paint will have come unstuck and curl back from any inadequately prepared rear surfaces. The weakest areas, such as the backs of downpipes and gutter-belly to bracket interfaces, will have been untouched and will be at risk of rust and failure. Cast iron has the potential to last a very long time indeed, but it has to be sensibly maintained otherwise it will need to be replaced. It is probably a false economy to opt for a quick decorative job in any circumstances since a thorough job could have more than twice the protective lifespan.

OPTIONS FOR SUSTAINABILITY

See chapter 7: Building services – Water management, harvesting rainwater and recycling.

Gardens and Trees, Vermin and Other Animals

As with an old house, it makes sense for a new owner to live with a mature garden through all the seasons to get to know it before wading in with spade and loppers. Gardens have a great potential to surprise and, with old-established, even neglected, ones there are often interesting clues from the past waiting to be rediscovered.

TREES

Sadly, trees are frequently feared and perceived as threatening to upset foundations and drains with their roots, or to fall down and destroy houses. While it is true that trees can occasionally present a hazard and that some combinations of position, ground conditions and species are more likely to cause trouble than others, there are nevertheless very many trees that have co-existed with buildings for many years without a problem. Local authorities usually have the services of a tree officer or landscape officer who can advise on specific situations. One issue with trees is leaf fall, which can block gutters and down-pipes; this does not have to come just from adjacent trees as leaves are carried on the wind (*see* chapter 3: Rainwater disposal).

Trees are automatically protected in certain situations: in Conservation Areas, for example, a tree with a trunk diameter of more than 75mm at 1500mm from the ground is automatically protected and may not be felled nor even pruned without permission (check with the local authority for the full current details of this and for direction to any further rules for houses in Areas of Outstanding Natural Beauty, National Parks and other protected areas). Individual protection – from Tree Preservation Orders – may exist to provide spot protection for specimen or

An old house rarely stands in complete isolation and a building can often coexist with a tree for a long time. Shade might be useful if climate change is severe.

important trees, perhaps where other protective measures do not exist (again, the local authority should have maps of these). It makes sense to consult the local authority to obtain their advice, not only on any protected status, but, if they can help, on the best way to care for a tree. Trees can be damaged during building work by the compacting of the soil over their roots, vehicle movements, tearing branches, changing drainage by the installing of patios or decking and by excavating trenches. A British Standard (BS/EN standards and codes can be inspected at public libraries) covering tree protection during building works exists to guide contractors. It is better to look after a tree and to have a healthy one close by rather than a sick one. There is a difference between the skills involved in felling trees and in pruning them so that they continue to flourish; the Arboricultural Association (www.trees.org.uk) may be able to help householders to select a qualified tree surgeon.

Just as building societies used to have a blanket fear of lending on properties without a damp-proof course, so some insurers find it easier to assume automatically that trees are trouble without assessing the actual risks on site. It is important to remain properly insured, yet it is also irresponsible to fell trees on an ill-considered whim, especially as the sudden removal of a long-established tree will most likely alter ground conditions for the house and that may itself adversely affect its foundations. Trees that are so old that they have become hollow in the middle are sometimes assumed to be dying or rotten, when this is merely a natural phase in their life: the condition ought certainly be monitored and drawn to the attention of a council expert or a responsible tree surgeon, but they might nevertheless pronounce the tree fit. Trees absorb carbon dioxide and provide the planet with oxygen; to be sustainable we need more of them, not fewer. If planting new trees, consider their impact when they are fully grown and allow plenty of space around them.

GARDENS

Many rural gardens attached to old houses were used for subsistence crops as well as flower growing, and this habit was imported into town gardens in the early twentieth century as former agricultural workers moved to urban areas. Grander old houses would also have grown fruit and vegetables, perhaps in a kitchen garden that was walled to keep out frost and rabbits, alongside space devoted to flowers and ornamental trees and shrubs. It can be possible to trace the outlines of former paths and beds, and some enthusiastic owners find it satisfying to grow only the varieties of plant that were available when their house was built, though in fact gardens would have developed over the years, absorbing new varieties as they became fashionable.

Larger gardens may have supported some fruit

Timber, cast and wrought iron gates; the step under the iron gate consists of stable blocks, a traditional slip-resistant paving that is still available.

trees, sometimes specially trained along walls to make the best of the sun's heat. Greenhouses have long been a way to modify the British climate to enable exotic crops such as pineapples, peaches, oranges and melons to be produced and long before they could be imported. The gardens of old houses are likely to contain some rudimentary archaeological remains of old greenhouses, privies, garden frames, compost heaps and rubbish burials. Some houses will have been built on the site of much older settlements and the local authority may keep records of neighbouring finds and perhaps be able to give advice on what to look out for when digging or excavating in the garden. Even without the aid of special surveys it is sometimes possible to see signs of former paths or buildings showing on a lawn after a dry spell.

Garden Walls

Garden walls are just as much part of an old house as the building itself. Sometimes, in the case of large rural properties, they have been left standing while the house itself could have been rebuilt long ago, thus the garden wall would be older than the house. In towns, old walls could mark the extent of a former plot that was later subdivided to provide space for several houses. The boundary walls of a listed property would normally be expected to fall within the listing, and walls may also be protected within Conservation Area and National Park boundaries, for example. Brick and stone walls that are very old can incorporate twists, and lean without cracking because they were built with movement-tolerant lime mortar (*see* Info pages: Movement in old houses) and probably on footings that consist of a few courses of masonry only a few inches wider than the wall itself. The same cautions apply to old garden walls as to old house walls if they are built with lime mortar: it would be a mistake to repoint them in cement (*see* chapter 4: External walls) and, if they are leaning or in need of repair, a conservation professional may be able to save and stabilize a wall, sparing the waste and expense of demolition and rebuilding.

Lime mortar meant that long walls could be constructed without bothering with the expansion joints that are required with modern, relatively brittle, cemented brickwork. In areas with a dry stone wall tradition, repairs to walls may need a local

The 'crinkle-crankle' wall uses lime's mobility and clever design to economize on bricks, as this is only 100mm thick.

craftsman to keep local walling variations alive (Dry Stone Walling Association: www.dswa.org.uk). While mature trees can live in harmony with a wall, it is probably better not to tempt fate and allow saplings to become established too close to walls.

This is the back view of some ivy removed from a brick wall; it has peeled off a skin of brick and mortar; ivy may look attractive but the surface of the wall will be affected.

Dry stone walling is a skill that survives.

Fences, Hedges and Ditches

Like walls, fences and hedges may be affected by Listed Building status, Conservation Areas and other designated areas. Traditionally, fences were appropriate to their location, and their construction reflected whether they were decorative or to keep out intruders or just livestock. A split chestnut fence or a vertical paling fence have become accepted as low-key rural and village fences, which can be supplemented by the garden plants behind. In towns, low masonry walls have long been used in conjunction with hedges or railings. Some shrubs are prickly enough to deter intruders. Painted fences need maintenance and hedges need regular trimming. The Hedgerows Regulations (1997, but may soon be reviewed) may apply in certain areas and, in a rural district, it would be a pleasant idea to try to re-establish local hedgerow varieties in a new hedge; the council arboricultural officer may be able to give householders guidance. Traditional hedge boundaries often had ditches alongside them, these may come under the control of the Environment Agency.

Gates

The wealth that has been applied to previously self-effacing old houses sometimes shows externally in a set of electrically-operated, welded steel gates that owe more to Beverly Hills than British traditions. Larger old houses may have once run to elaborate wrought-iron vehicle gates, but the majority of even quite large old houses may have had simple timber gates. Timber gates may be electrically operated too. By Victorian times small pedestrian gates were common in timber, wrought and cast iron (for repair and decoration notes *see* chapter 5: Doors and windows and Info pages: Paints. etc).

The Plot as Setting for a House

It is not just the old house itself that deserves special care. Its setting too should enhance the house. Some old houses belong on city streets and others in gardens, in either case the 'feel' of the landscaping is important. Too much hard, flat landscaping around a building can look like a car park. Perhaps it is actually necessary to park cars there, but there are many ways, gravel is one, to provide hard standing without sealing over the ground and sending rainwater into drains to overload them rather than to let it naturally replenish the water table by seeping into the ground.

Hard pavement surfaces too close to a house can trap damp against walls and cause rain to splash back up the walls as well. Soil or paving that is too high up the wall can also introduce unwelcome damp or block air vents intended to keep the internal voids dry. Paving, inclines or embankments that direct water

Field gates were once locally produced in timber with distinct designs in each region of the country; Common Ground has details www.commonground.org.uk.

against house walls will also accentuate dampness and some of these situations might be remedied quite simply by a variation of the French drain (*see* chapter 8: Damp, breathability and ventilation), provided that it is designed to discharge any water it traps away from the house.

Lighting

Lighting tends to be installed both for amenity and security (*see* chapter 7: Building services). Old houses in the country were built and used when artificial light was so poor that the moon determined many people's social lives. There are plenty of subtle, low-energy fittings that can enable the low-level lighting of dark areas instead of stark floodlighting. There are some genuine historical precedents for external lighting that pre-date the reproduction Victorian lamposts and coach-lamps of the 1970s, and a visit to the stable block of a stately home or village in the care of a conservation organization might provide some useful inspiration.

VERMIN OR PROTECTED SPECIES?

In terms of the wild animals frequently associated with buildings, rats, mice, rabbits and grey squirrels are considered verminous, while nearly all wild birds, all bats and several other wildlife species are protected. Even those old houses without timber floors immediately over soil may offer plenty of other access routes to outdoor creatures.

Rats and Mice

Rats and mice might be discouraged from rooms by electronic high-frequency noise generators, available from hardware shops, but neither these nor the more effective domestic cat, can get at them very well when under floors or inside walls. Mice can be small enough to fit though the holes drilled in joists, beams and studwork walls to admit electric wiring: the mouse who finds the hole just a little too small, or wants to sharpen its teeth, can gnaw through the plastic insulation, expose the live conductor and cause a short circuit and possibly a house fire. Installing appropriate circuit-breakers at the main consumer unit (*see* Info pages: Safety and building – Electrical safety) can turn

Strictly, it is illegal to handle bats. This one had to be quickly covered by a ventilated box, with the use of precautionary thick gloves, when it fell to the floor, still asleep in front of the cat; the local authority or Bat Conservation Trust can offer guidance on what to do next.

off the power speedily when certain faults are detected and this might reduce the risk of fire. Once a cable has been damaged it has to be traced for repair; be prepared for some disruption in uncovering cables in an old house. Rats, being bigger, can cause more damage and, while amateur traps and poisons are available, rats are considered a public health issue, so it is also appropriate to approach the local council for advice. Field mice, browner and more doey-eyed than house mice, sometimes enter rural homes singly; 'humane' traps allow their return to the wild.

Bats

Bats are frightening to some but can have the redeeming feature of purring when attached to a human (though handling them can be an offence and is inadvisable in case they are ill). Several different species may live in houses, and bats are much smaller than they look with wings outstretched in flight. They can access surprisingly tiny cracks around doorways or gaps between roof tiles at dare-devil speed, in the dark, with their famed echo-location. Fond of roof-spaces in old buildings, a bat colony can cause a temporary halt to building work to permit them to go about producing the next generation undisturbed. The bats do not enforce this themselves, it is done by the statutory Nature Conservation organizations (Natural England, The Countryside Council for Wales, Scottish Natural Heritage) as it is illegal to disturb or kill bats. The Bat Conservation Trust has information about the legislation and the varieties of bat that can be seen on www.bats.org.uk.

Birds and Squirrels

Birds and squirrels can be a nuisance in roof spaces, taking liberties with the loft insulation. Squirrels might chew wiring. It can be an offence to disturb most species of nesting wild birds, whereas grey squirrels, though cute, are regarded as vermin. Red squirrels are specifically protected as an endangered native species. Old houses were rarely built in a way that closed up the eaves thoroughly, and, as these gaps also provide useful ventilation, a practical compromise is to find a way of securing chicken wire as unobtrusively as possible across the openings. House martins can make an unhygienic mess under their otherwise ecologically-sound mud dwellings in the eaves. The Royal Society for the Protection of Birds (rspb.co.uk) offers suggestions for dissuading birds from nesting in critical locations. These measures need to be carried out well before the nesting season since all nests and their contents are protected by law. Wild pigeons have dropped in popularity from communal urban pets and rural pie-fillings to their present image as disease-carrying, aerial vermin; however, a licence is needed to dispose of them. Large public buildings seem more susceptible to feral

A wild bee swarm can gain entry through a small crack.

pigeon infestation than individual houses: netting and fine bristles are frequently installed to keep them off. An ingenious solution used in the USA is to install an artificial bird of prey to scare off nuisance birds. Presumably even a pigeon's brain can work out that a plastic predator is not a threat, but it seems worth a try.

Bees and Wasps

Wild bees, wasps and hornets can find old houses compelling nesting places. Wasps that cannot be ignored are usually despatched unceremoniously, sometimes local councils still offer this service. Bee swarms might be attractive to amateur or professional bee-keepers if they are reasonably accessible for capture, and it is better that their honey should be collected rather than trickle down cavities in roofs and walls. Bees were traditionally kept in many gardens from the Middle Ages well into the twentieth century, and with bee populations reportedly under stress due to disease or some aspect of the modern world, kindnesses done to bees now may benefit the future of our eco-system as they not only provide honey but are part of the mechanism for providing our fruit, vegetables and flowers.

Nests can cause a mess, such as this beneath some house martins, but it is illegal to disturb nesting birds.

CHAPTER 4

External Walls

HISTORICAL PERSPECTIVE

Walls have been just as much influenced by Britain's varied geology as have roofing materials. All types of stone, earth and clay have been pressed into service for house-building over time and, where the ground could not provide a material, then the trees, wild plants and crops that grew on it could be used. Stone and brick buildings tend to last, whereas many crude timber or unfired clay and earth houses have not survived to be counted. Timber is quicker to work than masonry, so it is likely that the earliest settlers would have used wood for their houses even if stone were close by. Areas with few trees would have had to reserve them for roof construction as nothing else would really do, so those people would have had to work harder for their walls.

Later, measures such as preserving forests for building ships or hunting may have influenced a shift towards stone and brick. By the Middle Ages stone was certainly available outside its home areas, but at a price that only the builders of churches and large fortified houses could afford. For everyday, vernacular buildings the local materials were almost always used – hence the presence of stone churches in the middle of otherwise all timber-framed villages.

The characteristic regional building shapes and details are determined by how the materials had to be put together and the lessons learnt, by trial and error over hundreds of years, about how the materials weathered and could be made to last: The mud-walled cob cottages of south-west England owe their chunky, rounded outlines and overhanging thatched roofs to the limitations and demands of mud building. The jettied timber-framed houses of much of England derive their shapes and framework design from the structural capabilities of wood. In parts of the country without stone or abundant timber the early necessity to develop brick, and with it roof tiles, has resulted in the sharper, modular patterns of brick-work building. The width, depth and height of houses were all determined by the structural spans possible in the timber floor beams and roofs, as well as the solidity of the wall materials supporting them. The pitch of the roofs in different areas was, in turn, a result of the ability of the roofing material used to shed water. Brick or stone houses were routinely built with solid walls, that is, without a cavity between an outer 'leaf' of masonry and an inner one (of concrete block, say) as for many modern houses. Cavities were introduced (gradually from about the beginning of the twentieth century) as a means to keep dampness

Traditional materials ageing gracefully.

Geology and landscape generate local building styles.

from internal wall surfaces, and it is counter to this idea to think of filling them up with anything that will allow damp to be transmitted to the inner leaf of the wall.

STONE

Britain has some fine building stones, but imagine taking a rough lump of stone and having to chip at it with hand tools to make it perfectly straight, smooth and square? Multiply that hundreds or thousands of times to build a house and this explains why it is

Small stones often appear in mortar (with regional names such as galleting and pinning-stones); these are either structural – helping to balance large stones – or decorative; some believed that they kept out evil; so there is no reason to remove them.

mainly expensive mansions and churches that used labour-intensive, dressed stone. Ordinary houses often made do with the sort of rocks and rubble that were left over from local quarries or found lying about in fields (or perhaps remainders of a dissolved monastery or a redundant castle). The quality and colours of British stones vary greatly, as do their properties; the broader categories are outlined below. The properties of stone – hardness, texture, colour, durability – can vary greatly within each category and local areas will have their own body of knowledge and reference that applies more directly. The local authorities' conservation officers would be useful starting points in any enquiry and there is very thorough analysis of the country's geology available from academic and scientific sources, including, naturally, the British Geological Survey.

Chalk, Flint and Limestone

Both chalk and limestone are formed principally of calcium carbonate (chalk being the softer version because it has fewer 'impurities'), and both have long been important not only as building stone but as raw material for making lime for building mortars. The rock is believed to have been laid down as deposits in early, shallow seas millions of years ago and contains the remains of tiny shelled sea creatures.

Chalk belongs principally to the south and the east of England, often too soft for building, it could contain flints. Composed of very hard silica, flint is totally different from the chalk that bears it. Flint has been assumed also to have originated from the remains of early sea creatures. Where the chalk was too crumbly for building the chalk-bearing counties of England resorted to rubble walls of flint and – when there was time and money – squared, cut flints as a decorative veneer.

Limestone is a more robust building stone than chalk. Many of the English quarries are concentrated in an arc approximately from the River Severn in the south-west sweeping up towards the Wash in Lincolnshire but missing it and veering towards the River Tyne in the north-east.

Chalk tends to be white and limestones range from white through yellows and browns. Portland stone and Bath stone are limestones. Marble, according to its strict geological definition, barely occurs in Britain but some native limestones are hard enough to be polished to look the same.

Sandstone

Like chalk and limestone, sandstone was formed by deposition, but in even earlier seas, and the principal component is silica or quartz – the same material as loose sand. Just as chalk is effectively strengthened by the presence of impurities, so sandstones may be stronger or weaker according to the other materials present. Clays, iron compounds and chalks are some of those useful 'impurities' and they also act to colour the sandstone. Sandstones have been quarried extensively in the central band of Scotland from the River Clyde to the Firth of Forth, at the very northern tip of Scotland, in central and southern Wales and in England west of the arc of limestone quarries

Chalk, being soft, is built cradled between brickwork; flints and field stones also use brickwork to keep them in place.

Flint: random, knapped and squared.

described above, that means much of northern England as well as central Devon. Also the North and the South Downs in south-east England.

Some sandstones, and some limestones too, split quite thinly along natural beds and so can be used for stone roofing slates (these are quite chunky and are not dressed so squarely nor split so thinly or smoothly as the more common grey/blue/green roofing slates so popular from the nineteenth century).

Sandstone varies in usefulness and colour according to its composition and the way it was formed. Colours range from yellow or grey, through browns to red. York stone is a popular name for a class of sandstones found in that county.

Slate

The common, smooth, roofing slate was once clay, the fine grains of which have been compressed into layers over time and then, at some point, subjected to even greater pressures (hence it is called a 'metamorphic' rock) to produce a very dense stone that obligingly splits into thin sheets, is reasonably waterproof and can be dressed precisely and punched cleanly with holes for fixing. Scotland (broadly, south and east of the line of the Caledonian Canal), Cumbria,

north Wales and Cornwall are among the most prolific historical producers of roofing slates, but there were other areas in the country.

Each area, according to its geology, could produce different colours, so Cumbrian slates are noted for being bluish or a distinctive almost verdigris green, while Welsh slates are famously an almost iridescent purple-grey that appears uniformly black when wet; many of the Welsh slates cleave thinner and smoother than other varieties. In its native areas slate has been used for building walls and was not confined to roofs (*see also* chapter 2: Roofs).

Granite and Volcanic Rocks

At two extremities of the British Isles, north-east Scotland (around Aberdeen) and south-west England (Devon and Cornwall) granite was commercially exploited, most intensively at the time of the building of nineteenth-century cities worldwide. In vernacular building the igneous rock granite, and its cousins the volcanic rocks, were exploited as they were found: principally in the highland landscapes formed by these hard, resistant rocks in Scotland, Northern Ireland, northern England, Wales, Devon and Cornwall.

ABOVE: *Rough and smooth sandstone.*

LEFT: *Limestone.*

ABOVE: A former Scottish slate quarry.

RIGHT: Aberdeen granite.

THE REPAIRING OF STONE

The hardest rocks – granite, slate and some sandstones, for example – are very resistant to most of the use that centuries of good or bad maintenance can deliver. With stone generally, badly cracked stones can be cut out and replaced if this is structurally necessary. Removing old cement pointing is sometimes difficult as it can damage the face of the stone, particularly the softer ones.

As with other aspects of the repairing of old buildings, a first question should be: is repair really necessary? Aesthetic grounds are not necessarily a valid reason for the disturbance and expense of replacement, and one person's 'worn ugly' is another's 'worn characterful'. However, with stones that have lost their function through wear – perhaps those intended as 'drip-moulds' to throw water clear of other stone faces below, it would be sensible to repair or replace them if they were no longer fulfilling their function, so putting larger areas at risk.

Softer stones – chalk, limestones and many sandstones – may suffer from being waterlogged, and then from freeze–thaw action which can fracture stone along the natural layers within its structure. Though building stones were selected and used for their durability, in time – much longer for some rocks than

Surface erosion on limestone.

73

Sandstone varies from soft to very durable; the erosion of soft stone opens cavities and accentuates the geological bedding planes.

others – the natural 'cements' that bind their constituent granules together can fail and the surface of the stone turn to powder.

Dressed stone looks worse, when worn, than rough stone, and if replacing a badly weathered piece of ashlar (smooth-faced and squared stone) there could be the problem of whether to align the new

In time, severe erosion removes the original face line; when that has happened, should any single replacement stones that become necessary match the eroded surface or reinstate the original face line?

face with the surrounding weathered stones or to replace it as it was when new, so that, in time, all the faces might be replaced and line up as originally. There is no correct answer to this, each case has to be judged on its merits. When replacing stone it is not simply a matter of sourcing the same geological type of stone, though that is the first hurdle; the properties of otherwise similar stones vary from quarry to quarry and factors such as relative strength and the orientation of the bedding plane of sedimentary rocks are relevant to future performance.

Lime-based Shelter Coats

Limestone walls, whether dressed or random, can be usefully protected from erosion, or consolidated if they are already suffering, with a shelter coat. Shelter coats range from simple limewash (*see* Info pages: Paints, etc.) with powdered stone added to match for colour (the fallen, weathered remnants might contribute to this) to more sophisticated lime-based mixes with additives such as casein (a derivative of milk) to bind them and increase their staying power. Since limewash itself dries to a composition that is effectively the same as limestone then the basic mix is very compatible. Supposed to have a fairly short life of only a couple of years, limewash has been known to survive in excess of five even in a coastal location (*see* photograph), but limewash is not universally suitable for all stone types.

'Plastic' Repairs

Although 'plastic' here might be confused with the noun describing the ubiquitous modern materials, the word plastic here is actually the older adjective meaning 'malleable'. Traditional 'plastic repairs' to stone simply comprised a lime-mortar based filling (in the case of limestone) which, like dentistry, made good the surface of the stone when it had become too decayed or worn. Sometimes these would involve an inner 'armature' (now stainless steel wire might be used, for example) to retain the 'filling'. A traditional lime-mortar plastic (non-synthetic) repair can often provide a way to fill and repair some of the functions of a stone as a better or intermediate option to cutting out and replacing it. It may be coloured to match by using stone dust, selected coloured sands or natural earth pigments.

Plastic repairs that use cement, real plastic or other chemical synthetics have been tried but are generally perceived to be less kind to the stone (*see* chemical interventions, below) and conservation opinion tends to be wary of these treatments because they can be too impermeable, too hard and ultimately damaging. Even lime mortar may not be suitable for repairs to some stone types, despite being the preferred medium for mortar joints.

Chemical and Other Interventions

The twentieth century came up with various water-repellents, cements, chemical consolidants and synthetic 'plastic repairs' for stone. Like many of that century's ideas for old buildings they seemed fine in

An example of a fairly obvious practical 'plastic' repair to some engineering masonry, but lime-based plastic repairs may be almost unnoticeable if done well.

theory at the time but have not always been a success when viewed with hindsight. The serious conservationist is unlikely to regard these techniques as a first or even second option in most cases now. Once the natural composition of stone has been changed its future weathering behaviour is difficult to predict and sometimes the side effects of these interventions have been unsatisfactory, particularly in terms of affecting the colour. A common cause for concern is that the introduction of unsympathetically impermeable solutions, patches or coatings can trap water inside the stone and simply accelerate the natural processes of decay from within.

Cracks and Cramps

Cracks should be inspected before repairing to decide what caused them and whether replacing the stone or carrying out a plastic repair would simply result in a new crack. One possible cause of cracking is the rusting of iron cramps. Before the relatively recent availability of galvanized and, far better, stainless steel, iron was introduced into pockets in stone to form connectors or to act as cramps to repair cracked stones or to hold stones in difficult locations. If thoroughly set in molten lead, these iron members might have survived without problems but they can become exposed to water and rust, the rust expands and 'blows' apart the stone that the cramps were supposed to strengthen.

Lime-based, shelter coat successfully protecting a random limestone wall in a coastal location.

Repointing

The rules that apply to brickwork (*see below*) about selecting mortars that are not too hard, and about not sealing up walls with modern paints and cement renders apply equally to stone. Even granite is porous to an extent, while super-hard flint seems to prefer being bedded in a relatively mobile mortar such as lime rather than being gripped by unyielding cement. As with brickwork, it can pay to make mortar 'sacrificial' since its job in traditional construction is to absorb movement and allow out moisture. Mortars have to be 'weaker' than the stone to do this, but at least they can be replaced when they fail. Mixing up a strong cement mortar is not a recipe for making the wall last longer, it will most likely hasten its demise instead.

The Repairing of Flint Walls

Building a flint wall is a balancing act and, with rounder flints, it would be tempting to believe that the original wall must have been cast inside shuttering rather than being assembled by piling flints on top of each other. What is certain is that the original builders would have proceeded slowly enough to allow the lower levels to set firm before much weight was put on top of them.

With poor foundations and no expansion joints, old flint walls benefit from the mobility of lime mortar to stay together without cracking. Mistaken cement repairs can stiffen up some parts unhelpfully and either cause the wall to crack or the repair patch to drop off in time. Repairing a 'blown' hole in a flint wall requires skill, patience and the right mortar for

Discreet, original-style pointing.

Discreet, modern pointing.

Modern 'weathered' pointing in cement that tends to upstage the stone, and may help the stone to erode.

Modern cement 'strap' pointing; this probably took more effort to achieve than discreet, slightly recessed lime pointing that would have also been kinder to the stone.

Apart from having lost the pattern of the flints, this repair patch is cracking around its edge, apparently because its mortar is incompatible with the original.

Cleaning Stone

Another stain on the twentieth century: stone cleaning was embarked upon right from the time that our cities were free from soot pollution. Techniques could be quite aggressive and abrasive, sometimes introducing chemicals to clean or attempt to consolidate. But as well as having dirt removed, the stone could be left permanently discoloured or deprived of detail, and even roughened to the extent that it went on to attract lichen growth or became vulnerable to water ingress and decay.

It is true that there are now remarkably gentle and effective ways to clean stonework, but the legacy of the late twentieth century is many stone buildings that are stained or suffering advanced decay as a result of inappropriate cleaning or simply as a result of having lots of cleaning water pushed into their walls. The drive to clean stone in the first place was no doubt pride in a fine building combined with a horror of dirt. These two emotions have been responsible for much other damage to old buildings; the misunderstanding here was that, along with the unfortunate soot staining, the surface of the stone may also have created its own protective skin over time. The blasting, abrasion, flushing and chemical intervention of cleaning have been held responsible for removing that protection and leaving buildings cleaner, but more vulnerable.

Technology may yet deliver innovative and less harmful ways to remove dirt from stone, but the lessons of the past suggest that it is wise to let others do the experimenting. A reasonably safe method that can be tried on an inconspicuous area is brushing with nothing more abrasive than a natural bristle scrubbing brush, using minimal water. A step up from this, favoured currently by some conservation organizations, is a proprietary process involving superheated water delivered, in trained hands, very controllably. Cleaning can be targeted to try to tone down the worst stains and to avoid vulnerable areas – it need not be a full-scale assault. It would be wise to check whether the building had been cleaned previously and by what method, since chemical stains from old, inappropriate methods might not now be removable and new attempts to clean may be incompatible or weaken the surface. So seriously do the authorities view the mistakes of the past that listed building or conservation area consents are normally involved for stone cleaning; in order to check contact the local conservation officer.

BRICK

Bricks are still made in relatively small-scale brickworks, but the majority of modern building bricks are made in large factories, using clays dug from deep pits. Old bricks, from the earliest times up to the Industrial Revolution, would have been made from shallower deposits of clay and very often close to the building site. Shallower clay is less compacted and has been leeched of salts by weathering. That, along with differences in firing, can produce a different, 'softer' brick from modern versions. Up to the 1930s in England houses were still being built with bricks from on-site brick kilns, though by that time centralized brick factories and rail transport will have been responsible for the great majority of the bricks used. Isolated brick houses, such as farmhouses, might still have an adjacent pond or pit visible, marking where the brick-earth was dug. Many locations retain names recalling brick fields or kilns. Differences in local clay account for whether a brick is red, yellow or nearly white, but, from the nineteenth century, bricks were

A fingernail can make an impression on lime mortar in sound, old brickwork, but that does not necessarily mean that it has failed, it is simply doing its job, being the 'sacrificial element' in brickwork.

Cement was used when repointing this wall; now the bricks have become the sacrificial element.

also made from other materials and these (often firing yellow or grey) would need to be identified before repair or matching. *See also* Bricks and mathematical tiles, under Timber Frame, below.

Bricks and Mortar

The pre-industrial, fired clay brick can be softer and more porous than its modern day counterpart. Perhaps the majority of old brick houses are built with straightforward fired clay bricks, but since the Industrial Revolution there have been more variations of clay brick available as well as some alternative materials to clay. Bricks function together with their mortar as brickwork so it is necessary that the bricks are in balance with the mortar. Traditional wisdom states that the mortar should be slightly weaker than the brick, in that way the brick is retained intact in the event of any movement and the mortar is less likely to trap water and water-borne salts in the brick (which can soften the brick or cause frost or crystallization damage). Old, soft, clay bricks laid in lime mortar have been a perfect combination. The fact that old walls have twisted and distorted without the bricks snapping shows how lime mortar is kind to brick.

Because the mortar is necessarily weaker than the brick, every so often the face of the mortar would traditionally have needed to be replaced (repointing), perhaps every century. Sadly, during the twentieth century many were repointed with hard cement. It may have seemed a good idea at the time: cement was tough, waterproof and would really last, they thought. But cement was too tough and too waterproof. It gripped the bricks unforgivingly hard and, if there was movement, then the bricks cracked. Cement enclosed the face of the bricks in a waterproof ring, trapping water in the brick ready for frost to expand it and pop the face off the brick.

A modern wall gets away with using cement because it is built on solid concrete foundations, has expansion joints every so often and because, everyone assumes, modern bricks will prove less vulnerable than traditional ones. But if there is movement then modern brickwork can crack, and if that wall has to be demolished the bricks in a modern cement-mortared wall cannot be salvaged because the cement sticks so aggressively.

Brickwork Repair

In the worst cases, traditional lime-mortared brickwork can be taken down, the good bricks cleaned and rebuilt in new mortar. It rarely comes to that as cracks can be 'stitched' together and decayed bricks can be individually cut out and replaced (turning them around is a cunning way to get extra mileage from the same brick and save having to look for a match). Good brickwork would have been designed with a coping or some other projection to reduce the

ABOVE: Past mortar refacing of damaged bricks has not halted decay and now repair options might include individual brick replacement or the selective turning of reasonably intact bricks to expose the uneroded face, although this has to be assessed structurally.

RIGHT: Decorative brickwork like this diaper work, also the bonding – the pattern of 'stretchers' (long sides) and 'headers' (ends) in a wall – should be preserved in any repair.

soaking of the face; where this has been lost by later redesign or decay it could be beneficial to consider replacing it.

Repointing

As lime mortar is intrinsically soft it is easy for the inexperienced to condemn old mortar as 'powdery' when there is nothing particularly wrong with it; such critics are confusing it with cement and expecting it to be as hard as the mortar in a modern wall.

Because the twentieth century saw many walls harmfully repointed in cement, it would be desirable for the cement to be taken out and lime pointing put

Care needs to be taken over the choice of materials and methods or repointing may remain obvious for too long.

Repointing can alter the look of a house by making the bricks appear smaller and the joints bigger.

Repointing, as here after ivy removal, can be limited to damaged areas and can be made to blend unnoticeably with adjacent, weathered brickwork, it does not have to extend to a whole wall or look 'new'.

This cement repointing has adhered so poorly that there may be a chance to replace it with a kinder mortar before too much damage is done to the bricks.

Using angle-grinders to prepare a wall for repointing can permanently scar the bricks.

A discreet repair should be unnoticeable through the correct choice of materials and the careful matching of workmanship, this falls some way short.

back. If the cement-pointers did a really thorough job and raked out the joints to a depth of 25mm or more and cleaned and wetted them thoroughly before putting in their (mistaken) cement then there is probably no hope of getting the cement out again without damaging the bricks. Try one or two inconspicuous ones to find out. If, on the other hand, the repointing was done poorly then the cement will probably be falling out already: a rare case of bad workmanship being an advantage. Even though it takes longer and the tapping drives people mad, the

use of hand tools risks less damage to bricks than power tools when preparing brickwork for repointing. The worst thing to use is a disc-cutter since these overrun and skim bricks or cut across them, leaving scars that never heal.

If an old house has not been repointed yet – and if its original lime mortar is genuinely in need of repointing – then it would be appropriate to use lime mortar to carry out this maintenance repair. Repointing, if badly done, can change the look of the house drastically. If it is really necessary, then there is likely to be a difference in appearance between old and new, but it should not be exaggerated. A terraced or semi-detached house may be expected to stand out slightly from the rest for perhaps a year or two, depending on the relative condition of neighbouring mortar, but, if done well, the difference should not be startling in the first place. The mortar should not be allowed to dominate the bricks or it will never blend in (*see* diagram). If the work is done in patches then an experienced hand can adjust the mix to weather to match. It is a big advantage, when repairing old mortar like-for-like with lime, that repointing can be done in patches just where it is needed, because the new should quickly blend in with the old. It can pay to get advice from a professional accredited in building conservation before embarking on such repairs, because it is unfortunately all too easy to pay good money to get repointing that screams, 'I'm new and different!' for years afterwards.

A word of caution: 'white cement' has occasionally been used as a substitute for lime mortar in the past, but it simply is not lime. It looks too white and, though not quite as strong as ordinary Portland cement, it has enough of cement's negative properties (in relation to old buildings) to make it worth avoiding now that lime is better understood again.

Joint Width
Time, or bad repointing in the past, may have taken all the sharp corners off bricks so they now have rounded shoulders. If the repointing is done back to the face of the bricks (a traditional style called 'flush pointing') then there will appear to be much more mortar than before and the bricks will appear smaller.

This does not need to be repointed, but the original distinctions in joint thickness should be respected if repointing such features.

So it may be necessary to keep the face of the mortar slightly back.

Some elements of brick buildings always had narrower joints. In particular voussoirs (the tapering bricks used to make round or flat arches over windows and doors). Sometimes called 'penny joints' (when pennies were chunkier), these look clumsy if remade with standard, modern-sized joints so these tasks need to be carried out with extra skill and care.

Mortar Mix
Phrases such as 'a little bit of cement will help it go off quickly' or 'this white cement looks just like lime'

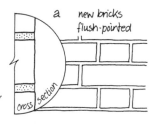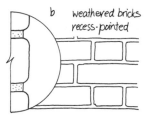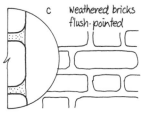

To keep the original appearance of brickwork it may be necessary to adjust the plane of new mortar when repointing.

are not helpful to a good repair and reveal an unfamiliarity with lime. Lime mortar is not a problem to those who know it, it needs no substitutes. But do not expect it to be used at any time approaching winter, it sometimes needs a long time to dry thoroughly and if it freezes first it might drop out. There are several types of lime available and the choice depends on the exposure and location of the property (*see* Info pages: Lime). Expert on-site advice is often necessary before deciding on the specification for areas with extreme exposure and difficult access to try to get the best balance of function and durability.

Mortar Colour
Lime mortar can be coloured, most simply by the choice of sand. For a repair, all that may be necessary to achieve a match is the use of truly local building sand or a good alternative. Mortar can also be coloured fairly reliably with natural earth pigments, but not at a high density or the chemistry of the mix may be affected. Builders used to match-in new mortar to old by sluicing the finished product with strong tea or soot, but it would have saved time, and tea, for them to have considered the choice of sand first and avoid those clumsy and potentially chemically inappropriate fixes. In addition to local sand, some now feel that some local mud would have frequently got into the mix from the sides of the on-site lime pit. Lime mortar will weather down, so, if the basic mix is right, it should match better by itself than if treated with colorants that may look good at first but might themselves weather badly.

White 'tuck' pointing and inscribed ('flat' and 'keyed') jointing are more frequent on old houses than one would expect; the white colour came from lime and marble dust or lime and silver sand.

Sometimes tucked pointing totally ignored the real joints and hides the real bonding pattern.

Fancy Pointing

For style and to impress the neighbours, some of our ancestors went in for intricate styles of pointing. For example, the profile of the joint might be given a decorative twist by finishing off with a specially shaped pointing tool. Alternatively, a thin line of extremely white pointing could be squeezed into a groove run in the main pointing which had been coloured down to match the bricks. This is 'tuck pointing', nineteenth-century 'bling'. Surprisingly, it is not difficult to find firms able to reinstate this today – but the choice of mixes still has to be carefully considered for the protection of old brickwork.

More Detail

This is a general guide rather than a DIY manual and there is more to the art of repointing than this book can cover: the variables of mixes and mysterious-sounding qualities such as the 'suction' of the existing brickwork need to be taken into account. The following is very general information and, if seeking further instruction on the subject, ensure that it is relevant to traditional lime mortar brickwork rather than to modern cement brickwork, the two are different subjects. Lime is caustic so gloves and goggles are essential and lime is extremely weather-sensitive (*see* Info pages: Lime). Lime mortar is naturally softer than cement; that is a useful property and does not mean failure and is not in itself necessarily a cause for repointing.

A basic repair mortar would be around 1 volume of lime putty to 3 of sand ('sharp' gritty sand and 'soft' rounded fine sand are often mixed; the colour of the sand can be chosen to help the mix to blend with surrounding original pointing). The old joints have to be carefully raked out to a depth of about two to three times the height of the joint, or more, to remove decayed mortar (obviously not so much at one time as would destabilize the bricks), using hand tools to avoid damaging the brick edges. Once the cleaned joints are dusted out they can be wetted to receive the mortar, which has to be of a smooth yet stiffish consistency, and pressed in without its spilling on to the face of the brick, then smoothed off with a pointing tool, usually to a millimetre or two behind the face of the brick (*see* diagram), but without over-working the surface. Once the mortar has begun to set it can be compacted slightly with a stiff brush, this closes up any surface cracks. Again, this is not a 'how-to-do-it' as much as a few ground rules showing what to expect. Those interested in learning how to do lime pointing properly could enquire about courses run by the Society for the Protection of Ancient Buildings and by some local authorities.

Cleaning

Many of the same problems that affected stone after its cleaning have been seen with brick cleaning (*see above*). As with stone, chemicals might have been applied after cleaning to attempt to reseal the raw, porous face that was revealed. That was not always successful and may have risked sealing in damp.

A bare piece of clay lump wall.

UNFIRED CLAY BLOCKS

The traditional recipe for 'clay lump' in Norfolk, where building stone was practically non-existent, went something like this: dig out suitable clay soil, free of vegetation and large stones and let it weather over winter, throw straw over it and then mix by trampling it with horses (a bit of dung probably helped). The resulting mixture was formed into moulds then air-dried in summer until set to a firm mass, reinforced by the straw stems. The blocks would have been built up like brickwork from a flint or brick base, at 18in by 6in high (approx 450mm × 150mm) and 6 or 9in (approx 150mm or 225mm) wide; the 'lumps' resemble modern concrete blocks. The walls were protected with sanded tar, often on outbuildings or maybe lime-rendered. Clay lump is found in several of the eastern English counties and may have been used anywhere where the soil was of a suitable composition. New lump buildings were being built at least up to the 1920s, but many older ones have been neglected and torn down.

Repair of 'Clay Lump'

Local research should provide information for reproducing new blocks, though generations of experience now has to be substituted by enthusiasm. Horse-free mixing, cutting and trampling methods can doubtless be found. Instead of replacing blocks perhaps a wet repair could be tried, with a similar mix to the original one, though it would need to be held firmly in place long enough to dry and bond to the original. Some mechanical bonding may need to be devised for this and developing these sorts of repair can be rewarding for those who like mud and mending things. Of course, an assessment should be made of overall stability first and the line between structural and superficial repairs understood.

What not to do is what, regrettably, still seems to happen: swathing the blocks in cement render held fast on metal mesh. That may seem a workmanlike repair from the modern builder's point of view, but it is not necessarily a successful or a compatible one. A harsh, modern repair with cement could simply accelerate the next round of repairs as the interior of the wall becomes wet and distressed and sheds the fixings holding the mesh and the concrete in place. Repair may have become necessary in the first place because the blocks were being dissolved by water due to a broken down finish, or inappropriate modern renders and paints trapping water within the wall, or a build up of soil above the plinth level, or faulty rainwater goods. All the usual building problems, so ensure that these are dealt with before repairing.

EARTH WALLS

There are traditions, and survivals, of mass earth-walled houses in parts of Scotland and Wales, but perhaps the most photographed are south-west England's 'cob' cottages. Using recipes quite similar to the unfired clay blocks described above, the mix would have been trampled in place by human foot direct on to the wall, either free-form 'by eye' or between wooden boards, as formers, that were moved up the building as work progressed. The method depended on local tradition while the materials varied with locality; soft chalk or fine gravel might be added to the mix.

Whereas the unfired clay lump blocks could be used to create fairly precise, square buildings, the consolidated earth method tends to more plastic shapes, particularly with unshuttered cob construction. The walls are thick and they need a protective weathering coat on the outside, just as for clay lump, which is further protected by a good overhang to the eaves. Since thatch was the roofing material often associated with cob construction, and thatch is less reliable at flinging water clear of the wall (rain soaks into the thickness of the straw), the overhangs have to be really generous to protect the wall beneath, adding to the special appearance of these buildings.

Repairs would be similar to those for the unfired clay blocks, above, either *in situ* or perhaps by making up special repair blocks to dry off and insert into place, with a thin, wet mix, into holes carefully cut in the original wall. Again it is necessary to be flexible in approaching this type of repair and to get rid of the notion that doing a proper repair must mean going to the builders' merchant in a van and buying lots of manufactured things in polythene bags. Buildings built with mud can be repaired with mud, there would need to be some research first to establish how the wall had been built, but, in repairing, the normal rules of building safety and organization apply, but the magic ingredient is skill and that can be learnt or hired.

TIMBER FRAME

Timber frames could be made up at some distance from the house site and transported to it. The transporting of large timbers was not easy, so the distances were not great but were influenced by the necessity to use fixed, manual, sawing pits, once they were invented, to cut the larger timbers. Trees would inevitably have had to be transported from their felling positions. Oak and elm were the favoured building timbers in Britain, softwood was also used,

An earth wall deprived of its broad roof and protective render will quickly decay.

Thatch successfully protecting an earth-walled cottage.

and timber was evidently imported from the Baltic area and Scandinavia for building long before the Industrial Revolution.

A popular image of a timber-framed house is the black and white cottage. The black part is, however, probably only a Victorian preference as medieval timber frames were originally most likely left to weather silver or be limewashed over the same as the rest of the wall. Timber frames were also commonly plastered over (rendered with a lime and sand mix) to conceal and protect the timber frame – so they can be indistinguishable from rendered brick buildings from a distance. It is a generalization, but some areas, such as the west of England bordering Wales, have a tradition of highly decorative and robust timber-framing left on display while other areas, such as East Anglia, used timber less ostentatiously and frequently covered it up.

Exposed timber-frame: [this page top] East Anglia, [bottom] Surrey; [facing page top left] Kent, western England.

Green Oak

Timber used for fine joinery is usually 'seasoned' – that is, the natural fluids present in the timber are allowed to dry off so that the wood has finished its twisting and cracking before it is worked. But for building, oak was used 'green', that is, unseasoned, since oak is so dense that seasoning can take decades and, once seasoned, the wood is harder to work. Seasoning then takes place naturally as the building ages – the cracks and twisting that are seen in old timber frame buildings are a result of that process. Because the wood contracts as it loses its internal moisture, it shrinks and, because it shrinks width-ways more, relatively, than lengthways, joints may appear to open up and dowel pegs stand proud. These things ought to have been anticipated by the original builders, who would have been drawing on generations of experience, so they are not always as bad as they look. When using green oak for repairs, the amount of moisture with which the wood starts life in the building can at least be limited by speci-fying winter-felled timber, which should contain less sap. Oak can release a dark tannin stain when washed over with water, and for this reason green oak frames need to be kept dry and out of the rain. In the past timbers may have been left in a fast-flowing stream to flush out the tannin, part of a long seasoning process and unlikely to have been entirely eco-friendly.

Green-oak woodworkers, who can provide authentic, handmade building components, may be known to local conservation officers.

Decay

Oak is remarkably durable and can even survive being totally immersed in water in certain condi-tions, but, like any wood, cannot survive the type of dampness that softens its fibres and turns them into an attractive source of food for fungi and insects. Softwoods can also be remarkably durable and harden with age, but they tend to be much more susceptible to softening by damp. The great majority of traditional building materials and paints, being made from such things as limes and earths, were generally not impervious to water vapour and so were less able to seal up the timber to a harmful degree. While wetting did happen, the timber was able to dry out and, with luck, rot never got a permanent hold. More recently, cements and plastic and oil paints have been applied over timber-framed buildings and caused them to remain damp inside, and so rot can have been accelerated over recent decades (*see* Info pages: Rot and decay). Once a timber-framed house has been decorated inside or out in modern, imper-meable paints or covered with new waterproof renders and plasters, then the chances of rot occur-ring are multiplied, although rot can still happen without this help.

Repairs

The advantage of timber frame is that it is sectional and so relatively easily to repair. However, the components are knitted together in a matrix that prop and hang from each other and so a failure is not always apparent. Once one member fails alternative support may have been taken via another network of members. This is useful but can make for surprises as things are not always held up by the obvious route. Houses have usually been subject to careless surgery over the years – and it is not unusual to find roof timbers sawn apart to install a dormer window or beams shaved down to almost nothing to let in a newer door or stairway or accommodate some long-forgotten piece of furniture. Needless to say, it pays to understand what is actually holding things up rather than just to assume that the obvious members are important.

There are several conservative methods for repairing timber and the choice would depend upon the circumstances. Access for new lengths of wood,

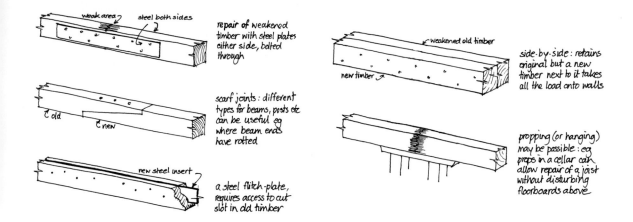

Some of the many options that exist to repair weakened or broken timbers; these are diagrammatic, actual repairs need structural design.

access for working, sensitivity to damage of the adjacent fabric and the degree of visibility of the finished repair are likely to be deciding factors. Timber works as a structural material both in compression (you can try to crush it) and in tension (you can try to stretch it). In a conventional, horizontal beam supported at each end, the top half of the beam is working in compression at the same time as the bottom half is working in tension (this is why it is a bad idea to drill holes though a beam at all, but, if pressed, then a structural engineer can define a narrow band between the compression and the tension zone where a hole will have the least impact).

Steel Plates, Flitches, Cramps, Sleeves and Straps

Iron and steel have long been used to reinforce and repair timber. Traditionally left to the blacksmith to scratch his head over, now a conservation engineer would be called in to calculate sizes and fixings and to assess which option would cause the least disturbance to the old fabric.

Scarf Joints

Because of the tension/compression set-up it is possible to cut out rotten timber in such a way that a new piece can be cleverly locked in its place and take up the load without needing to be glued into place.

This involves analysing the structural loads and carefully cutting the replacement to fine tolerances. Old woodworkers had this to a fine art, so there are established patterns of joint, but no one pattern to suit all situations. A combination of conservation engineer and skilled carpenter is required. Usually these joints are also bolted or clamped, since it is never certain how the replacement timber may shrink over time and possibly loosen its grip.

Simple Props, Hangers and Side-by-Side Repair

If the timber is of special interest but broken or weakened, it could be unfortunate to have to cut it to make a repair. Propping or hanging the timber might offer a solution. Alternatively, a 'splint' could be inserted next to the weakened member to which all the load would be transferred (it may or may not be necessary to attach the splint to the original). As with all repairs, any decay needs to be stopped in its tracks (*see* Info pages: Rot and decay).

New Timber Repairs

Sometimes there is no option but to install a complete new timber member. Where size and stability are critical it might be preferable to source a seasoned piece of oak (ideally, not one that has been pillaged from another old building). This is to avoid a 'green'

A new roof in green oak to replace one lost in the past.

piece of timber seasoning itself inconveniently out of place over time and setting up unwelcome stresses in the existing structure to which it will be joined.

CLADDING AND INFILL TO TIMBER FRAMED WALLS

Timber Weatherboarding

This is a quick and simple way of cladding a timber frame, which some areas, such as Essex and Kent, have used extensively. The weatherboards were simple, quite thick planks or 'feathered' boards and not the intricately-machined, thin, interlocking profiles that were used in 1960s speculative housing. Nor were traditional designs necessarily 'secretly' nailed, as modern profiles might be. The local traditions ought to be apparent by observation, but later replacements can create a false impression, so it is worth some research before embarking on an over-haul. As in other areas of houses, weatherboarding has usually, and mistakenly, been coated with non-breathable paint, although it has to be said that, particularly in coastal areas, weatherboarding may have been painted with pitch, as were barns or boats.

Lime Render on Timber Laths

This is as described in chapter 6: Internal Walls. Once the render is in place it may be difficult to determine whether the house is timber frame or brick underneath except by thumping it. Usually plain, the render was, however, sometimes incised with lines to give the impression of stonework and sometimes it was patterned with inscribed or stamped decoration or even richly decorated with moulded plasterwork, pargeting (lime render sets slowly enough for this to be done). Later Victorian repairs may have applied a pebbledash finish. Expanded metal mesh (at first bitumen coated, then galvanized, later stainless steel) has often been used to repair this cladding rather than to reinstate timber laths, and, though it can be successfully used with lime mortar, there is no reason not to use traditional timber laths, of suitable durable timber properly fixed with non-corroding nails or screws. Old repairs may have introduced later layers of cement over the original lime render and this, combined with the negative effect of plastic masonry paint, can often lead to failure (*see* Info pages: Paints and paint removal).

Bricks and Mathematical Tiles

Many timber-framed buildings can be found with their framework infilled with brick. It seems counter-intuitive to have built a timber building and then gone to the trouble of fitting in a jigsaw of bricks if there were bricks available to build a brick house straight away, and some investigation of the inner parts of the frame should confirm whether or not there are holes or grooves indicating an earlier infill of wattles (*see below*) for daub. Brick can also be found laced with timber members in a way that suggests that brick was being tried out as a new material locally, but, just in case it did not work, there were

ABOVE: *Traditional weatherboarding was rarely interlocking and often completely flat; much of that which survives often has a beaded lower edge.*

RIGHT: *Lime render has dropped away from its timber laths because it was sealed over by a cement top coat and plastic paint; once it became permanently damp the lime render disintegrated.*

Panels between timber framing were made by daubing mixes on to a grid of some sort; often a basketwork wattle was woven for this purpose from thin, springy stems specially cultivated by coppicing young bushes and trees.

some good pieces of timber to make sure. Naturally, these have rotted and weakened the brickwork as later generations sealed them up with impervious paints. Another explanation for timber inclusions in 'finer' houses is that the external and the internal brickwork were laid by different gangs and the timber was to make up inconvenient mismatches in courses.

The Georgian period saw many medieval timber-framed buildings refaced in brick, sometimes just the elevation facing the street. Another feature of this fashionable upgrading of timber buildings, where circumstances would not allow for a new brick wall, was to hang on to the timber frame some new clay tiles specially shaped to resemble bricks, which, once they were all in position, could be pointed-up in mortar to complete the illusion. These were called 'mathematical tiles' and sometimes fool no one as they clad a jettied and obviously timber building, but sometimes the illusion can be entirely effective.

Wattle and Daub

Wattle and daub is perhaps the best known of the early survivals of methods for cladding timber frame. Whippy sticks, specially cultivated, of trees or shrubs such as hazel or riven strips of oak or chestnut, were woven into a coarse basket with their ends wedged into holes or grooves made in the sides of the timber frame's main members and trimmers. There were variations on this theme, but all amounted to forming a grid of sorts fixed to the timber frame so that a formless, setting material – mud, hair, dung, straw, lime, clay, chalk, grass are frequent constituents – could be pressed on to it, so that what was a space became a wall. The wall might have been self-finished in mud or lime rendered, and lime-washed. When carrying out repairs look at the evidence for what was originally there, it might even be possible to grind up and reuse the original material. In the recent past there seemed to be some embarrassment about trying to use mud and sticks, let alone dung and blood, while men were being sent to the moon, so all sorts of plastic foam and metal mesh were tried instead, finished off with cement. They were frequently not flexible enough and could also be difficult to seal at the edges. Currently, conservationists are trying to find ways of keeping the benefits of the traditional methods while also introducing insulation.

Movement in Old Houses

Walls and roofs out of true can be part of the character that people like about old buildings. But there can be a temptation, once one owns an old house, to try to straighten things. Unless there are sound structural reasons to do this, it can end up as an expensive and disruptive way to destroy an old house's character. All old houses were new once – and it is likely that most were built more or less straight and true. What has happened over the years is perhaps that timber has seasoned, shrunk or twisted, walls have settled into soft ground on their simple footings, and elements of the fabric have relaxed into a 'comfortable' position.

HISTORICAL PERSPECTIVE

Old houses were built, for the most part, before any official building codes existed and certainly not to modern standards. This does not mean that they were poorly built, but it does mean that more reliance was placed on tradition, experience and honesty than is the case today, with all that implies, good and bad. Generalizations are not universal truths, but one can understand how a family farm intended for generations and built by neighbours might be more carefully put together than a speculatively built town house erected by travelling workers.

Time will have seen at least a little movement occur in old properties and most have adapted well.

93

Time has tested the construction of surviving old houses sure enough, but time also brings changes like decay so one cannot be too complacent.

Structurally it is usually quite obvious how the upper parts of a building rely upon what is underneath to hold them up, but, in any group of old buildings, no one building is necessarily structurally self-supporting: one building may rely on an adjacent one for direct support. For example, its floor joists may have been built into a neighbouring wall, or one building may have suffered structural fatigue centuries earlier and is now leaning on a neighbouring building, and putting extra stress there. An entire block of old houses built at different times could be structurally interdependent and removing or altering one may make the others vulnerable.

MOVEMENT – OLD, NEW, SERIOUS OR ROUTINE?

Cracks and subsidence in any property can be a cause for concern. In some cases these may indicate a problem that needs to be addressed by structural repair. In others, movement in an old house can be part of the way that the building copes with its environment. New, clean cracks and other new symptoms, such as doors and windows binding, may be a signal to get a conservation-accredited professional inspection (*see* chapter 9: The Professionals). Some apparent cracks might be scars from very old structural battles. Owners should not attempt their own diagnosis, but it is worth introducing some of the issues that might be discussed with a professional. Rules of thumb used in building can appear temptingly simple: some might say that a superficial crack up to a only a millimetre or so is 'acceptable', particularly if there is evidence that it has happened before and seems to 'come and go' with the seasons – thermal expansion and contraction, perhaps. But even the most serious fault has to start somewhere and rules of thumb do not take that into account, some serious expertise is also needed to look at other factors.

Professionals and contractors unfamiliar with old buildings – possibly driven by insurers or anxious occupants – can sometimes overestimate the extent of a structural problem and carry out unnecessary work. Where old houses are concerned this can result in invasive repairs, loss of original fabric and the introduction of incompatible modern materials. For example, underpinning or over-stiffening a part of an old house that has subsided relative to the rest can lead to that new repair staying rock-solid but ignores the fact that the rest of the house is going to carry on moving slightly, as it has always done; new cracks can appear at the junction of the repair and it could look as though the underpinning had failed. Repairs have to be in tune with the existing fabric and take into

The familiar tie-bar spreader-plate indicates early remedial work aimed at holding a building together; long iron rods accompany these inside the building, sometimes crossing it completely.

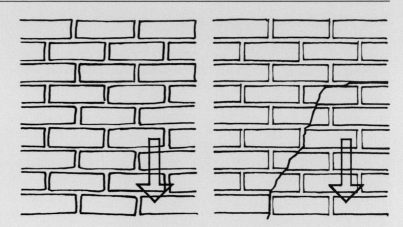

*When slight movement occurs …
[RIGHT] … bricks in lime mortar
can 'shuffle' better than …
[FAR RIGHT] … bricks in hard
cement mortar which can crack.*

consideration how the whole house works, not modernize a small part of the house and expect that to work.

MOVEMENT – SOME VARIATIONS

Foundations

Old houses, unless built direct upon a solid bed of rock, did not generally have rigid foundations. The deep, wide strips of concrete that are the footings for most modern houses were generally unknown a little over a century ago. Walls may often have simply penetrated a foot or two into the soil – beyond the layers rich in decomposing, shifting vegetable matter. They may have been widened a little at the base in order to spread the load. Our ancestors sometimes used not to bother much with elaborate or deep foundations (unless they built cellars). They had no concrete anyway, and the alternative materials available were the same ones they had to build the walls. If these were materials that were just going to decompose, there was no point putting these too far underground.

When comparing these with modern foundations, it may seem surprising that old houses are not rocking all over the place. A modern house's foundations penetrate beyond much of the heaving and shifting that goes on in the top layers of the soil. They are also spread out underground to distribute the load of the house more evenly. It is probably true to say that modern foundations are designed to cope with the worst reasonably likely case, whereas old foundations

have continued to manage average conditions, allowing some movement from time to time. Old foundations that have survived until now have been tested in a wide range of extremes, but we may be heading for new extremes of climate.

Ordinary movement could be due to the subsoil's drying out and shrinking, or swelling in a wet season, or freezing, or being affected by the growth or removal of trees, or by the underground water table, or various complex, sometimes man-made, underground conditions leading to soil movements in any direction. Fortunately, the materials most often used to construct old houses were able to cope with some of this movement reasonably well. They can cope much better than when the equivalent modern-day materials are placed on old foundations, which is why it often makes little sense to incorporate modern fabric in an old house.

Brick or Stone Walls

One usefully accommodating material used in the past was lime mortar, as used in old masonry (*see* Info pages: Lime). It has the ability to 'creep', that is, to allow the bricks or stones it binds to shuffle slightly when movement occurs. This explains why sometimes an old brick wall can be seen with its courses rising and falling. The bricks were probably laid reasonably level but the ground has shifted slowly over time and the lime mortar has allowed the bricks to follow. A hard, modern cement mortar does not do this nearly so well and the wall is likely to crack instead of accommodating the movement.

Buttresses have been popular for propping walls but can have a life of their own – if this had been better bonded to the wall it looks as though it might have pulled the wall over.

This beneficial mobility in lime is not just confined to the mortar in masonry. Lime was also used as a render (for the external and the internal 'plastering' of walls). Where a relatively hard and brittle cement render might crack under stress, lime render can take a certain amount of deformation and small cracks tended to be 'healed' by repeat applications of limewash at redecorations. Cracks admit water into the wall, a cement coating is impervious enough to trap the water but a naked or limewashed lime render allows the water to evaporate, reducing the chances of decay taking hold. This breathability is part of the way that traditional buildings coped with the effects of structural movement.

A 'crooked' wall need not automatically be a cause for concern, but there may be other factors that make it so; for example, the wall could have settled into a condition where, without yet breaking, it is in danger of becoming unstable. If repairs are necessary to an undulating or leaning wall in an old house they might usefully be carried out with like materials. This avoids the further complications that can arise from introducing modern materials with their different and sometimes incompatible, movement and breathability characteristics.

Timber-frame Buildings

In addition to subsoil movements, timber frames have to cope with their own internal movement due to long-term seasoning and also their responses to variations in temperature and humidity during the year. A timber frame might have knitted together to produce some surprising and potentially confusing situations (*see* chapter 4: External walls – Timber frame – Green oak – Repairs), if what appears to be a simple, post-and-lintel construction actually turns out to be complex structural grid or network. This may be evident where members have been cut or reduced beyond their apparent functional limits – the loads may have been transferred along a different route. However, it would be best to get them checked, and missing or weakened members can usually be discreetly reinforced or otherwise compensated for.

The panels of material infilling the spaces in the timber frame have had to cope with these changes too. Once again, traditional materials (for example, hair-reinforced lime render over a framework of fine timber) have shown themselves able to adapt where more rigid, modern materials might fail. But in all probability they had been refilled and patched several times over the life of the building (*see* chapter 4: External walls – Timber frame – Wattle and daub).

Roofs

The similarity between a roof of tiles or slates and the scales of a fish helps to explain how well a traditional roof covering can allow for movement in the timber skeleton of rafters and purlins underneath the tiles. As the timbers flex, the tiles can slide by tiny increments across each other. Between each tile a current of air can flow and, provided the roof has not been 'underdrawn' with an impervious roofing felt ('sarking' or 'underlay'), then that air should help to condition and ventilate the timbers in the roofspace.

Lead 'flashings' around chimneys and against walls allow for a flexible joint between the relatively rigid stack or wall and the roof. Lead is usefully malleable and can take some deformation, while its weight is usually, with luck, enough to reseat itself after slight movement. Should the lead be too rigidly fixed or be laid in sheets that are too large then its own thermal expansion and contraction can cause it to crack and admit water. For this reason leadworking has its own commonsense set of rules and guidelines to enable the material to flex and still function.

Ceilings

Ceilings are a case where a crack can be a useful alarm signal. Modern house ceilings are usually made with sheets of plasterboard which tend sometimes to crack in straight lines between sheets as the ceiling flexes. The ceiling of an old house, when made of plaster applied to timber strips (laths), can crack for a number of reasons and is worth inspecting. The hair-reinforced plaster sticks to the laths by having been pushed between them when wet, forming a bulge on the other side of the laths, which, when set hard, keys the plaster in place (*see* Info pages: Lime – Render)

Sometimes damage or wetting from a broken pipe or leaking roof can detach or soften those locking bulges from the rest of the plaster and make an area of ceiling loose. In other cases the nails holding the laths to the ceiling joists may have rusted and failed. The ceiling can often be repaired again according to its original construction.

Doors and Windows

The occasional sticking or jarring of doors and windows must be familiar to anyone who has lived in

Cross-section through a lath and plaster ceiling showing how the plaster, reinforced with hair, is mechanically keyed to the timber laths.

an old house. Just as with the timber frames of wooden houses, the timber used for joinery purposes responds to changes in temperature and humidity by expanding and contracting. Joinery timber usually started out well-seasoned and so there should be less scope for dramatic movement, but this can be distorted by new sources of dampness due to a leak, condensation or through the drying effects of central heating.

Even in ideal conditions, exterior doors and windows have to cope with one climate on their inside surface and a different one outside, so some seasonal movement is almost inevitable. In addition, doors and windows need to be able to adapt to the larger structural movements that can be inherent in an old house. Fortunately, traditional wooden doors and windows can be adjusted with simple hand tools (more difficult to achieve satisfactorily if the frames are complex sections of plastic or aluminium). Some very old houses have moved so much that the doors and windows have slowly become very distorted. But they have been adjusted to fit and the glass replaced to ever more bizarre shapes. This shows how sustainable traditional construction can be. What can be a source of delight in an old building would be a source of alarm in a new one.

MODERN RIGIDITY MEETS TRADITIONAL FLEXIBILITY

Partial Underpinning

Every case of subsidence will be a totally unique combination of circumstances and only on-site inspection can address the actual problems that are at work. Buildings can suffer from localized subsidence due, for example, to exceptional ground conditions, causing severe cracking as a part of the wall sinks. The automatic response with a new building would be to restore the ground support that has been lost by inserting a specially designed beam or piles or extra-deep foundations under the affected part of the building. That might be a reasonable measure because originally a modern building would probably have started out with quite rigid foundations which that repair seeks to reinstate.

But if those same measures are applied to an old building then the new section of foundation – to modern standards of rigidity and strength – might be much firmer than the remaining old foundations that support the rest of the building. Consequently, when the rest of the old house continues its centuries-old tradition of gentle movement with the seasons, the part supported by the new repair could stay relatively immobile. The result can be a new set of cracks. One way of tackling this in an old building would be simply to try to restore that amount of support which had been lost in the first place rather than bring the repair (or, indeed, the whole building) up to modern standards of rigidity. If a sympathetic restoration of lost support can be achieved with like-for-like materials, rather than over-rigid or too-impervious modern ones, then there is a chance that the performance of the building in other respects will not be upset by the repair.

Extensions

Mixing old and new does not only occur when underpinning. A new extension to an old house involves similar considerations. The old house wants to carry on in its old ways – gently shuffling about on its footings – while the new extension, designed to modern building rules, sits firm on a rigid concrete base. In those circumstances it would be appropriate to consider how the two might be carefully detailed to move harmlessly against each other. Alternatively, the rules might be explored with professional guidance to see whether a new foundation actually has to be so inconveniently incompatible with the existing one. However, even if very similar support were used for an extension as for the original house, there would still be the potential for differential movement between the two as the new would tend, at least, to need to indulge in an initial 'settle', to a greater or lesser extent depending on its construction materials, the composition of the ground and the way it had previously been used. In any event, the preference for new extensions to historic buildings to be 'reversible' (that is, potentially removable without leaving a scar on the original – *see* Info pages: Conservation terminology) can make it inappropriate to anchor a new extension aggressively to the existing walls, so the requirements of good conservation are in line with structural common sense.

When a building has been around for a few years it may have been altered several times, so the result may lack some of the structural logic of the original.

Paints and Paint Removal

Old houses can be put at greater risk in a shorter time by being 'smartly decorated' in some of the materials now in use than they ever suffered over centuries from indifferent maintenance with traditional finishes. Given the damage that inappropriate paint finishes are now recognized to do, future owners of old houses are more and more likely to want to strip them. But paint is not the only culprit – other features such as modern cement render are also a problem. That, and some paint finishes, might be difficult to remove without causing even more damage.

HISTORICAL PERSPECTIVE

Paint has always served two functions: to protect and to decorate. In Britain protection means coping with a damp climate. Traditional paints, for the most part, helped to shed rainwater, but were not waterproof by modern standards so they could not keep walls and joinery dry by simply keeping rain out. They did the next best thing, being – in most cases – 'breathable' they were able to allow any damp that got past their surface to dry out later. That is doubly useful because damp does not just get in by rain (*see* chapter 8: Damp, etc.) and all damp needs to be allowed to dry out.

Some Traditional Paints

All of these are available again today, most in their original formulations:

Limewash
The basic, traditional external finish but also used inside. Naturally a soft white but could be coloured with earth pigments or vegetable dyes. Regional colours were derived from local vegetation or local minerals. Limewash could be modified with ingredients such as oils or tallow to improve durability, but this does reduce its useful breathability. Limewash is readily available and becoming more widely used on old buildings again (*see also* Info pages: Lime).

Natural-oil Paints, Varnishes and Lead Paint
Painted exterior and interior joinery would have been finished in a natural-oil-based paint (principally linseed oil from flax, but other oils had different and useful properties). This paint once contained lead in the form of a salt such as lead carbonate which provided body and a basic white pigment. Lead paint was eventually restricted in use and withdrawn from

'Boiled' linseed oil is a simple way of preserving external oak, here being applied (at top); it weathers back to show silver oak again after a few years.

general sale (*see* Info pages: Safety and buildings), and its place taken by less breathable modern oil alkyd paints. Lead paint was coloured with a variety of additional pigments and dyes but also, sometimes compounding its toxicity, metal salts – even arsenic – were used.

'Boiled' linseed oil, diluted with natural turpentine, could be used to give a clear protective and breathable coating to timber. Interior floors and hardwood panels might have a natural wax (such as beeswax), if they were finished at all. Alternatively, a natural-oil-based varnish finish for fine hardwood joinery could be used.

Natural-oil paints and varnishes are not complex to manufacture and are becoming popular in old building conservation and other sustainable building projects; they are on general sale. The lead content has been substituted by salts of other metals for safety. Lead paint is still available by special licence for use on the higher grades of historic building if its use can be justified.

Distempers

An established internal finish, still surviving in many old houses, 'soft' distemper (chalk and animal glue) or variations of that incorporating oils or milk (casein from milk is a natural binder) for durability. All these are relatively simple, still available, satisfying to use and give a gentle finish that can be more compatible with the 'feel' of an old house. Most are available in basic, 'breathable' formulations that have the potential to assist the drying out of water vapour from within the fabric. Because of the lack of varnishes, soft white distemper stays crisply white and it is easy to clean up splashes. It also visually 'heals' minor cracks in old walls and ceilings as it is applied.

Other Traditional Paints

More rigorously waterproof finishes such as pitch or tar have been used, most especially on agricultural buildings, though sometimes even these can be relatively breathable compositions. It is rather more difficult to obtain modern versions from everyday suppliers.

Traditional Colours

Pigments have moved with the times and, before chemical dyes, there were always elusive and expensive colours such as blue. Traditional paints tend to work best in traditional colours because they are linked to the make-up of the paint: limewash and distemper are by no means now restricted to pastel colours but, because of the chalk content, pastel colours have always been easiest. Modern paints are now marketed in traditional colours; that does not mean that the paint is necessarily good for an old building (*see* Info pages: Old house style and lifestyle – Paints old and new).

The Change to Modern Paints

By the late nineteenth century chemical and industrial skills were beginning to be applied to some of the perceived deficiencies of house paints. At the same time, buildings were becoming more rigid, with concrete foundations, and effective damp barriers were being introduced in the construction of houses. New paints catered for this growing market and gradually the needs of old buildings were sidelined.

Masonry Paints

Limewash was gradually abandoned in favour of new preparations which were more convenient to sell pre-prepared in tins and with a long shelf-life and which could support a wider range of colours. Since limewash could not be used successfully up to or during winter, or in any other extreme weather, and because it is quite caustic until first dry, it did not adapt well to a faster, all-year-round, modern building industry that was beginning not to nurture skilled tradesmen. Perhaps the most popular exterior wall paint today is masonry paint that, with a resin formulation, is sometimes referred to in conservation circles as 'plastic' paint. This has been widely used on old buildings and, sadly for their survival prospects, is nowhere near as breathable as the limewash it has pushed aside.

Gloss Paint and Other Joinery Finishes

Lead paint was re-formulated by gradual steps during the twentieth century into glossier and more colour-fast oil gloss paints, eventually becoming lead-free and containing different, petrochemical-derived oils, solvents and pigments until arriving at the modern gloss paint, which is now less toxic when dry (without lead in it) but whose vapour emissions (from the solvents it contains) when still wet stand

Modern paints do not always have a good record in protecting timber on modern houses; these, pictured new in the 1960s, have now lost most of their original exterior joinery.

accused of threatening the environment and health. Alternative water-based and solvent-based versions of mainstream gloss and other finishes have been, and continue to be, developed. Modern joinery paints have, in general, abandoned the one important feature that helped old buildings to survive: breathability (what the paint industry might call microporosity or water-vapour permeability). There are some exceptions in that there have been for many years vapour-permeable paints and stain finishes that would have been less damaging to underlying timber, but these seem to have been more popular with architects than the retail trade. It is important to understand that, while some new and usefully breathable modern paints are water-based, many aggressively non-breathable paints are also water-based – so being water-based does not itself mean compatibility with old buildings. Also, because breathability is relative, a paint might legitimately claim to be breathable without actually offering the quality to a useful enough extent to benefit an old building. Traditional oil varnishes were effectively supplanted by polyurethane varnish by the late 1960s. This, like many modern joinery paints, forms a plastic skin that resists breathing and is prone to crack at points of stress.

Emulsions

Interior distempers were replaced by emulsion paint, the forerunner of today's vinyl and acrylic emulsion paints that have become a standard modern interior finish for walls and ceilings. Again, these plastic emulsions were developed primarily for the convenience of the modern building industry and are fine in that context, but they are sadly lacking in the breathability required to keep old houses healthy. An occasional exception can be found in low-vinyl emulsions that modern builders used to paint plastered walls before they have dried out fully, these are available in a limited colour range but suppliers might be persuaded to experiment with automatic colouring machines at the customer's risk.

HOW PAINTS PERFORM AND WEAR: TRADITIONAL VERSUS MODERN

A big, technical subject and this can only be a general guide:

Breathability

Traditional paints were 'breathable' in the first place, which meant that they let out the damp that inevitably found its way into the fabric from a variety of routes, even when everything was newly built and in good order. Modern paints on the whole have been less concerned with letting out damp, because modern houses are constructed with a variety of design features intended to keep damp, absolutely, out. Old houses cannot do this and it is generally a flawed idea to attempt to make them try because there are so many routes and so much will always be unknown about the inside of any one old building (*see* chapter 8: Damp, etc.).

Old lead paint can often still be seen with its characteristic 'fade away' wear pattern rather than the 'crack and blister' of much modern gloss paint.

Wearing out

Benign Failure of Traditional Paints

Traditional paints tended to 'fade away' with wear; this can still be seen on the occasional outbuilding where a lead-painted door looks dusty and matt.

There is no longer any barrier to deflect rain so the wood gets a little wetter than when newly painted but, importantly, it can still dry out again.

Damaging Failure of Modern Paints

Modern paint tends to hang together as it ages, but it does crack or part company from the background, keeping the illusion of solid colour in place once the paint has failed. But those cracks are admitting water, the blisters are acting as reservoirs and the damp fabric behind has little chance of drying out properly because it is screened from sun and wind by a sheet of waterproof paint half-stuck and half-loose. This applies both to plastic masonry paints and to conventional oil gloss paints. Both old and new construction suffers from this, though generally modern houses are more rigid, but old houses inevitably move a little and so any modern paint can quickly become compromised.

The Compatibility of Paint with the Performance of Walls

An old house needs to breathe to rid itself of the low-level dampness that is inherent in its construction. It needs a paint that breathes a lot. Traditional paints do this, but many, if not most, conventional modern paints do not. An old house moves, more than most modern houses. A paint that behaves more like a surface deposit (many traditional paints) rather than a brittle film that cracks (many modern paints) can be easier to repair and redecorate as there are fewer

This hatch had lasted upwards of twenty years unpainted without serious decay because the wood could always dry out after rain (and it has minimal ledges to trap damp), but within a few months of being painted with modern paint the film has cracked, admitting water that may now become trapped under the surface, risking advancing decay.

blisters and curled-up broken edges to cut out and smooth down. Traditional paints, such as limewash for walls and distemper for walls and ceilings, tend to 'heal' the minor cracks of earlier layers relatively effortlessly. Even true linseed oil paint (the modern descendent of lead paint) rebuilds the surface of its earlier coats (though cracks in joinery still need to be filled).

Over time, most old houses will have acquired a mix of layers of several types of paint. Sealers may have been applied to force old limewashed or distempered walls to accept a coat of non-breathing, plastic masonry paint or emulsion. Toxic lead paint may be lurking under failed modern gloss. The benefits of traditional paint can be won again, but there is usually little technical gain, apart from visual appeal, in applying them over modern paints.

CONSIDERING PAINT REMOVAL

Is It Worth It?
Owners of old houses have become aware of the importance of letting the building fabric breathe as freely as possible and are turning to paint-stripping so that they can reinstate more breathable traditional paints, and ones which actually enhance the period appearance of their homes. Professional advice is necessary to identify what the paints are, whether removal would be likely to benefit the house, whether there are potentially harmful substances present (for instance, lead or asbestos) and whether paint removal should be linked to other measures, since old houses may have been altered in a number of other ways that might add up to affect their performance. Ideally, an old house should be happily returned to a bright future with a tasteful coating of traditional paint, but unfortunately in some cases an old house can have been so thoroughly abused by the twentieth century that a programme of intelligent damage-limitation is a better course than trying to restore its original finishes.

Legislation
Though it may seem intrusive to some, legislation provides for controls or consultations in painting, cleaning, stripping and recolouring houses and other buildings if they are, for example, listed or in a Conservation Area, National Park or other designated area (*see* Info pages: Red tape). Private agreements or covenants may exist in relation to some houses or communities. These are all in place to preserve the maximum aesthetic value for the majority and should not be seen as a hate-campaign against people who might, for example, strongly like the colour purple.

Health, Safety and Damage
Some of the processes used to remove paint, for example, some chemical strippers, burning, abrasion and grit-blasting, can be hazardous to health as well as damaging to the surfaces underneath, and to adjacent surfaces, such as glass. Chemicals may be caustic as well as toxic. Fumes from burning paint can be toxic and irritant. Dust particles, especially where underlying layers of old lead paint or asbestos-textured paint are disturbed, can also be a health hazard. The use of blowlamps can risk igniting unseen pockets of straw, debris and timber fragments that are often associated with old houses. After some bad experiences, some conservation organizations have almost completely banned hot paint stripping.

Destroying or Changing History
While it may be acceptable to remove the modern layers of paint from an old house, removal methods are not readily able to discriminate between what is new and what is old. Taking off all the paint from joinery down to bare timber permanently removes

Each mark tells a story.

the historical record of the paint colours and types used ever since the house was built. Along with that will also disappear the scratches, scrapes or burns that testify to the history of the building (*see* Info pages: Old house style, etc.). Many surprisingly humble, medieval buildings have valuable ancient wall decorations hidden under old paint which can be wiped out forever by aggressive paint removal.

Surfaces Intended to be Painted or Covered

In the 1980s there was a regrettable fashion (sometimes in contravention of listed building legislation) for stripping paint and plaster to reveal bare wood and masonry that the original builders had taken great care to conceal. Georgian and Victorian softwood joinery was usually originally carefully filled and painted to hide an 'inferior' timber, or it may have been fake-grained to look like a more expensive timber (this skill can still be found). The timber and workmanship of a basic, panelled, pine door may seem extravagantly luxurious to us now, compared with a modern door stamped out of compressed fibreboard, but that is no reason to make it stand there naked.

Painted-on fake woodgrain surviving inside a cupboard door.

Surfaces Intended to be Bare

Timber moulding, carving, panelling and doors made from hardwood were originally more likely to have been left unfinished or simply waxed or oiled. In recent years they may have been stained or thickly varnished and professional advice may be needed to restore these. Fine work may have been selectively gilded or highlighted with colour, so look in cracks and crevices for clues.

Ambiguous Surfaces

Medieval structural timbers internally and externally may have been left to weather naturally, or may have been limewashed along with adjacent areas of wall or ceiling or even painted with decorative designs or pictures. The modern image of a timber-frame building with jet black timbers is, in some areas of the country, largely a feature of the last hundred years or so and applications of black paint could be harming the wood beneath.

Cost

Successful paint removal is usually a skilled and labour-intensive operation, particularly if every last scrap of the paint is to be removed (and sometimes that is not realistic nor desirable). Removal of harmful paint layers can be thoroughly worthwhile in helping to preserve an old house for the future, but there may be other more pressing areas needing attention or other things that can now be done to reduce the problems caused by the wrong paint.

Medieval decoration followed a different logic from ours and may be found anywhere and not respecting boundaries and obstructions; this can be destroyed forever if care is not taken to look under existing finishes when redecorating.

This house was in a bad way, plastic paint was one of many problems, but, because of the rough and cement-repaired surface, removal was unlikely to be very effective so the existing surface needs to be kept in good order.

REMOVING PLASTIC PAINT FROM EXTERNAL WALLS

There is little technical point removing plastic paint that is over cement (rather than lime) render since the cement is also a barrier to breathing; professional advice needs to be taken on whether the cement can be removed. It may not always be possible to remove modern paint from some surfaces completely, but it may be possible to remove enough to replace with a benign finish such as limewash. If some of the breathability of limewash is restored, along with its unique appearance, then an old house should look and work more like it was intended. The method depends upon how well the paint is adhering, how delicate is the background (the 'substrate') to which it

has been applied and how thorough the paint removal is required to be. The conservation officer at the local council should be able to guide house-holders on any relevant planning issues and may have up-to-date local knowledge of contractors. The following includes methods that may be inappropriate, but it is useful to understand why as they may be offered by contractors.

Scraping

Poorly adhering paint may be removed with a wall-paper scraper, perhaps starting with a nylon one rather than metal, possibly assisted by a simple wall-paper steamer. Care should be taken not to damage the underlying surface since old, traditional bricks and renders are by their nature soft and easily

Paint removal is usually a dramatic affair.

scored. Even if it were too labour-intensive to apply to a whole house, this method might expose some sample areas to enable decisions to be made.

Chemical Strippers

Some manufacturers offer to match an effective stripper to a sample of paint sent to them. Find out what effect the stripper may have on the fabric underneath (the 'substrate') to avoid damaging it, try samples if necessary. It is important that chemical strippers are neutralized or they could attack any new paint. Chemical strippers work by attacking either the paint itself or loosening its bond to the substrate. New formulations and techniques cross into building use from other industries from time to time and the future may offer better solutions. Chemical strippers should be treated with respect following the appropriate health and safety guidance.

Pressurized Hot Water and 'Steam'

This is almost always carried out by specialist contractors. It is reasonable to ask for a test sample beforehand (find out first whether this is free or whether a charge will be made). The success of these techniques depends largely upon the skill and experience of the operator, not least because the jets of pressurized hot water are capable of burrowing into mortar and render as well as just stripping paint. A skilled person can cause less damage and take less time. It should be carried out only when there is adequate time and weather to dry out the fabric before winter, otherwise

the walls can be frost-damaged as a result of the water pumped at them. Some proprietary processes are better, more effective and less damaging than others – a conservation professional or conservation officer may be able to help choose.

Grit-blasting

Although there are sophisticated gentle variants of this approach (*see* Specialist abrasive techniques below under Joinery), straightforward sand or grit-blasting is usually far too abrasive for the removal of paint from an historic fabric. This is because, when trying to remove plastic paint from old and soft substrates, such as brick or lime render, the paint presents quite a resilient target and the grit fired at it tends to bounce off, whereas the blast of grit can enter gaps in the paint surface causing deep scars in the more easily attacked wall behind. Some blasting is dry, other processes use water as well. Dust or slurry will result and that can be an inconvenience with an occupied building.

To benefit from total breathability, it may be necessary to remove not only plastic paint but cement render as well; success depends on how much damage the cement does in parting from the wall and on how durable any replacement lime pointing and render might be in the prevailing conditions; it is advisable to seek local feedback on similar work as there is not yet much experience to go on; it is always possible to try a test area, but bear in mind that a small test patch could act as a conduit and sole outlet for trapped damp from a wider area.

Problems with Pebbledash

This finish, small stones half-embedded in a coat of render, can be particularly difficult to strip, either because the stones may be dislodged or the rough surface helps the old paint to cling on. If the pebbledash is in a cement mortar (fashionable in repairs from around the 1920s on) there is little point in removing the paint since cement also creates a relatively impervious surface; if the pebbledash remains then its paint needs to be kept in good condition. If pebbledash is in place only on parts of a house that can otherwise be stripped, it can be limewashed to match by using admixtures to make it stick (this makes the limewash non-breathable, so is only for use locally on patches of wall that are already irredeemably non-breathable; *see* limewash below). As pebbledash is difficult to repair invisibly, it was often painted early on to conceal patches.

PAINTS TO USE ON STRIPPED RENDER AND MASONRY

Limewash

Having made the surface breathable again, anything that seals it up is to be avoided. Limewash can be the perfect finish, but beware that some mixtures are less breathable than the basic. (For the background to building lime and courses *see also* Info pages: Lime.) Limewash is lime putty diluted with water, sometimes coloured with natural pigments. It can be relatively cheap and its technical and visual qualities that suit old houses are:

- breathability in conjunction with the original traditional construction to which it was applied (it cannot make a non-breathable underlying surface like cement render breathe);
- compatibility with many traditional materials, especially lime mortars and renders; it is made from the same material, shares their ability to creep under conditions of movement and can help to 'heal' those surfaces on reapplication;
- appearance – it has a softer look than modern paints; without resorting to artificial paint effects it can take up subtly graduated shades and textures according to the method of application, background and exposure.

ABOVE: Limewash is simply a traditional weathering surface for walls – here the limewash covers both render and timbers, which is thought to be a more accurate reflection of medieval practice than the 'picture-postcard' black and white.

BELOW: Limewash is also used to decorate and protect stone and brick walls; it was traditionally used as natural white or coloured with locally available 'natural earth' or vegetable pigments.

Application

The use of limewash is straightforward and satisfying, but tuition is necessary to avoid misunderstandings over the different types of lime and to avoid reinventing the wheel. It requires an understanding of its properties (for example, it does not tolerate frost until it is properly dry) and respect for its caustic state when in use (gloves and goggles are essential minimum protection). Limewash can be bought in large plastic tubs ready-mixed and coloured, which can save time and ensure a reasonable degree of consistency, although, as with render and mortar, the mixing is critical but not overly complicated and limewash can even be made on site: simple limewash can be made by gradually, and carefully, diluting lime putty until a brushable liquid results. Purists say it should be applied with grass brushes, but a coarse 'distemper' brush (or any type that holds a lot of liquid) should work. The wall should normally be wetted well immediately before application and the ideal surface is, of course, the absorbent, soft lime render.

Pigments and Coverage

Pigments can be added to limewash up to a volume of about one-tenth of the total mix and would ideally be natural earths, but vegetable dyes were traditional too and, provided there are enough fruit or plants to finish the job, there is an opportunity to research and experiment with truly local colours. The number of coats is whatever is required to cover the background; the finish will rarely be totally uniform or totally opaque and may, for some reason, obstinately leave patches which need lightening or darkening. The beauty is in the brush marks (so it might be applied with panache) and in its subtle imperfection, like handmade paper.

Other Additives and Variants

Additives are usually strongly avoided as they can compromise the breathability. Even traditional ones such as tallow or oil (for additional waterproofing) act to reduce this useful aspect of its performance. Some contractors reckon they can make limewash stick to stubborn areas of concrete or old sheets of plastic paint by adding PVA (a universal, water-soluble building adhesive). However, this additive makes limewash non-breathable so it is strictly only for matching-in limited areas that are non-breathable anyway. Ordinary limewash is made from lime putty that comes from non-hydraulic lime (or sometimes hydrated lime). There is growing interest in using hydraulic lime to make a limewash but as yet not a great deal of experience to draw on.

Limewash can be white or pigmented and not only can it allow old walls to breathe but its subtle surface shading can express the background material, the method of application and even respond to the weather.

Modern Breathable Paints for External Walls

Limewash can be remarkably durable in sheltered or moderately exposed locations, a thorough redecoration can sometimes last for more than five years. But this cannot be guaranteed and allowance should be made for recoating every few years. As a result of the possible difficulty of regular access to high-level painted areas, an approach adopted by some conservationists has been to use modern breathable silicate paints (also known as mineral paints). Their cost may be offset if they live up to their reputation for durability in difficult situations. As they are claimed to bond with the background, they would seem to be non-reversible and so should not be used without some thought. Silicate/mineral paints vary in formulation between manufacturers and so it is worth checking how breathable any one is. As always, independent advice is needed to interpret manufacturers' 'blurb'. Silicate paints are favoured by some conservationists for their long life, but they should not be confused with other coatings, also marketed for long life, but which may not be breathable to any useful degree.

REMOVING PAINT FROM JOINERY AND TIMBER

If, having considered the potential damage to history (*see above*) and also the potential hazards of disturbing old lead paint (*see* Info pages: Safety and building), it is thought appropriate to remove paint from joinery then a suitable technique needs to be found. But whatever the technique, some rubbing down is inevitable and this risks losing fine detail unless it is carefully controlled. Old glass can be easily scratched by abrasives and so masking, wet rubbing down or the use of softer abrasives such as wire wool may be preferable. Not all the following are appropriate to old houses but they are discussed, with some pros and cons, as they may crop up in discussions with professionals and contractors:

Chemical Strippers

Many of the observations made above about chemical strippers and exterior masonry paint also apply to the chemical stripping of paint from timber doors and windows. Paint strippers for joinery may come as a paint-on solvent or for application as a thick poultice. Some chemicals can permanently colour the timber. Water-based strippers, and flushing, preferable in many ways, does risk raising the grain of some timber (making it look hairy).

Burning-off and Hot Air Guns

Although the use of intense heat from an oil, gas or electric source has become a conventional solution for melting away paint, it is not regarded as appropriate to the conservation of historic buildings since it can permanently alter the timber by scorching and crack adjacent and valuable old glass. Burning old paint can release a cocktail of toxic fumes, from old lead to modern petrochemicals. 'Hot works' are usually automatically banned by conservation organizations because of the fire risk since old buildings frequently have too many inaccessible voids filled with debris that can smoulder and then catch alight when the building is unsupervised. The owner of an old house would be wise to follow their cautious example.

Dipping

Items that can be taken off a building, such as doors, and stripped of their accessories can be stripped of paint by dipping them in a bath of chemicals. As with chemical stripping *in situ*, the process may change the natural colour of the timber – bleaching or darkening it. Any water-flushing can raise the grain of the timber. A more serious potential drawback is that the chemicals can also dissolve glue so that, in extreme cases, what emerges from the tank is a kit which may not fit together as well as when it was first made.

Specialist Abrasive Techniques

As with walls, fierce abrasive blasting risks destroying the item being stripped as well as the paint, it is all too easy to turn a fine example of joinery into a piece of driftwood. Any form of abrasion, however gentle, from sandpaper to sandblasting, risks releasing toxic lead dust into the air if there is lead paint present. Gentle proprietary processes of grit-blasting have been developed by using a relatively subtle, oblique application via a vortex of fine grit that strikes with a glancing blow rather than head-on. The success of these depends on the skill of the operator (who works in a protective suit inside a perpetual cloud of dust), not just the system. Hardwoods are likely to produce a better result than softwoods, but a skilled person can clean paint from softwood with very little furrowing of the grain. The earliest of these sensitive techniques has been favoured by conservation organizations for removing paint from internal and external structural timbers as well as from some joinery, though total stripping is rare for conservation reasons.

None of the Above

The complete removal of paint from joinery is questionable on conservation grounds as it can destroy good historical layers along with bad modern ones (releasing lead and toxins is also an issue, *see above*). Complete removal is only functionally worthwhile if a breathable paint system can then be applied and kept. Strippers may one day be able to reliably remove modern paint and leave old breathable layers, but until then one practical solution is to keep the existing build up of paint in good order to minimize the entry of water; some modern gloss paints are usefully more robust and flexible than others, but all paint is liable to crack on joinery that moves and so needs regular attention. Any damp that enters the joinery via its unpainted surfaces, say where it is attached to a wall, can still be trapped, however. An alternative strategy is to find a breathable paint finish that is compatible with what is in place and simply begin to use that – on the basis that preparation for subsequent repaintings will inevitably expose a little more bare wood here and there in vulnerable areas, which, over time, may add up to a modest increase in breathability.

PAINTS FOR STRIPPED TIMBER

There is no point in stripping non-breathable paint from joinery unless it is replaced with something more benign. The options are: lead paint, but only for appropriate locations on higher grades of listed building and subject to special licence; natural-oil paints, such as linseed oil paint, that are similar to lead paint but use substitutes for lead (such as zinc), these, like traditional lead paint, can take longer to

dry but some can be simpler to apply and to repair in the future; limewash was traditionally used over exposed structural timbers and sometimes on the more 'rustic' door and window frames, so any stripping of external timber might be followed by limewash or alternatively 'boiled' linseed oil thinned with natural turpentine, according to local traditions and conservation advice.

Several of the big paint companies have produced 'vapour-permeable' paints and stains for some time, though it is difficult to compare the degree of useful breathability offered with that of the traditional (that is, historic) paints. Conventional modern paints that rely, for example, on petrochemical-derived VOCs (volatile organic compounds) are likely to have to be reformulated to reduce or eliminate them; as a result, some conventional modern paints are becoming available in water-based options, but this feature alone does not in itself make them any more suitable for old houses.

REMOVING PAINT FROM IRON AND STEEL

With cast-iron gutters and downpipes, iron window frames and cast and wrought iron fences the options for stripping are generally similar to those already described (and so are the cautions about removing history). With the exception of some delicate wrought-iron work, iron is generally tough enough to resist the scraping and abrasion involved in paint-stripping and preparation for a new finish. However, heat can crack cast iron and can 'unlock' some wrought-iron joints, while chemicals have to be chosen with care so as not to attack the metal. Care must also be taken not to leave stripper residue in crevices where they may attack new paint.

PAINTS TO USE ON STRIPPED FERROUS METAL

For painting cast-iron gutters and downpipes *see* chapter 3. For iron and steel, where old paint has been removed down to bare metal, rust can be chemically treated and then the bare metal primed with a good quality metal primer that also chemically protects the metal (zinc-based primers claim to do

All surfaces benefit from thorough preparation and application of an appropriate paint system.

this). Manufacturers' guidelines differ, but typically two coats of primer are applied as soon as practicable; these can be followed by several intermediate coats of the marine-quality paint known as 'micaceous iron oxide'. MIO can be bought in glossy versions which offer finishes in themselves, but, as the colours are limited, may also be used in their rougher finishes which would then be given a couple of coats of conventional gloss in the desired colour. MIO is a special thick paint that helps to protect from knocks, but it can obscure detail on decorative ironwork and so sometimes a more conventional primers/under-coats/gloss coats system may be appropriate (MIO, like other paints, may be subject to reformulation to reduce the VOC content and this might affect performance). Rust is caused by splits and cracks in the paint film admitting water, and, since metal has no need to breathe, it is more important that the finished paint film is well attached, is continuous and can flex or expand with the metal as required. Too thick a build up of paint layers can be inflexible and split.

With all paints, but especially multi-coat systems, ensure proper preparation and cleanliness, compatibility between coats and correct, safe handling and application by referring to the manufacturer's directions. A properly prepared and executed job can far exceed the life of skimped work.

REMOVING EMULSION PAINTS FROM CEILINGS

The traditional chalk-based finishes, such as distemper, had a powdery finish which could reduce the ability of modern emulsion paints to adhere over the top. Any stabilizers applied in the past to overcome this can now make the paint harder to remove. Emulsion might also be difficult to remove in kitchens and bathrooms due to the effect of years of water vapour. Steam strippers are sometimes used, but with mixed results. Usually, however, emulsion parts company from distemper willingly by using a wallpaper stripping hand-tool angled close to the ceiling, being careful not to gouge the plaster. Stubborn patches of emulsion might remain and these may have to be accepted and painted over when new distemper is applied to the ceiling. They can be made less noticeable by 'feathering' the edges with light sanding or the application of conventional filler to 'ramp' the edges. If the existing emulsion is not readily removable and there is no urgent need for the ceiling to breathe, then distemper can usually be successfully applied over clean, sound emulsion; in addition to preparatory cleaning (with sugar soap), the surface might usefully be keyed by light sanding or wire brushing (while wearing suitable protection against dust and having confirmed that there are no hazardous materials present in old finishes; *see* Safety in building – Asbestos).

PAINTING STRIPPED CEILINGS

See below under Removing emulsion paint from internal walls.

REMOVING PAINT FROM CEILING CORNICES AND CENTRAL ROSES

These features may have been blurred by layers of paint. How successful removal will be depends upon the material from which the rose or the cornice was made. Plaster (often gypsum for these items) is fragile and very porous, and along with the other materials used for ornament, such as gesso (a compound that is like hardened putty) and papier-mâché, can be softened and damaged by steam. It can be a time-consuming job in an uncomfortable working position to give these items the attention needed, trials are advisable first. Perhaps the easiest problem to deal with is a build up of soft distemper – which might be gently wetted and wiped away. Where emulsion has been painted over distemper, it may come off by gently peeling back the paint with a flexible, flat-bladed plastic tool, taking care not to score the base plaster. If not, then chemical strippers or steam might be investigated, but neither these methods nor scraping is advisable on very old or valuable examples – that is a job for an expert conservator. It is better to leave the item badly painted than to risk destroying it (*see below*).

PAINTING STRIPPED PLASTER ORNAMENTS

Sometimes a view has to be taken on the degree of improvement that will be visible and the likelihood of damage to these, sometimes irreplaceable features, with current stripping technology. If stripping is decided against, then the least aggressive paint with which to freshen up existing painted features like this is plain (soft) distemper. This can be removed quite easily in the future, whereas applying more emulsion can make a future strip more difficult.

REMOVING EMULSION PAINT FROM INTERNAL WALLS

Where modern, non-breathable emulsion paint has been painted direct on to a 'traditional' distempered wall it is likely to bubble as damp will be still trying to escape from within the wall but will be blocked by the new paint. The simple act of painting an old wall with emulsion has been enough to draw attention to low-level dampness, which grew as it was trapped, then someone came along with a damp meter, gave a quotation and installed a damp-proof course and replastered the wall with 'special' renders and plasters. As a result, the wall may not be traditionally constructed any more, so have this checked first. If there is a damp problem more serious than the normal background transpiration inherent with old buildings, then that needs to be addressed (*see* Info pages: Damp). Sometimes the only route out for damp is the wall surface and replacing a non-breathable paint with a breathable one is the best option. Stripping emulsion from walls is as for ceilings above, but in some circumstances chemical strippers may be appropriate – these would be selected by experimentation or submission of a sample to the manufacturer, as already described (*see above*: Removing paint from external walls).

Emulsion applied over old wallpaper or lining paper can be removed if the paper is removed with it. But be careful that, if removing old wallpaper, layers of history are not also being stripped. Be aware too that the 'sizing' (priming with paste) of a wall can reduce breathability and old size needs to be cleaned off. Washing down stripped walls can help to dissolve some wallpaper paste residues, but care over hygiene is advisable as some pastes contained fungicides to prevent mould.

Some modern plasters that may have been used in repair or remedial works (for example, in connection with chemical damp-proof courses) do not work as part of a breathing wall. Some other, sometimes pink-coloured, plasters (used for repairs, perhaps) which absorb airborne moisture may react unfavourably with distempers. It may be worth assigning a small sample area to check and this is where some professional advice may be useful in order to look beyond just stripping paint. Damp can take a long time to dry out fully. It can be worthwhile to allow as long as possible – months even – before redecorating, but resist the temptation to over-heat rooms in the meantime to speed things up.

PAINTING STRIPPED INTERNAL WALLS AND CEILINGS

Limewash has been used internally, but for centuries distempers have been the popular traditional materials. These are available nowadays in ready-to-use tins and a range of colours:

'Soft' or Plain Distemper

A gentle-looking finish which, in white on ceilings, stays fresh and bright looking on a dry surface; application can produce a soft-brushed effect or a smooth surface; it is also available in colours, mainly pastels because of the chalk content, and is a highly breathable internal finish (check that the binder is a glue that, like traditional rabbit glue, permits breathability, some modern alternatives might compromise this). Soft distemper can rub off as a chalky powder, not a problem on ceilings but for walls some people prefer to sacrifice full breathability for:

Oil-bound Distempers and Milk Paints

These distempers, which are less breathable but more durable and can sometimes support darker colours, are 'bound' with oil, ideally, traditionally used natural oils. Alternatively, distempers are made up with casein, a natural binder found in milk (hence 'milk paints'). Modern plastic binders may be too aggressively waterproof for old buildings.

Non-vinyl or Low Vinyl Emulsion Paints

Not as traditional-looking and probably not as breathable as distemper. These modern paints are sometimes used by builders for a first decoration while a new building's gypsum plasterwork is still drying out. These may be appropriate in certain circumstances in an old house since they will permit at least some breathing. It is possible to have these paints tinted in a wider range of colours than those normally offered. For more on colours *see* Info pages: Old house style and lifestyle – Paints old and new.

SUMMARY

Paint removal on a large scale is expensive and time-consuming. It is labour-intensive and requires skill. It may be inappropriate where the result would strip the building of history but is otherwise to be encouraged where the removal of inappropriate modern finishes will help to arrest the decay of hidden fabric by allowing the insides of walls and other elements to dry out by breathing.

Therefore, for many old houses, the greatest benefit is likely to be from removing modern, exterior, 'plastic', masonry paints and replacing them with traditional limewash together with some parallel work on interior walls. In other cases, where old houses have been significantly altered, it may be sensible to retain modern paint systems and keep them in good condition pending a thorough reassessment.

Changes to the breathability of elements of a building should preferably be considered in relation to the whole building to avoid moving damp problems elsewhere, rather than solving them. As it is difficult to predict the behaviour of hidden, unknown, fabric, then paint removal to achieve breathability should be approached in a spirit of experimentation rather than the expectation of a final solution.

In medieval houses wall paintings were often painted on timbers and the in-filling panels in between so extreme care must be taken when dealing with walls that may have early decorations on them. In all houses the patterns of wear on joinery particularly are part of the signature of history, so beware of removing them in efforts to make the building over-perfect.

Changes of colour or finish may require local authority consents.

An old house painted in limewash that darkens in patches after rain and is softly varied in colour is a different, and arguably much more authentic, old house from one painted in a uniform, chemically-pigmented, modern, 'plastic' paint. If all the other conditions ensuring breathability are correct then that house may also be expected to last longer too.

CHAPTER 5

Windows and Doors

HISTORICAL PERSPECTIVE

Glass and Windows

The earliest windows would have been shuttered openings with no glass, the supposed origin of the word from 'wind' and 'eye' says it all. They may have been shut much of the time, but with glass came convenient and reliable natural lighting inside buildings, though the first window glass was costly and so windows were small. Until the twentieth century, when the manufacture of large sheets of glass was possible, windows were made up of small panes in frames ingeniously made to gather maximum light.

Medieval glass tended to be thick, not very clear, small 'quarries' of glass and these are what survive in

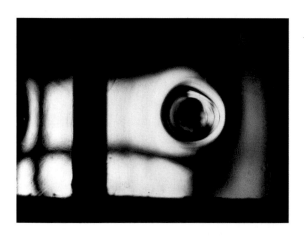

Though much prized in the 1960s and even much earlier, the 'bulls-eye' was really just a cheap off-cut from early glass-making.

early leaded-light windows. The earliest glass windows were valuable and so might perhaps have been portable between the dwellings of the super rich of the period. Georgian buildings exploited 'crown' glass, made by blowing a balloon of molten glass, flattening it by spinning (the part attached to the blowpipe was the waste 'bull's eye') and, after controlled cooling in an oven, it could be cut to size. 'Cylinder' glass formed the balloon into a tube which was slit and flattened. These hand-made glasses retain some of the curve and striations of the process, which can still be seen in Georgian windows. Relatively thin and light, they were an ideal partner to the fine Georgian and early Victorian glazing bars in their sash windows. The Victorians developed mechanically-blown glass which could make larger sheets.

Glass has also been made by casting and rolling, with the potential to imprint patterns on the surface (previously glass was rendered obscured or patterned by acid etching) and to incorporate wire reinforcement within it. Plate glass was made optically more perfect by starting thick and polishing down. Later Victorian and Edwardian buildings adopted larger panes and frames became a little heavier to take the weight. By the early twentieth century glass was made relatively cheaply and in large sheets by drawing it down towers; its optical qualities varied and more perfect large sheets could be made by floating molten glass on a bed of molten tin – the basis of modern glass production. Glass is now available with coatings and interlayers to boost its performance and appearance. Special applications have also improved – modern fire-resisting glazing looks more elegant than the old, wire-reinforced glass.

Joinery is the expression on the face of an old house.

For centuries since the first use of glass in building the technology for making glass windows has been accessible to anyone, sufficiently determined, with a bucket or two of sand, a few handfuls of limestone and soda ash and a really good fire. In the present century all the processes required to make a modern, highly-insulated glass window would almost certainly be impossible without industrial back-up. A modern, triple-glazed, gas-filled, reflective-coated window assembly leaves traditional windows standing in terms of thermal insulation. But there are other ways to insulate window openings in old buildings (*see below*).

Side-hung casements have always been popular, in timber or iron. Iron was an excellent partner for leaded lights since the metal made for thinner frames than wood, admitting more light. In Britain casements traditionally open out (so were rarely paired

Matching parts to houses is not always taken as seriously as matching parts to machines, the original identity can be lost.

FAR LEFT: Present-day double-glazing is too thick and heavy for slender glazing bars.

LEFT: The Georgian sash was an elegant blend of contemporary science and art – maximum light through height, fine glazing bars and state-of-the-art glass sizes – all in harmonious mathematical proportions. By contrast the white strips embedded in modern PVC windows seem a poor showing for two centuries of further human development.

with continental-style external shutters). Vertically-sliding sash windows became popular with the Georgians and this continued until the early twentieth century: their height gave better light penetration into rooms, but the lower ceiling heights in modern housing saw a preference for 'picture' windows.

Doors

Timber does not remain stable in door-width planks, even if it grows that wide, so the introduction of vertical boarding was the first step in wooden doors and this has been the basic utility door ever since. A lighter and more elegant solution was the panelled door, a joinery frame filled with boards, which braced it. Some of the panels could be replaced by glass. Unlike natural wood, processed boards such as plywood and hardboard do come in door widths and so were mounted on a hidden frame; this is the basis of modern doors – even though many of them are stamped out in fake panelled designs. In the past, a door that became redundant would be reused elsewhere, not scrapped. Today's old houses may contain doors cut-down, or made-up, from ancient salvage.

Both doors and window frames would have once been made from native hardwoods or slow-grown, well-seasoned softwoods for reasons of availability

Traditional doors are usually either boarded or panelled, depending on their age and status.

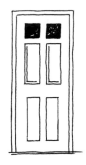
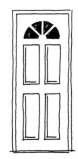

Traditional fanlight
(as 19th century).

Traditional UK toplight
door (as 19th century).

Modern replacement door
(as 20th century USA).

*Modern, mass-produced timber doors, as right, are often inspired by European and
American traditions not Britain's own familiar designs.*

and durability. Imports of softwood and tropical and
other hardwoods from the eighteenth century on
introduced species of varying durability into the
country. Changes in paint technology away from
traditioinal, breathable paints, coupled with the use
of fast-grown, non-durable softwoods meant that by
the mid-twentieth century new doors and windows
might be expected to last for only ten or twenty years
when traditional joinery had lasted ten times that.

GLASS

Repair

It is difficult, but not impossible, to release old glass
intact from its frame, and this is a reason to try to
repair, rather than replace, a frame as it is more
likely that the charming old glass can be kept.
When repairing and decorating old windows it is
worth knowing that, apart from being thinner and

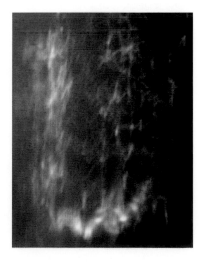

*Until the first half of the last
century, ordinary glass panes for
housing were often mildly
distorting, their busy reflections
and refractions of sunlight can
make modern, optically-perfect
glass look sterile.*

117

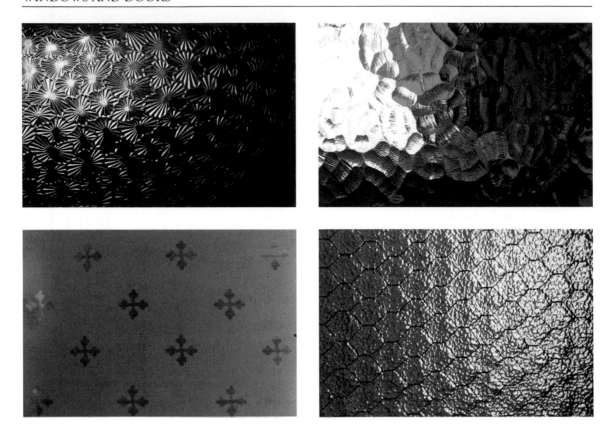

Patterned glass can be associated with a variety of dates; these are early twentieth-century. Replacements may not be current from British manufacturers, but can sometimes be sourced from overseas.

more fragile, pre-Victorian glass can be easier to scratch than that produced by modern processes, so care is needed when rubbing down adjacent paintwork.

Glass has usually been replaced rather than repaired, but broken panes were once made reusable by being cut down to a smaller size. It may be tempting to try to repair old panes of valuable, characterful glass that have a very minor crack by using a modern glass repair adhesive that works into the crack by capillary action. This is unlikely to restore its strength, the glass would remain weakened and so would be appropriate for tiny cracks in small panes. Adhesive films have been produced for upgrading existing panes to meet safety standards, though they are not usually intended as repair options (addition-

ally, the adhesive is suspected of altering old glass permanently). Glass made by historical methods, or to match period glass, can be bought (but beware of overworked examples). Mid-twentieth century 'reject' glass might have ended up as 'horticultural glass' which, usefully, could have similarities in appearance and thinness to some Georgian glass. However horticultural glass is made differently now, and does not resemble old-fashioned glass so well. Moreover, modern safety and other regulations can place more restrictions on what is deemed acceptable for replacement glass.

Modern regulations and sensible safety precautions dictate that glass in certain locations should present minimal hazards in the event of accidental breakage. This calls for the use of safety glass (glass that is toughened to break less dangerously or is laminated with plastic inside to resist disintegration). It may not be necessary to sacrifice any existing old glass in these locations as other measures, such as the application of a plastic film or secondary glazing, may be deemed to provide an acceptable level of protection. But, if replacing broken glass in these locations, it can be possible to obtain toughened or laminated panes made using reproduction period glass. Ensure that these are identified as meeting the necessary standards.

Regulations may also tend to the use of reflective-coated ('insulating') glass or even double-glazing in some window replacements. These requirements can technically apply to repairs or alterations in old buildings, but they are not intended to compromise them so it is worth discussing them with the local authority's building control department, and, if the building is listed or in a conservation area, with the local conservation officer. If single glazing is crucial to the external appearance of an old house but double-glazing is mandatory, it might be suggested that single-glazing is backed-up with suitable secondary glazing.

Leaded Lights

The repairing of leaded lights is specialist work. Very old, inscribed or coloured glass (painted, stained and grisaille designs) is not as resistant as modern glass and can be damaged by mastics, adhesives and cleaning fluids. Traditionally, a broken 'quarry' (pane) might have been mended by joining it along a break with a further 'came' (shaped lead strip) rather than with a new quarry – and this, or a modern conservation version of this repair, may be an option for a quarry that is specially coloured or part of a design. Opening and resealing the lead cames is not as easy as it looks and a poor repair can be an invitation to intruders. Lead does not usually last as long as glass, so really ancient leaded lights are likely to have been releaded several times. If renewal is necessary the cames are unlikely to be standard sections, so they may have to be specially made (consider recycling them from the existing), while the glass may need to be sourced from a specialist supplier to match for colour, texture and thickness. The traditional diagonal pattern was probably better able to resist buck-

The sparkle of real leaded lights is absent from modern glazing.

ling than the square grid, but the latter is better able to conceal metal rods (ferramenta) that strengthen the cames.

A 'cement', to hold and waterproof the glass edges, was not always used, but, if it was, an old mixture might have included plaster of Paris, linseed oil, red lead and lamp black. Some modern work uses special non-setting mastic. Leaded lights are frequently criticized for leaking, vulnerability and being draughty, but it would not be appropriate in most cases to seal

Diamond leaded lights, with wooden bars in place of 'ferramenta'.

up leaded lights into one half of double glazing, because they are not airtight and because the glass or lead may be damaged by the persistent condensation that could result. Installing secondary glazing sensitively, behind the leaded light, is a kinder way to improve thermal insulation and security and keep the special sparkle alive outside.

WOODEN WINDOWS AND DOORS

Timber doors and window frames are practical and almost infinitely repairable. Wood is a 'sustainable' product and capable of periodic adjustment when, as is inevitable in an old house, the walls make small movements on their shallow foundations or expand and contract in tune with the seasons.

Repair

For some time a 'proper' timber repair has been regarded as cutting out the affected timber plus some more to achieve a sound, straight or profiled edge suitable for bonding in a new piece with mechanical joints and glue. Recently, fillers have become more versatile and, even though they are not strictly compatible with timber's inherent breathability (but

then, neither is the glue-line of a pieced-in repair), they can offer scope for a repair that minimizes the amount of timber that has to be removed since a straight edge is not necessary. Fillers are more likely to be able to be applied without the removal of a window frame for a bench repair, helping the glass to survive. Fillers might use metal armatures to strengthen and tie the repair while cut-in new timber might be additionally supported with metal brackets, normally of stainless steel or brass to resist corrosion. Putty should be kept in good order and cracks in its surface and against the glass kept filled and painted. If this can be done between redecorations then the eventual repainting of the whole window should be easier as decay should be reduced.

Paint

Paint is critical to the performance of external joinery. But the gloss paints used for much of the twentieth century tended to seal damp in, especially once they began to wear. Traditional paints could be neglected with less damage to the wood. *See* Info pages: Paints and paint removal for more about paints used on joinery, including the hazards of finding old lead paint.

the bottom rails of sashes are prone to decay, along
with cills (so keep all paint and putty in good order)
a : loose tenon joint can be re-glued/re-wedged - or
b : a brass or stainless steel bracket let in
c : decay, or entire rotten members, can be replaced
d : a,b&c can be adapted to mend frail glazing bars

Some basic window repair techniques.

A timber sash can respond to straightforward repair techniques.

Paint fails at the joints in joinery, which is just where the protection is most needed; more traditional paints tended to powder or flake away all over, not only at joints, giving failed areas an extra chance to dry off.

Sash Windows

Vertically sliding or horizontally sliding, these were suitable for opening on to busy roads and footpaths and became popular in towns, since the British have never taken to inwardly-opening windows. The vertical sliding types rely on a box on either side to contain pairs of weights on cords or chains that counterbalanced the sashes. In Scotland many lower sashes are traditionally adapted by simple, clever ironmongery to also open inwards for maintenance and cleaning.

The channels to either side of vertical sliders should be preserved with an oil such as linseed or a suitable wax to avoid paint build-up jamming them; horizontal sliders may have alternative protection.

121

After some hundred years of sash cord replacement, the access panel for the sash weights may be a little ragged, but some designs have clever access doors.

A wrought iron and leaded window.

Replacing Sash Cords

Sash cords break from time to time. They last quite well considering that they are exposed to daylight and made from natural fibres, but breakage does mean that some dismantling of the sash box is necessary. Finding the prepared opening in the frame to access the dropped weight can be difficult as there might be fifty years of paint applied since it was last opened. Experience shows that new sash cords of natural fibres, waxed, pre-stretched and specially made for the job perform well. Man-made fibre cords were tried in the 1960s and, like so many twentieth-century ideas, seemed to be a durable repair that would last forever – but they stretched.

The replacement of sash cords is a ruthlessly logical operation and benefits from experience, correct equipment and an extra pair of hands. The job can be frustrated by the pulley wheels at the top of the window frame having seized. Ideally, time should be allowed to repair these as well since the modern replacements are frequently of different sizes to the eighteenth- and the nineteenth-century versions. As sash-weights are to counterbalance the sash, they may need to be adjusted to balance extra paint or thicker glass acquired over time.

Sash Draught-proofing

Any measures that remove or permanently alter the original components take away authenticity, while proprietary systems can introduce special seals and other components that might not be available for ever. In good condition, an original sash window can usually be draught-proofed effectively by simple, reversible, DIY measures. Remember that even brand-new, triple-glazed windows are required to be accompanied by ventilator panels so that occupants can breathe, so over-sealing a window is pointless.

IRON AND STEEL WINDOWS

Wrought Iron and Its Repair

Iron frames have been widely used for windows since the earliest times and in Britain are particularly associated with early leaded-light windows. An early, pre-industrial, metal frame would have been made of wrought iron, a product of the blacksmith's forge, and theoretically should be repaired in the same way.

The central piece of wrought iron shows the laminations in its structure that result from working the metal and which give it resilience.

But this would mean removing the sash from its frame, de-glazing it and disassembling the frame. Sometimes modern welding repairs can be carried out without such disturbance – it all depends on the balance of risks and the value of the features. Welding using mediums that are of relatively pure iron is said to make for a reasonably compatible repair, in terms of material. Intense heat from welding might risk the breaking of glass and might also risk releasing some mechanical iron-to-iron joints. *See* Info pages: Paints and paint removal – Paints for stripped ferrous metal.

Cast Iron and Its Repair

Cast iron was much used for Victorian 'cottage' window frames, and, surprisingly, even for large, vertical, sash windows. Cast iron was the wonder material of its age. It was manufactured by casting iron into the impression left by a timber 'pattern' in fine sand. A superficial repair can be reasonably straightforward, but, if structural integrity is compromised, specialist techniques might be needed for repair and reinforcement. If repair is not possible, recasting is an option. Sometimes, to avoid the expense of making a new timber pattern to cast from, recasting is done from a mould made by using an identical component from elsewhere on the building (one half of a pair of gates, for example). In that case the finished product would be fractionally smaller than the original due to the contraction of the

cooling metal. Cast iron can be reasonably durable without painting (as in old manhole covers), but was usually painted for household applications and it lasts better if properly painted. *See* Info pages: Paints, etc.

Steel

Twentieth-century steel windows were popular replacements for worn-out iron frames in cottages during the last century, and were often accompanied by fake 'stick-on' lead on their glass. Though relatively recent, these have acquired a degree of nostalgic respectability: Standard-sized casements, fittings and some of the steel sections for use in repairs can still be found new or second-hand. From the 1950s steel windows were offered galvanized and this helps them to survive. Painting direct on to new, galvanized steel requires a special priming treatment. For painting ordinary steel as well as cast and wrought iron *see* Info pages: Paints, etc.

IRONMONGERY

The hinges and catches of windows are important in holding the window properly closed to stop draughts. Modern hinges are usually made of stainless steel or brass, but older ones were often iron; they need oil or grease to slow wear and to stop them seizing if unused over winter. Hinges and catches should be adjusted to operate freely so that no undue stress is

Cast iron was able to provide standardized decorative windows for nineteenth-century cottages.

Pet access can be confined to new features rather than irreversibly damaging old ones.

put on frames and glass when operating them. Locks, particularly the finer mechanisms, may be clogged by grease or oil which can attract abrasive grit, so instead, use graphite (scraped from a soft pencil and inserted on the key).

The fittings on old houses have frequently been painted over so many times that they can look unappealing. Careful cleaning can reveal delicately moulded brass, bronze or cast iron. Old iron hinges and latches may have been the work of a local blacksmith and, rather than throw them away when they are worn out, they can be repaired or perhaps preserved on the door and supplemented with newer working versions alongside. Letter flaps are only potentially as old as the postal service and these items of brass or iron are collectively known as 'door furniture', along with bell pushes, knockers, knobs and kick- and finger-plates.

Cat Flaps

Owners of old houses need to think carefully about siting these. Cutting a hole in an old door is destructive and weakens it against intruders. If there is a new door on the property perhaps it has a lower panel that can be temporarily substituted with another panel for the cat flap. Or perhaps there is a new section of wall that can be harmlessly adapted. Some lateral thinking is needed: cats are agile and sufficiently motivated to use any reasonable route.

SECURITY

Security Fittings

Insurance requirements and common sense dictate that some new locks and security fittings should be added to doors and windows. With older properties, insurers may need to be asked if their stipulations can be adjusted since some styles of door and window cannot be fitted with the recommended locks and fasteners without being seriously weakened in the process. Get approvals for such variations in writing. Break-ins would seem now to be by force rather than by skilled lock pickers, nevertheless, a sophisticated lock is worthwhile since the more novel features the lock design offers, the less chance there is that one of a big bunch of keys will fit. Locks are always being improved, but try to stick with ones that fit pre-existing mortices and 'backsets' (the distance of the keyhole or handle from the edge of the door), since the strength and historical integrity of the door will suffer from too many alterations. To make a door more unattractive to a lock picker, fit secure bolts internally and, to the main exit door, consider fitting two entirely different types of lock. Security products come in various patterns, so take the trouble to select those that look best and do the least damage as well as being effective. The local crime prevention officer should be able to offer general advice and experience on providing physical security and on useful deterrent measures (*see* Info pages: Trees, gardens, etc. and chapter 7: Building services – Security lighting).

Alarms

Intruder alarms are now an almost standard back-up to physical security and these might relieve the necessity to make too many physical changes to an old house in pursuit of security. However, detectors and contact points on doors and windows can also involve drilling and cutting that may weaken the timber. Wireless intruder alarms, whose detectors communicate with the alarm's base unit by radio, not wire, can offer a useful compromise that limits any damage during installation. Batteries will have to be changed (usually indicated by the control panel). Some wireless and hard-wired systems can usefully be extended to provide remote sensing of fire and smoke.

DOOR AND WINDOW REPAIR VERSUS REPLACEMENT

Replacement Doors?

Doors are large and so mostly out of reach of the damp ground, thus complete replacement is rarely necessary. They can certainly be severely compromised through rot and inappropriate paint, but timber doors can also be extensively repaired. A replacement door is probably indicative of a successful sales pitch rather than an irreparable old door, and an old house is usually more desirable with its original door than without it.

Replacement Double-glazing?

Around the same time that applying fake stone cladding to buildings became popular, putting entirely modern double-glazed window frames into old houses was also seen by some as a good idea. Since then there has been an increasing awareness of historical accuracy, a demand for unspoilt, period property, and also an awareness that some double-glazing is not living up to all its promises of longevity. The twenty-first century is now more likely to see efforts made to repair old, single-glazed windows, often in conjunction with secondary glazing (*see below*).

However they may look to start with, old doors are rarely beyond repair and often just need sympathetic decoration that does not sacrifice character – that is the green solution. The survival of the blue doors seems to have been helped by their traditional paint.

Building conservationists favour retaining as much original material as possible, so that a building keeps its valuable historic authenticity. Environmentalists would recognize that the material, energy and transport costs involved in a modern industrial replacement are wasted if a simple, localized repair were part of measures that upgrade performance significantly. Traditional timber windows have lasted for hundreds of years when correctly maintained, newcomers such as PVC and aluminium have shown technical promise, but can look out of place, may not tolerate the movement in old houses and tend to require more specialist repair should they fail. PVC may need no decoration, but it clearly weathers enough for there to be a special paint marketed for it.

Repair Options

(*See also* under individual materials, above.) Old windows were made with simple technology by the hands of village joiners and blacksmiths, so, whether the frames are of timber or iron, mending them does not have to involve high technology. Of course, windows and doors can be draughty if they have not been properly maintained, yet the wooden windows of old houses can be repaired, adjusted and smartened up. If necessary, simple, self-adhesive

gaskets or draught-strips can improve some designs (they should be removable without damage if they wear out). Sometimes sashes can be thoroughly jammed by old paint, risking damage to free them; if there are other serviceable windows in the same room there may be no necessity to free them all. Old houses tend to move slightly and timber has traditionally been simple to adjust to fit again, but complex plastic or aluminium sections may not tolerate adjustment. The components (such as gaskets and hinges) on which some modern windows rely are often non-standard fittings that may be difficult to replace now let alone in the future. But for traditional windows, ironmongers still stock putty and a useful range of hinges.

Reinstating Old Patterns of Windows

Undoing any disfiguring past installations of double-glazing ought to have visual benefits and the local authority should be consulted for guidance on the planning and building regulation issues. It might be possible to reinstate authentic single-glazing plus secondary-glazing to provide the insulation, or it might be possible to make an *authentic-looking* window that is double glazed in one sheet, but with fake glazing bars planted over each side of the glass.

The original timber windows [right] were designed to minimize the framework and maximize the glass area, but plastic replacements have thicker frames so windows tended to be enlarged, and this changes the architecture.

The latter may be applicable to new extensions where the planning department could be looking for a perfect match, while their building control colleagues are requiring modern performance. To get a good match between old and new, look at several joinery firms since each will have preferred component styles and sizes, one of which may better match a particular window.

Around the early 1980s, for economy or possibly tax reasons at the time, there was a tendency to make replacement windows a different size or to use standard sizes, so altering structural openings. Reinstating traditional windows in these cases means carefully making good to the wall with matching materials and possibly some structural work to revise or repair lintels, which will need professional advice. A much older tax, the window tax, famously limited the number of windows on houses to different numbers at different times. This tax ran for about 150 years up to the middle of the nineteenth century and relating its requirements through time to a house can provide interesting clues to that house's development.

Regulations

Old windows are a valuable part of an old house. In Britain window replacements – and some window repairs – to listed buildings or those in Conservation Areas and National Parks usually need consents. Window replacements are also required to meet certain administrative and performance criteria which local authority building control departments should be able to advise on. Ask both planning and building control departments at the local council what regulations and other factors apply locally and generally before considering carrying out any such work.

There are safety regulations affecting glass vulnerable to breakage and energy-efficiency regulations requiring special 'insulating' glass (coated to retain heat) (*see above*, this chapter: Glass – Repair). The ability to use certain windows as fire escapes may have formed part of past approvals for attic conversions, thus it may be worth revisiting the subject with the local authority's building control department to see whether changes in regulations or technology can make for improvements in safety or in use, or whether any new proposed alterations will reopen these issues.

Secondary glazing can often be discreetly designed to match the original frames, be invisible from outside and also totally removable in summer.

SECONDARY-GLAZING AND INSULATION

For many old houses, electing to combine existing traditional windows with well-designed secondary-glazing may be one way to satisfy the requirements of both building and fuel conservation. Some grander historic buildings had cleverly designed secondary-glazing that was hard to spot because the inner and the outer frames married up so well. More recent standardized kits in plastic or aluminium tended not to be adaptable enough to make a good looking job and were flimsy or awkward to operate. However, it is perfectly possible to provide a discreet, good looking and functional secondary glazing solution tailored to individual windows: insist that both design and materials match up with existing frames and sashes and that, if the secondary-glazing is not removable in summer, the windows can be used fully. Conservationists like to see 'reversible' solutions – meaning that a modern intervention ought to be ultimately removable without trace and without leaving damage. Secondary-glazing, with a good air gap from the original outer window, has conventionally also

been considered a worthwhile form of acoustic insulation that performs better than with the small air gap present in regular double-glazing.

Other Insulation Measures

Draughty windows can be weatherstripped to cut down the worst of the draughts. This need not be a complex process, the sensible use of ordinary DIY products can work well. Even state-of-the-art modern windows are required to have trickle-ventilation to let us breathe fresh air, so there are diminishing returns in stopping draughts altogether. To lessen draughts and improve the insulation offered by old windows, shutters can be refurbished where they exist and curtains used whenever possible, perhaps lined with metallic, heat-reflective interlayers. A cost-effective method for evaluating the potential of secondary- or double-glazing can be found in DIY kits using stretched plastic film on double-sided adhesive tape. This would not be expected to perform identically to a permanent installation, and effectiveness depends also on any remaining, perimeter draughts; it is not intended as a full-time solution and potential problems with condensation may make it inadvisable.

Entrance doors without lobbies were common and clever, automatically-lifting curtain rails were once seen on the backs of such doors – the remains of these may be seen in many old houses and there seems no reason why these should not be installed today.

Using shutters can boost insulation and security.

Conservation Terminology and Ideas

HISTORICAL PERSPECTIVE

When old cottages, farmhouses and urban terraces were new there were always grander houses and palaces with comforts that were, for most, unattainable. So, despite the inadequacies and sometimes squalor, people had little choice but to love their homes, however humble, cold and inconvenient they would seem to us now. Owner-occupiers were in the minority until the twentieth century. Maintenance, if it happened, would once have routinely been with time-tested, traditional methods that worked with the original fabric rather than fight it, as could happen later with twentieth-century methods. For anyone interested to find out more, glimpses of real life in nineteenth-century old houses are written into Thomas Hardy's novels: he was brought up in a

cottage built by his own family, who were builders, and then became an architect. By the twentieth century, new urban housing was offering ordinary folk some of the comforts previously reserved for palaces, but in the country things changed slowly.

A Ministry of Housing and Local Government publication *New Homes for Old – Improvements and Conversions* (HMSO, 1954) says of rural areas:

> Country cottages usually lack modern amenities, and the standards of accommodation are often low. By no means all rural areas have piped water supplies and electricity. In those that have, their full benefit can be enjoyed only if the cottage is modernised generally. Even in areas still without piped water and electricity, worth-while improvements to the cottages can still be made. One advantage is that the

Cottages that are now highly sought after may have been at risk only half a century ago.

modernisation of country cottages which are structurally sound and have a life of more than fifteen years will help to preserve the character of the rural scene.

The paragraph was accompanied by a photograph of a stone house in what since has become an extremely sought-after Wiltshire village, and which would probably now command a price well in excess of that of the average modern home – possibly two or three average modern homes. Our attitude to these 'cottages' has changed dramatically and the value of 'preserving the character of the rural scene' has not been lost on the market.

But more interesting is the idea that a further life of fifteen years would be good. Faced with a stock of virtually 'disposable' old buildings that only had to be good for less than a couple of decades, it is not surprising that people then did not always bother to consider what repairs would be best for the full potential life of the building. Admittedly, there were other physical pressures on post-war Britain and modernity was in vogue. But this government booklet was introducing improvement grants for private owners: some old houses it may have saved from demolition, others it could have condemned to, in our view, inappropriate modernization.

It is now rare to find cottages that are un-modernized.

Conservation can make long-term sense in all societies, but it is something that a relatively wealthy society has the ability to put to the fore, perhaps as a reminder of the good old, bad old days. A pair of photographs in the same 1954 publication show a demonstration kitchen in London before improvement: scrubbed pine table, marble fireplace, cast-iron range, brass gas lamp, panelled wooden dresser – and then after: gas cooker, plywood table and drawer unit, Belfast sink and a sliding-glass, wall-cupboard. It says a lot about us that the scrapped contents of the 'before' kitchen would probably now fetch a handsome price at auction while the modernizing contents of the 'after' kitchen would now, except for the sink, probably be thrown into a skip.

A BRIEF GLOSSARY OF CONSERVATION CONCEPTS

Adaptation versus Alteration

Adaptation takes what is there and works with or around it to serve a new need. Alteration takes what is there and chops it around to serve a new need. The former can have the advantages of full 'reversibility' and 'minimum intervention' (*see below*), while the latter can be a more destructive path. Adaptation has to truly mean adaptation and not be just a word applied to a proposal drawing in the hope that it creates the right impression.

Breathability

One of the most quoted words in conservation, it means the ability, shared by most traditional building materials and finishes, to allow water vapour to exit from building fabric by natural drying rather than, as conventional modern products can tend to do, seal it in. Old houses that have acquired later sealed-up surfaces may be trapping moisture that is feeding decay. Moisture vapour permeability or porosity might be more scientific terms, but 'breathability' seems to have caught on. There are no doubt scientific measures for the amount of breathability of various gases and liquids through various materials, and almost anything made up from atoms must be breathable to some extent. What is important to old houses is that, on average, they should be permitted to dry out quicker than they get wet, which means 'very breathable'. Modern materials that are waterproof and modern construction that is sealed-up can work well if they are part of a modern building that has been designed from scratch to be waterproof. It is generally several hundred years too late to redesign an old house to work that way, and the two systems may not live happily side by side in the same house. Breathability often goes with adequate ventilation, which is something that modern houses pay lip-service to, but tend to block up when no one is looking (*see* chapter 8: Damp, breathability and ventilation).

Conventional versus Traditional

In this book 'conventional' is used mainly to denote the products that we are used to seeing in DIY stores, builders' merchants and stacked in builders' vans. The 'traditional' products are those that come from the past and were used to build our old houses. Traditional products are very likely to be appearing alongside conventional ones more and more as they are commercialized and marketed in the wake of the heritage industry. Some modern conventional products look very similar to the traditional ones they are descended from but may perform differently, bricks would be an example (*see* chapter 4: External walls).

Historical Periods

This book is mainly concerned with the practical issues of old houses, most of which will have been 'vernacular' rather than 'schooled' designs. The development of building styles in Britain and in relation to external influences is too broad a subject to record fully here, therefore some liberties have been taken in the interests of simplicity: medieval here means anything up to around the end of the seventeenth century, when most domestic buildings were built pragmatically (strictly this encroaches on what archaeologists call post-medieval and which many histories of architectural style subdivide into Tudor and so on). Georgian refers to a period mainly in the eighteenth century when architectural style was self-consciously being applied even to smaller domestic buildings. Victorian was the mid- to late-nineteenth-century period in which industrialization began to affect the look and materials of buildings. These regal, shorthand names are already well established with the 'look' of their periods. Of course, Georgians

Building up lost fabric with tile fragments in lime mortar makes for a sensitive and reversible 'honest' repair to masonry; but there are limits to its extent and eventually like-for-like replacement becomes sensible.

did not become Victorians overnight and there were still essentially 'medieval' buildings being put up well into the Victorian period.

Honest Modern Repair

A repair popular with early conservationists when faced with badly weathered stonework was the 'tile repair' where several layers of plain clay roof tiles were cut to fit and laid with their edges facing out in a wall to replace a missing stone. It is still a respected repair but there is a limit to how much of a wall can be replaced with tiles. Honest modernity is sometimes also preferred by conservationists where it is impossible, or prohibitively expensive, to repair extensive damage to a building – or it is impossible to know exactly what the design of long-missing components might originally have been. 'Modern' in this context usually means more 'simplicity' than 'high-technology', so a modern but genuine panelled door to replace an unknown old one, not a modern plastic one; a modern timber floor to replace an unknown timber floor, not a modern concrete one. But there are no hard and fast rules and a particular building might benefit from a truly inspired modern design to lift it out of ruin in appropriate circumstances.

Like-for-like Repair

If repairing items on an old house that are completely worn out, say pointing to brickwork, then it makes sense to replace them with what has served well for years and fits the way the house works rather than something new and different. Like-for-like repair really refers only to surviving 'original specification' items in old houses: it would obviously not mean replacing failed cement pointing with new cement pointing in an old house originally successfully built with lime mortar. In that case, cement would have been someone's poorer replacement for lime mortar – a repair that was not like-for-like and would not be wise to repeat (*see* chapter 4: External walls). Even when the original picture is masked by later repairs, searching the structure for clues or examining local buildings of a similar age and type can provide leads. This has to be proved with forensic thoroughness or it could lead to 'conjectural restoration' (*see below*: Repair, refurbishment, etc.).

If an old house is made of wood it usually makes no sense to replace a post or a beam with steel, because steel can be stiffer and more abrasive where it joins the timber, it would look out of place among the timbers and may not share the timber frame's willingness to shift about with the seasons. A timber replacement, preferably in the same species of timber seasoned to the same state, would be physically and visually in keeping. But if the post or beam were merely broken it would make more sense to mend and keep it. In that case, a steel repair plate, bracket, splint or whatever could be valid in conservation terms.

Minimum Intervention

The same is true as in human surgery: the less disruption an old house has to endure, the fewer the scars and the better recovery it is likely to make. It is sometimes necessary to design quite cleverly to achieve minimum intervention, and this may involve persuading several other contributors to the building effort to also think laterally. But it can be done.

Non-invasive and Non-destructive Investigations

Allied to minimum intervention, these are the opposite of where an old building is 'surveyed' by using a 2lb hammer, crowbar and a big drill (it happens). It is usually possible for an experienced, professional building conservationist to make a reasonable guess at what a hammer can reveal. Their fee would probably be less than the cost of the making good necessary after the hammer work. And, if it is necessary to take a look inside a wall, there are subtle and discreet methods to achieve this. If they do not work, then miniature fibre-optic probes can be hired from builders' suppliers.

Repair, Refurbishment and Restoration

Among conservationists repair is considered the purest of these three Rs, since it can be taken to mean sensitive 'minimum intervention' work. 'Refurbishment' and 'restoration' might be words used innocently by the public and the media to include the idea of preservation, but, to a building conservationist, 'refurbishment' can imply gutting and modernizing an old building and 'restoration' can be taken as stripping off more recent history with the hope of exposing a notional past appearance that is unprovable and probably over-romantic. Conservationists call this 'conjectural restoration' because it is based on guesswork and, as it disguises the property's actual journey through time, it can be destructive of real history. It is probably best to avoid phrases such as 'restoring it to its former glory' when talking to a conservation officer.

Repair or Reuse versus Replace

Repair can be justified on environmental as well as preservation grounds: it is better to retain not just the original, historical fabric but, along with it, its 'embodied energy' and so save the environmental cost of manufacturing and transporting a replacement. In conservation terms, replacement is unfortunate because it can remove some of the history of a building. If repair is absolutely out of the question for sound practical reasons (and if the item is not riddled with rot) then it can make sense to reuse it within the building (for example, a broken timber can be reworked for use elsewhere) or to keep the broken pieces for future repair (technology may develop ways of mending what we cannot). In either case, it is worth labelling the item so as to enlighten its future owners.

Reversibility

Few people want to live in an old house exactly as it was intended. It is one thing to respect traditional ideas about breathability and ventilation but quite another to live without a bathroom. Old houses need to be adapted, but the act of adapting them can destroy parts of them for ever. If it is possible, and it usually is, new additions – from installing light switches to building whole extensions – can be designed so that one day, when they become redundant, unfashionable or the need for them has passed, they might be removed from the original old house with minimal scarring.

Righting Wrongs when There Is a Bad Mix of Old and New

Undoing past and inappropriate work can be desirable for aesthetic or functional reasons – to protect the building from decay. But sometimes the cost of rectifying past 'wrongs' can be too high, as in causing more damage than it will save. For example, old brickwork that has been thoroughly repointed in cement mortar might not be stripped of that mortar without removing much of the surface of the bricks as well. Ugly features such as flat-roofed extensions might be too expensive to rebuild (but could be disguised or improved relatively cheaply). Technically incompatible repairs that threaten the fabric, such as inappropriate damp-proof courses, may be impossible to reverse, and so any perceived harm may have to be limited by other measures.

Salvage – Help or Hindrance?

Reuse is better than destruction. The question is whether the old items being reused have been removed from their original home for some sound and unavoidable reason or just for profit, leaving the donor old building vulnerable. Salvage can introduce inappropriate components into old buildings, confusing their history and distorting their design with non-contemporary and non-local items. An alternative to salvage is to use new but traditionally-made versions of what is needed. This can stimulate crafts and help traditional, sustainable products to be revived for use in new buildings.

Though it is regrettable that people throw out old fixtures and fittings from their houses, provided that they have not done so in contravention of planning law, their short-sightedness can benefit another old house whose previous owners have done the same thing. However, introducing building components

from non-local or even overseas historical traditions is opening up that cycle too much. If incorporating salvage, labelling the items discreetly or making some other record of the fact can help future owners.

The Replacement Window Paradox

Ask anyone who loves old houses what is the worst visual blight of recent years and they may say that it is modern replacement windows and doors (with particular venom reserved for PVC). Take the same

Reversibility in action – originally this house had no external door to its stone-lined entrance lobby arch, so to make the new installation reversible, the new, traditional-style, wrought-iron hinges and lock plate were extended to fix only into the brickwork beyond the stone; the stone would not be altered by drilling fixings and one day the original layout might be restored without damage.

person along one of the many hundreds of ancient streets in British towns or villages and show them Georgian sliding sash windows in medieval buildings and they will probably admire them. But to the Georgians these were modern replacement windows that were forced into venerable old walls, without any care about what size or design the originals were.

Does this mean that plastic-framed double-glazing might become attractive after being around for 250 years? People may, of course, think differently in the year 2225, should any have survived. PVC as a material is not intrinsically ugly, but it has its own structural, design and assembly needs which are in a different manufacturing league from all the handmade timber and iron window frames that have ever been put into old houses. So it is going to look different, and, to many of us, out of place. PVC and its relatives are useful materials and might one day be modified or reassessed to address the many environmental criticisms directed at them. But even the supporters of plastics would be hard-pressed to argue that the average PVC window installation incorporates the classical mathematical ratios and harmonious proportions aspired to by Georgian windows. Georgian windows do not look out of place in medieval buildings because, yes, we have got used to them, but also because both traditions used the same materials and handcrafted them in the same way.

The 'Museum' Criticism

There can be little doubt that change and innovation over the centuries have been significant contributors to the variety and interest of old buildings. If that is so, why do conservationists and planning authorities seem to resist change now? Part of the answer is, as for replacement windows, that until the Industrial Revolution virtually all dwellings were built by taking local materials and handcrafting them. Old houses related in their scale to human capabilities, in their colour to the local landscape and in their form to both. By contrast, much of the housing built in the twentieth century in Britain has no sense of place and there is less handcrafted input: by the 1950s and 1960s new houses in Cornwall might be very similar to those in Antrim, Essex, Argyll or Gwynedd, they were all built from the same materials and with components from the same factories. Planning guidelines for new buildings and the preservation of old buildings have helped to preserve some local style – perhaps artificially. But if sustainability means, as it must, a re-evaluation of local materials and reinvestment of some craft-based labour in our housing, then preserving a record of how people managed it in the past, before fossil fuels were consumed by machinery and transport, is going to make preservation and conservation one of the most valuable investments our society has made.

Progress in Conservation

The ability to conserve buildings well has progressed from the mid-twentieth century – when some traditional crafts and knowledge were at the point of dying out – until the present where there is active interest in the subject and a growing body of recent experience.

Conservationists themselves have acquired confidence; for example, it is now an automatic assumption that a lime mortar mix is to be preferred for repairs to most buildings that are old enough, while as recently as the 1990s many still used a small proportion of cement. As an example of how the custody of traditional methods has survived the industrial age, the author's great-great-grandfather headed a family of bricklayers who would have been among the last to use lime mortar as a matter of course. An architect of the time would, we guess, not have presumed to know more about the subject, at least not in front of them. But since most modern bricklayers have been trained to use their skills with cement, it has recently been up to people such as architects in conservation to try to promote the use of lime where it seemed necessary for the protection and sustainability of old buildings. So generations pass, things move on and one gets to be retailing the same information as one's great-great-grandfather; '...*plus ça change*, son', as he might have said. All sorts of other areas of traditional expertise are being rediscovered and might eventually make their way back into the mainstream, in many cases due to their inherent link with sustainability.

CHAPTER 6

Internal Walls, Floors and Ceilings

HISTORICAL PERSPECTIVE

Early medieval houses were occupied by households that appear to have traded privacy for warmth in that they gathered about a central fire in one main room. Upper floors were not as we know them, there was little point until a chimney was installed since smoke filled the upper part of the house. In the earliest surviving such houses, internal walls and floors are likely to be later additions. Later medieval houses built with upper floors and divided into rooms may also have been altered as staircases replaced ladders.

Early internal partitions may have been much less substantial than external walls – little more than curtains or woven screens or 'hurdles' of sticks or rushes. Floors in ordinary vernacular houses, as can still be seen in some survivals from as recently as the nineteenth century, were simply the floorboards on timber beams. No ceiling underneath. Ceilings could be an application of lime render under the floorboards on timber laths – literally a 'sealing'.

The internal faces of external walls may have been left in the unfinished stone, brick or timber frame during some of the medieval period, perhaps limewashed, but by the eighteenth and the early nineteenth century an internal 'plaster' finish would have

Builders and householders more familiar with modern plasterboard may not realize that a ceiling can be attached to the floorboards above.

135

been common, not the gypsum plaster we know, nor, in humbler old buildings, plaster of Paris, but a smooth render of a lime and sand mix. During the twentieth century, proprietary gypsum plasters were being marketed, each with its own properties.

FLOORS AND CEILINGS

The size of rooms we have become accustomed to is directly related to the size of the timbers available. A span of 4 or 5m (12 to 15ft) was a comfortable balance of availability, cost, span and loading for an 'ordinary' house or cottage. Grander houses had to buy bigger, more expensive timber if they wanted wider rooms and structural tricks were devised to stretch their rooms, such as 'double floors' where a row of floor joists spanning one way was overlaid by a row spanning at right-angles, so that they supported each other.

Roofs could span wider spaces by using the structural qualities of the triangular roof truss. A very large room might then be possible on the first floor, with its floor sitting on the dividing walls of smaller rooms underneath.

Floor Boards

Hand-finished
The earliest surviving floor boards are of native hardwoods, such as oak or elm, and, without machines to saw them, would have been in whatever width the tree delivered. The thickness would be determined by the structural need to span between the floor joists and the ability of the timber to resist twisting. The boards would not be uniform in width or thickness; they would have had to be packed or notched on to the joists, themselves uneven, to level them. A really old floor is a bit of a jigsaw puzzle. These hand-sawn, or even adzed, planks have a distinctive worked look to them, further smoothed by centuries of wear.

Machine-cut
When machine sawing and imported softwood had become established, boards and joists became more uniform. The regular pattern left by the teeth of machine saws might be visible. Boards were still 'butt-jointed' at this stage (that is, square-edged and

pushed up close to each other), shrinkage caused gaps to open between them, but this was useful in ventilating the under-floor and most of the inconvenient transmission of sound, light or heat would be dealt with by a ceiling underneath.

Modern
Floorboards narrowed along with the fast-grown softwoods used to make them and because there is a balance between thickness, width and twisting. A regular eighteenth-century board might be nearer 200mm wide (about 8in) while, by the late nineteenth century, 150mm (about 6in) was common. Later, more modern boards were joined together at the edge by a 'tongue-and-groove' joint which braced the whole floor together, resisted the twisting of individual boards and allowed their thickness to be reduced to a minimum. When applied retrospectively to an old house this cuts down ventilation as well as stiffening up the floor structure (not necessarily always a good thing).

Repair and Redecoration of Floorboards
For interest, and to comply with listed building legislation, old floorboards belong where they were first fixed. It is a simple carpentry job in most cases to reinforce a broken board without removing it or to splice in a new piece to repair a weakened board. This applies to Victorian sawn softwood just as much as hand-hewn medieval oak: the floorboards help to trace the history and development of the house.

Modern houses have been designed to do without underfloor ventilation, but old houses were not: it is a mistake to seal these up as damp and decay can result.

The 1980s saw a craze for stripping floorboards of all their history and patina with a hired industrial sanding machine and then sealing them up with a heavy-duty varnish until they looked just like a sales floor in a department store. Floors lucky enough to have escaped that are well worth looking at rather than being hidden with fitted carpets. Modern varnishes are difficult to remove sensitively, but it is not impossible (*see* Info pages: Paints and paint removal). A crusty build-up of old wax polish might respond to a small-scale experimental application of household solvents, such as white spirit or methylated spirit.

Most old floors that lived through the nineteenth century would have been stained around the edges (that is, beyond the large central rug). This may not clean off, so one solution is to get a carpet or rug of the same size as the old one, which could save having to trim the bottoms of doors to accommodate a fitted carpet and underlay. A natural and breathable wax or light natural oil that wears away gracefully and can easily be reapplied is usually a preferable finish for old timber floors. Modern, very hard, varnishes, such as polyurethane or two-pack epoxy varnishes, can wear very starkly and tend to require more preparation to reapply, while having the disadvantage of sealing up the wood.

Gaps between Floorboards
It is not a sound idea to block all the gaps in an old floor, partly because these are useful for ventilation (and would have been effective in feeding the old open fires with air) and partly because the gaps are useful for the house to flex and stretch. However, there may be quite wide gaps in rougher floors that need a carpenter's repair to fill with matching timber. In some cases the cosmetic filling of gaps is often desired and this has been achieved with papier-mâché or strips of cork, the advantage being that the boards can still move a little.

Woodblock Floors
Popular around the early twentieth century, blocks of pitch pine or other, more exotic timbers were laid in a tar-like compound. Sometimes the blocks were designed to interlock. After acquiring a hundred years of patina and mellowing in daylight, these have

Starting from here, many would be tempted to machine-sand and varnish but the patina would be swept away; instead it can pay to experiment with washing or the use of a suitable solvent to remove old, built-up polish and a light manual sanding, followed by a traditional oil, wax or polish as appropriate to the traffic and use.

been vulnerable to the same ruinous modern sanding and varnishing as some floorboards (*see above*). Instead of that, a light sand followed by an oil or wax would have kept the glow and interest alive and it is much easier to re-wax or oil a floor than to revarnish it. Loose blocks can be reset and matching timber replacements made for missing or damaged blocks.

Gaps between Floors and Ceilings
Lifting floorboards can reveal a surprise. There will be dust, there may be reminders of workmen's lunches (from nineteenth-century oyster shells to cigarette packets). Some floors were 'pugged', that is, filled with some mix of sand, earth, straw or similar, presumed to deaden sound transmission. Any ancient grass or cereal seeds present could be of interest to botanists.

New Carpets and Floor Coverings
Some modern carpets come with a non-breathable, rubber backing, sheet-flooring and foam underlays may also be inherently unbreathable. The choice of any new floor covering needs to be made with reference to an old house's floor construction.

137

The floor between the master bedroom and the servants' hall beneath in this Georgian house was filled with a solid, earthy mass reinforced with grass and doubtless intended for privacy.

Some Historical Floor Variations

Sanded Floors

Timber floors are thought likely to have been sometimes left bare in the Georgian period, even in parts of some reasonably formal town houses. Perhaps sprinkled with sand, they would be 'self-cleaning' as people walked over them. Eventually this sand may have built up in the underfloor space.

Oilcloths, Linoleum and Carpets

If the Georgians wanted to make a plain floor look smart, but a carpet was not appropriate, then canvas could be stretched over the timber and the effect of tiles, stone or a geometric pattern painted on. These are called oilcloths. Linoleum is a later invention, still available, and has a better environmental reputation than much modern, plastic flooring. Carpets have long been around as a luxury item. Fitted carpets in large rooms used to be made by stitching more manageable rolls or panels together. Rugs were almost certainly the mainstay of those who could afford carpeting until mass-production and man-made fibres made carpets big and cheap, central heating removed dusty open fires and vacuum cleaners provided an alternative cleaning option to beating.

Lime-ash Floors

A mixture containing a variation of lime mortar with wood ash can produce a floor that, while still being breathable, is harder wearing and less liable to turn to mud when wet than a beaten earth floor. This could be used in ground-floor 'utility' areas, but was also used semi-structurally with various forms of natural reinforcement to form a solid floor filler between timber joists to make upper floors (that might be mistaken for modern concrete). They are durable, but not so hard nor so resistant to water as concrete and repairing them is a specialist job.

Stone, Bricks and Pavers

Laid direct to earth or on a bed of sand or lime mortar, these were a step up from a bare, trodden, earth floor and, in very old properties, probably a conversion from that. In the twentieth century many of these floors were taken up and replaced with concrete, then carpeted or covered with a hard flooring. If a replacement concrete floor is now giving trouble and is about to be removed, it is worth investigating to see whether the concrete was laid on to a plastic sheet damp-proof membrane over the original floor. If it was, then the original stone, bricks or clay tiles may have survived their interment in a reusable state. If they have partially decomposed in the damp they can at least be identified for an authentic replacement. Resisting sealing or waxing these floors will enable them to wear gracefully – and, of course, let them breathe; for the most part they really need only regular, mild washing; feet will buff them.

Structural Stone or Brick Floors

Though not as common as timber floors, masonry arches, tunnels and vaults may occur over a cellar space. The structural principal is that all the stones or bricks act together in an arc to transfer the load from above to the walls at either side. Usually those walls are being buttressed (supported laterally). The whole structure is interdependent, so cutting holes and removing areas of supporting wall can risk collapse or weakening. Arches (this also applies to window and door arches whether 'flat' or curved) would have been assembled over a supporting former, usually of timber, that was left in place until the mortar dried. Repairs may need to adopt the same process and it would be wise to involve a structural engineer.

Ceilings

Ceilings started as ways of sealing the gaps between floorboards, when the floorboards were the only barrier between an upper and a lower room: gaps would have leaked light, noise and dust between rooms.

The mainstay of old house ceilings was the lath and plaster ceiling which survived in British house construction until the 1950s, when it was superseded by large, quickly-erected, sheet finishes such as plasterboard. Lath and plaster for ceilings would have

Traditional clay pavers are fashionable again for internal and external surfaces and various regional patterns and colours can be sourced; externally they can be laid, not grouted, on sand for drainage and internally any grouting – avoiding thick, pasty joints – might be with a suitable lime mortar.

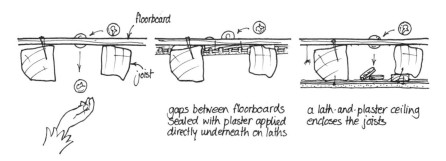

Three possible stages in the development of a ceiling.

been developed in a similar way to their use for cladding for external and internal walls. Old houses might have ceilings of nineteenth-century sawn timber laths nailed to the ceiling/floor joists, or earlier split oak or chestnut, in each case coupled with lime plaster (as shown in the diagram in Info pages: Lime – Repair considerations for lime render). In ordinary domestic work each of the plastering coats would quite likely be a lime/sand mix (hair in undercoats). In finer, traditional work (and early twentieth-century house-building) plaster of Paris might have been introduced in the top coats for extra smoothness.

Cornices and Decorative Plasterwork

In grander old houses and many Victorian and Edwardian houses, pre-cast plaster of Paris cornices, ceiling roses and other embellishments formed over timber or hessian reinforcement might be fixed to the ceilings. Heavier items might be nailed, spiked or screwed through to the floor joists above; lighter members like cornices could be simply stuck on 'dabs' of plaster. This reinforced, 'fibrous' plasterwork became established from about the end of the eighteenth century. Before then, and for some time after as well, cornices and other features could be 'run' *in situ* in similar lime mixes to the walls and ceiling. They were formed by running a profiled metal sheet over a ridge of wet plaster to shape the feature and were made by craftsmen on site rather than prefabricated in a workshop. Both of these techniques have survived in conservation and fibrous plaster still has a strong market in new-build despite competition from plastic and plasterboard products.

Repair of Lath and Plaster Ceilings

Old ceilings can suffer abuse. As can be seen from the diagram, a lath and plaster ceiling relies upon laths for strength. If these are cut (say, to install an inset light fitting) the ceiling is considerably weakened at that point. If the laths are sound, then the ceiling can be put at risk by leaks, which weaken the 'nobbly bits' that key the plaster to the laths. That key can be broken by vibration from machinery or building works or, believe it or not, by people going into the attic, knocking them all off and sweeping them up to make the attic look neater (this sometimes happens).

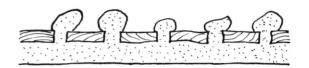

In a lath and plaster wall or ceiling the hair-reinforced lime plaster is locked to the timber laths by being pushed through them while wet; the timber laths need to have a solid fixing at the end of each one, spanning horizontally between joists or rafters (ceilings) or studs (walls).

If damaged ceilings are suspected, carefully lift the floorboards or explore loft spaces. It is possible to re-key old lath and plaster ceilings locally by reinforcing them from above or – depending on whether the plaster, the laths or their nails have failed – by introducing extra, specially designed, fixings from below. This is delicate work and needs to be properly understood to avoid making matters worse, so, once again, proper professional advice and skilled tradespeople need to be involved.

A badly damaged lath and plaster ceiling might be remade like-for-like. It might be possible to reuse any existing sound, and soundly-fixed, laths – depending on the way the ceiling failed. Then replastering is fairly straightforward. This might also be applicable to patches, so that repairs can be limited to failed areas, while any cornices can be retained undisturbed. The twentieth century was unsure about timber laths and so would often carry out belt-and-braces repairs, perhaps adding an expanded metal mesh. There is usually no reason not to consider using new timber laths for a traditional repair, provided the expertise of the building team is up to it.

Adding plasterboard under a failed lath and plaster ceiling was a common, quick, twentieth-century repair, but this risks putting the load of any further collapse of the old ceiling on to the nails holding the plasterboard. Sometimes an old house has been stripped of its original ceilings and plasterboard substituted. This is unfortunate, not just historically but acoustically since, subjectively, traditional lath and plaster can appear more soundproof than modern plasterboard. This may have something to do with the plaster in lath and plaster being thick and stopping up any air gaps, or just that it is heavy and does not vibrate so freely, whereas plasterboard is a taut sheet, like the skin of a drum or the diaphragm of a loudspeaker.

INTERNAL WALLS

An internal finish might be the same as that applied to the outside of a wall, so lime or earth and clay renders might have been used historically inside and might still survive. As with other traditional finishes, finding an old, clay-plastered wall presents an opportunity to research the material and establish whether repairs are feasible in the original local mix or by using proprietary clay plaster mixes. Where partitions are not made from the same stone, brick or even earth as the external walls of an old house, internal walls were often framed in timber 'studs'. Studs are a series of vertical timbers spanning floor to ceiling, perhaps braced with horizontal timber 'noggins' between. Some stud walls are just partitions, others are very much structural and are, for example, responsible for directly supporting (propping, bracing or even hanging) surrounding floors, roofs and walls. Studwork is a technique that lasted into the days of sawn timber and plasterboard, but older houses used other means of covering the studs.

Lath and Plaster Walls and Their Repair

As came to be the case with ceilings, the aim in wall construction was often a seamless expanse of plaster, and, for this, lath and plaster came to be a staple of British house construction methods. The thin timber laths were nailed to the timber studs of partition walls. In some cases, instead of plastering direct to the inside of a solid masonry outer wall, laths would be fixed to vertical timber battens on the masonry – to provide a gap as protection against damp.

Its properties and the repair techniques applied to it share much with lath and plaster ceilings (above), although, because walls are usually two-sided (as well as being less directly threatened by gravity) repairs to their back surfaces would rarely be an option. Corners are a problem even for modern plaster because they are vulnerable to damage and now there are metal beads that reinforce them. Lime plastered

walls often used a round timber corner staff which is left on show. Traditional plaster walls are unlikely to be perfectly straight or regular, even when in perfectly sound condition; it would be a regrettable loss of character to try to smooth them out when redecorating.

Fixing to Lath and Plaster
Ideally, any fixings into lath and plaster would pass through it and direct into a sturdy timber stud (or joist, in the case of a ceiling) to which the timber laths are themselves fixed. Laths cannot be relied upon to carry loads greater than that of light picture frames, and even then it may be advisable to predrill a fine pilot hole and use a narrow screw into a lath

A timber frame of studs, noggins and braces forms the skeleton of many old house walls and is a method of construction that is still used; this is a 1960s' partition being stripped from a much older building.

The reverse of a lath and plaster wall in good condition and a bundle of new timber laths ready for a repair job.

Softer traditional finishes, like lime render painted with distemper, were protected at corners with timber beads to help resist wear.

rather than to knock in a pin, since the act of hammering into a lath 'bounces' it, can fracture the plaster nibs attached to it and weaken the wall.

Timber studs may be locatable with an electronic stud detector. Beware of pipes and cables that may be inside the wall if drilling or nailing (pipe and cable detectors can be deceived by thick plaster). The timber studs may not be conveniently located, so in old houses a traditional solution was to attach a batten along the wall, fixed at the stud positions, and then fix the shelf, or whatever, to the batten. The batten can be scribed to the contours of the wall to take up any unevenness in the old plaster surface.

As mentioned above (*see* Repair of lath and plaster ceilings), cutting out a section of lath and plaster leaves the lath ends unsupported and any load imposed at that point will be transferred to the plaster and may cause cracking or failure.

Boarded or Panelled Walls

A stud wall or a masonry wall might be faced with regular planed and moulded boards or simpler, butt-jointed boards, similar to floorboards. These might be arranged vertically or horizontally and, on a masonry wall, fixed to timber bearers. A Georgian house might have rough, vertical studwork faced with fairly regular boards, set horizontally, that are filled and painted over. A Victorian house might have studwork with noggins spaced to allow the fixing of vertical planed boards, with a graceful 'bead' moulding along each joint. The moulding was a practical way of disguising the joint and any irregularity in the plane of one board and its neighbour. Moulded boards came to be tongued and grooved for a more reliable fit. Modern 'V'-jointed matchboarding is descended from this, but bead-jointed boards can still be ordered.

The ultimate in boarded walls was formal panelling. This was not just nailed on to studs but 'secretly-fixed' to background timbers. So secret can these fixings be that it can be difficult to work out how to disassemble them without damage. There is much folklore about the reuse of timbers in old houses from ships and other old houses, some of it is fanciful but it seems clear from poorly fitting examples that panelling was often recycled.

A panelled room can have forgotten, concealed, sliding doors and window shutters, popular with the Georgians and right up to Edwardian times. If found, they need to be coaxed out with care since they may have succumbed to damp inside the wall and swollen or fallen apart. Panelling from these periods is likely to be in softwoods and finished with a paint or faux woodgrain finish. Earlier hardwood panelling, such

as carved oak panelling from the sixteenth and the seventeenth century, would likely have been designed to display the timber and all the carved detail. If plain, it could have been oiled or waxed once and may have lost some original coloured painted or gilded highlights.

SOME INTERNAL TREATMENTS AND FINISHES

Stretched Hessian Wall-lining

An irregular wall, or perhaps one created from several adjoining different constructions (a brick chimney breast adjoining timber boarding perhaps) might be made more uniform by stretching hessian over it on thin timber frames. The hessian was not usually a finish itself but a useful background straightener for wallpaper.

Bead-moulded boarding is available in modern tongued and grooved softwood, often as a standard off-the-shelf item.

The reverse side of panelling seen from outside a stripped wall; the panels are secretly locked in place and can be difficult to release for repair.

Wallpaper

Wallpaper started life as small printed squares, progressing with printing and papermaking technology towards the standard rolls we know today. Early wallpaper paste was animal or vegetable glue and generally much more 'breathable' than modern pastes. Sizing a wall (preparing it with paste in advance of papering) can seriously reduce breathability if carried out with an impermeable adhesive. Modern, washable, vinyl papers and finishes are also usually non-breathable.

Specialist manufacturers keep old designs ready to manufacture, or can specially copy a one-off if required, though this is not cheap. Embossed wallpapers, and panels of embossed composites, were produced for the Victorians, with whom they were very popular. Some designs and materials have survived to the present, though owners of old houses need to be aware that some modern versions are made with impermeable plastics and therefore incompatible with a 'breathing' wall.

Tiles

The Victorians took to glazed tiles possibly because they provided a robust finish for dados, which would take a lot of wear from voluminous dresses and outdoor coats and, in turn, would not deposit chalky distemper or whitewash on clothing. The Victorians

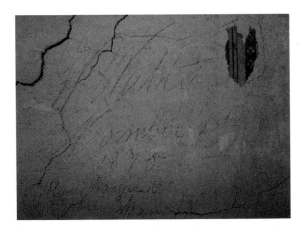

Pride in one's work, a decorator leaves his mark in 1875 and may have been surprised to know it would not be discovered for over a century.

were entering the era of cement in building their houses, so the fact that tiles are an impermeable surface may not have been so incompatible for all of them. But now tiles are routinely applied to kitchens and bathrooms of much older houses when they would often be better isolated from the structure by being installed on a board held off the original wall with a ventilated air gap behind.

Period Decoration

In the past, fashions swung between simplicity and clutter, much as they do today. The Georgians had simple, bright interiors partly as a result of having to see by candlelight, whereas the Victorians introduced all the paraphernalia of their rising materialistic world and even dressed their furniture and mantlepieces in 'clothes', but they did have oil and gas lights to help them navigate all this at night. Period interiors responded to technology, fashions and need; for example, easy chairs would be high-sided to keep draughts off the head and neck, the Victorians favoured the dado to keep big dresses from rubbing the walls, door widths and heights responded to human dimensions and fashions over time. To get an insight into the times and their buildings it can be worthwhile to join an amenity society that relates to a particular period, such as the Victorian Society or the Georgian Group. Research can be carried out at home into the former decorative schemes of a house by looking in places where old paints and papers may not have been removed or by carefully scraping to reveal old colour layers (remembering that some of them may be undercoats).

Medieval houses would have been rather sparsely furnished by modern domestic standards and, of course, non-medieval finishes would inevitably be part of a modern home in a medieval house. Those non-medieval finishes need to be chosen with care. Apart from the technical problems that can result from sealing up the fabric (doing things such as varnishing old beams and posts or putting vinyl finishes on original walls), thought needs to be given to retaining the surviving genuine period flavour or otherwise a charming, old, crooked cottage can quickly be turned into something that looks more like a badly built modern house (*see also* Info pages: Paints and paint removal).

CHAPTER 7

Building Services

HISTORICAL PERSPECTIVE

Water, Drains and Sewers

Water and sewerage were originally, historically, do-it-yourself utilities: a well or a river for extraction while nature did the rest. In sparsely populated countryside this worked, but in towns civil engineering operations became necessary to avoid disease such as cholera, linked to contaminated drinking water. Almost accidental cultural habits, such as boiling water to make tea, have helped British towns to reduce contamination. In Cambridge a main street is still served by a man-made, open, water channel alongside the road (Hobson's Conduit), installed for the benefit of the townsfolk. This used to be luxury.

Gas and Electricity

Gas and later electricity began to appear in houses in towns and cities, sold direct from local gasworks and generating stations where the raw material for both was generally coal. Some towns supported several supply companies, and, by modern standards, a robust disregard of some of the dangers of these commodities. When gas was intended for lighting only, the supply might be shut down during the day and simply restarted at night. There are still iron gas pipes underground, prone to rust. Electricity was supplied according to generating conditions and voltages, and whether the current was AC or DC varied with location. A few large Edwardian country house estates generated their own electricity, some

This commercial installation of boilers in an old fireplace shows the clash of cultures between old buildings and modern plant; in the decade since this picture was taken equipment and regulations have changed so it is always useful to design-in flexibility.

manufactured their own gas. Britain settled on a (potentially lethal) domestic point-of-use voltage of 240V, later adjusted down slightly to harmonize with other countries; a higher voltage suffers less loss in transmission and so do overhead cables. Pylons were installed in the countryside in the rush to meet demand and at the time newspapers carried advertisements promising to put them out of sight one day.

Communications

Telephone and radio were introduced under the control of the state through the General Post Office. The postal system, and letterboxes in front doors, were only a generation or two old when telephones first appeared as luxuries. Postal services, in combination with the railways, had developed to a highly efficient state before telephones became universal: until the early 1960s a country builder might order materials via postcard and they would be delivered that afternoon. Telegraph, telephone and power cables proliferated. Even radio was distributed in some towns to household loudspeakers by overhead cables, accounting for some interesting fittings on a few old houses. Large, wire aerials for radio developed into more familiar radio and television aerials that have

Satellite TV dishes are officially unwelcome on listed buildings and in conservation areas but they can work just as well sited on the ground as long as they can 'see' the satellite.

now inhabited chimneys for generations. Now satellite dishes all point to the same spot in the heavens and TV aerials are becoming larger to cope with fickle digital reception.

Utilities in the Street and in the Home

Water, gas, sewers and electricity and telephone cables have been under the streets for some time and were put there by local service companies and later nationalized boards, each of which had an interest in their long-term management, some of which still remain engrained in their privatized commercial status. Fibre-optic cables are the latest addition, but new and rapidly changing communications and media companies do not have this heritage. Tree roots and existing services can suffer from the cramming of new ducts into streets or to serve individual houses; the complexity, and in some cases disorganization, of underground services can complicate new connections to all services.

Inside the home utility installations were at first openly visible: perhaps people were just as proud of their new-fangled pipes and wiring as later folk were of the first satellite dishes. Water and central heating pipes were fixed to internal walls, winding their way through ceilings and floors; electricity cables originally came in 'conduits' (metal pipes) that served switches and fittings, as gas pipes had done beforehand. A GPO telephone was installed with its wiring nailed across walls by the shortest possible route. Sometimes the surface application of services was beneficial to old houses because it avoided the obsessive modern channelling, digging and drilling of old fabric to bury cables and pipes. Old houses now desperately need wireless systems to become fashionable for home entertainment and telecoms because the wiring for current systems can be damagingly excessive.

Heating

Space heating and a hot water supply were designed into old houses in open fireplaces, the occupants harvested and burnt wood in a sustainable way. Towns turned to coal fires and the countryside followed; these were labour-intensive systems: shovelling, stoking and poking of fuel and the clearing and disposing of ash. The clean, automatic production of heat and hot water came with the introduction of gas, oil and electric boilers with radiators and a hot water cylinder – having started in larger houses with coke-fired boilers tended by servants. In the 1960s nuclear electricity briefly promised to be a cheap source of power and some old houses went straight from open fires to electric storage heaters. Later, natural gas altered the economics. All these moves were considered 'sustainable' in their time and served well enough for decades. Now fuels are having to be reassessed once more and this time there is, perhaps, no cheap option until we can harvest natural energy efficiently.

MAINLY ABOUT HEATING

Some Effects of Heating on Old Houses

Drying
Most old houses have already established their relationship with central heating. For those that have not yet, the speedy over-drying of the air can lead to joinery and timbers taking a sudden twist, while the temptation to block all ventilation passages can lead to dampness and decay setting in despite, or even because of, the increased warmth.

Fuel Storage and Meter Boxes
Coal bunkers and oil and gas tanks are likely to be joined soon by wood stores or even biomass stores as timber is likely to be the low-carbon heating fuel of choice for some. Old houses may have oil and gas tanks sited and designed according to old regulations and standards. Renewing or resiting them can involve new requirements, for example, a 'bunded' oil tank – one that can contain its contents if the main tank leaks. Meter boxes and pipe and external cable entries to houses can be a visual blight; better options than the standard white box-in-the-wall include low-level, in-ground meter boxes and internal meters, perhaps with remote displays. Overhead cables can be replaced by underground supplies; it can be difficult to persuade a supply company to do this, but the local authority might be able to add weight to requests for underground supplies in a conservation area or National Park, for example.

Pipework
Radiator and other 'wet' systems rely on pipes, which need holes to worm their way around an existing building. The damage that can be done by installing these is often overlooked in applications for listed building consent and floor joists can be perforated and weakened by drilling for pipes and vulnerable old walls hacked when some careful forethought could have routed them less harmfully. Many installers limit themselves to conventional, rigid, copper pipes, but there are other options which might help out: copper piping of very small diameter and plastic pipes of regular diameter can be reeled off without access needing to be cut to make joints; the small copper pipes might also save the compromising of the structure by the drilling of holes in beams. Plastics might, however, be vulnerable to the teeth of rats and mice. Both copper and plastics are likely to become less cheap and plentiful, so more thought is going to have to be given to system design; minimizing the effect on an old house should be part of the brief.

Modern Gas and Oil Boilers and Water Heating
Boilers are now required to be replaced with energy-efficient, condensing boilers when they are due for replacement. So far these have tended not to be as long-lasting as conventional modern boilers, partly because of the way they operate and partly because they are technically complex and can reach 'uneconomic repair' status. Not a perfectly sustainable option, but they do use less fuel. Modern boilers have offered options of 'indirectly' heating a hot-water cylinder from which hot water is delivered by gravity, or heating water only on demand and under mains pressure. There are space savings in the latter, though solar water heating tends to be readily adaptable to the indirect cylinder method. Solar water heating has to be backed up by conventional methods for sunless midwinter days. Whatever the heating method, hot water cylinders need to be highly insulated to conserve energy.

Old Iron Pipe Systems and Radiators
The earliest central heating found in larger old houses used large diameter iron pipes that were fed by 'gravity' (the natural circulation of hot water). If

Cast-iron radiators, once associated with schools and hospitals, have acquired nostalgic affection and may also be optimal for future ground source heat pump installations in old houses, so it is doubly fitting that English Heritage has identified them as an important feature in listed buildings.

these are in good condition they have the advantage of already being installed, of potentially being durable for longer and of being adaptable to modern pumped systems. Old cast-iron radiators are now considered a visual asset for old houses and, happily, they are a more reasonable option than modern, pressed steel radiators for use with heat-pump technology (*see* Heat pumps below). Radiators can be helped a little by suspending a reflective metallic foil behind them (not touching the radiator to stop conduction and, if possible, not touching the wall to let it still breathe).

Room Heaters

A room heater can be anything from an electric or gas fire to a solid-fuel stove. Many can be turned on or off according to occupancy and were a popular, convenient means of heating that replaced open fires. The convenience and luxury of central heating in turn replaced them, but, with modern timing and thermostatic controls, they may be a sensible option for the future – producing heat at the point of need rather than pumping it around a whole house. They may also be considered for backing up another system, and, as old houses usually have plenty of chimneys available, there is generally a degree of flexibility when installing room heaters. Portable gas and oil heaters have been much used in old houses but are unsuitable, not only because of the risk of fire but because they generate a lot of water vapour which can condense on cold surfaces.

Electricity

Electric systems, without the need for pipes and boilers, are perhaps the kindest from an installation point of view, but storage heaters or direct heating panels have been expensive to run and, while some old houses have sufficient thermal mass to work well with storage heaters, others do not and the ventilation necessary to keep such a house healthy can waft away stored heat too quickly.

Potential for Heating in a Sustainable Future

Fossil Fuels or Biomass?

All are carbon fuels that release carbon dioxide into the atmosphere when they are burned. The difference is that the fossil fuels – coal, oil and natural gas – release carbon that was absorbed and locked up millions of years ago when the vegetation that was their precursor was growing. The CO_2 that they produce on burning is therefore 'extra' and the use of these fuels is likely to be discouraged, unless their emissions can be cleaned. On the other hand, wood and other biomass-derived fuels merely re-release carbon that was absorbed from atmospheric CO_2 relatively recently, while they were growing, therefore they might be considered as 'carbon-neutral', if burning them makes no net difference to current atmospheric levels of CO_2.

Of the three main fossils fuels, there is progress towards offering a substitute for heating oil (and transport diesel) by using oil-rich crops, though this would compete with food production and so may not be sustainable in that respect. In theory, methane could replace natural gas, the technology is relatively simple and methane is naturally generated by decomposition, landfill and farming, but the exploiting of this seems a long way off. Burning wood was once universal but is now largely abandoned because of the inconvenience of gathering, storing and controlling the burning of logs. Volume for volume, logs do not generate as much heat as coal and the problem of storage combined with urban smoke control has discouraged wood-burning in towns and cities (for a guide *see* www.uksmokecontrolareas.co.uk). Pelletized wood or other biomass are reckoned to have the potential to be more efficient, cleaner-burning and are also more adaptable to automatic feed into boilers, so these 'added-value' products may be what are delivered to homes in the future.

Combined Heat and Power

Domestic CHP installations use surplus heat from a central heating boiler to drive a simple generator (some use a Stirling engine, a type first developed 200 years ago) to produce electricity. Relatively new to Britain, the idea is likely to gain ground as units become available in a greater range of capacities. An advantage of generating electricity direct in the home is that transmission losses are eliminated.

Solar Heating

All 'renewable' energy ultimately derives from the sun, but at present solar water heating, for domestic use, is about the limit of marketed systems, as space heating needs the highest energy input at times of the year when sunshine is weak. Solar water heating panels are variations on the theme of a fluid taking up heat from the sun and transferring it to the domestic system. Old houses may be more adaptable because their plumbing was likely to have been retrofitted in the first place and not crammed into a special cupboard with no room for extra equipment. But old houses are also problematical as they are specially vulnerable to possible disfigurement by roof panels; however, collectors can be sited elsewhere as the main requirement is an open, sunward outlook and a solar panel can also work at ground level provided that it is unobscured. It is only recently that houses have been designed with solar panels in mind,

and, unless a roof happens to be oriented and pitched to face the maximum sun full-on, rooftop collection can be compromised. A garden collector can, if there is room, be adjusted to face the full sun more of the time.

Orientation, Passive Solar Heating, Management

Many older houses were built alone so some did take the opportunity to relate to their sites, using sun, shade and shelter to advantage – the principal rooms facing south while kitchens, bathrooms and pantries faced north. Deciduous trees planted for summer shade assist cooling, the leaves are not present in winter to obstruct the light, while a thick hedge to windward can reduce winter chill. These are the sorts of idea being revived to be built into modern homes that use passive solar heating. Old houses had no automatic controls to open and close curtains and shutters, but these things can still be managed manually to take the best advantage of the situation and reduce fuel consumption. Managing a conventional

A log-burning boiler for country folk, but perhaps not towns due to fuel storage and smoke emissions; wood-pellet boilers offer an urban alternative.

149

fossil fuel heating system properly can save on CO_2 emissions, this can be done by manually programming basic switchgear and timers as well as with full automation. Fully automated controls can be counterproductive if they are used where unnecessary: a thermostatic radiator valve may be fine in a modern house with efficient heating, but in an old house that struggles to come up to temperature a thermostatic valve may never be called upon to operate and represents a wasted investment in materials and energy. Automation that relies on electric monitoring, pumps and motorized valves should also be appropriate to the task to minimize maintenance and replacement costs and energy use.

Heat Pumps

Heat pumps provide a magical-sounding solution that seems to create heat out of nothing at all. These systems are sometimes also called 'geothermal' heating, but, in Britain at least, they do not tap into the heat of the earth's core. In Britain heat pumps would work on a similar principle to the domestic refrigerator, drawing low-grade heat from the garden soil (or from a borehole, the air or a stream) and concentrating it into higher-grade heat to release indoors: imagine the contents of the refrigerator as the garden and the mesh of black pipes at the back as a radiator inside the home. Just as a refrigerator uses electricity to extract this heat so a heat pump needs to have electricity invested in it to produce heat from the garden. It has been quoted as a rough target that one unit of electric input should deliver three units of heat if a system is running properly. For most old houses – because they are less well insulated – the technology may struggle to do this and earn its green credentials all the time; back-up could be required from another, more expensive source. Nevertheless, many old houses have big enough gardens for the necessary network of underground pipes (archaeology permitting – ask the council for information) so there are hopes that this technology will continue to adapt and improve.

Some other European countries are ahead of the UK in delivering this system, using it regularly to power underfloor heating in new, highly insulated homes. Much of the expertise being sold in Britain has originated from that experience. In Britain's old houses,

large, old-fashioned-style, cast-iron radiators may be preferable to underfloor heating on the grounds of conservation, since installing underfloor systems could risk disrupting foundations, obscure or destroy old floor finishes and alter the balance of damp management in floors and walls. The heavy, old, iron radiators seem to cope better than modern pressed steel ones with the lower water temperatures offered by heat pumps.

A Foot in Both Camps

In their present form heat pumps and solar water heating may not always be applicable to old houses for practical and visual reasons. Even some more modern houses will not be able to take full advantage of them. Where installations are possible they may not always be able to replace the full capacity of fuel-burning boilers, but they might be able to boost their performance, and save fuel, by working in tandem with them.

Some Organizations Relevant to Heating Installations
- Heating Equipment Testing and Approval Scheme (www.hetas.co.uk)
- Solid Fuel Technology Institute (www.soliftec)
- National Association of Professional Inspectors and Testers (www.napit.org.uk)
- Oil Firing Technical Association (www.oftec.co.uk)
- Confederation for the Registration of Gas Installers (www.trustcorgi.com)

ELECTRICAL ISSUES

Power Generation

Electricity has to be generated on the back of another source of power: fossil fuels, nuclear or natural. It cannot yet be harvested direct from atmospheric electric storms, but it can be generated using renewable natural power sources. Hydroelectric power is a proven technology that delivers 'clean' electricity, wind farms are established, generators using the power of tides are promised and photovoltaic solar panels (*see below*) are developing fast into the domestic market. These will all take some time to meet a significant part of demand and governments may fill the gap with a new generation of nuclear power stations, which, though hardly 'green', avoid direct fossil fuel and carbon dioxide emissions. One of the drawbacks of electricity production is the power loss in transit, so either electricity has to be generated in big enough quantities to stand the losses or it has to be made close to the point of use. The existence of the National Grid means that small generators can potentially sell their surplus into the system. If microgeneration (home generation from renewables) can ever square up to the demand, then the problems would be solved. But that does not look like happening in the near future and efforts are also being focused on reducing demand through efficiency and husbandry.

Microgeneration

For turning natural energy direct into electricity (*see* Info pages: Sustainability); the systems currently available are at an early stage and will probably appear clumsy and inefficient in only a few years' time. On offer are photovoltaic panels for turning sunlight into electricity, wind turbines for harnessing wind power and, for those lucky enough to have a fast stream on their land, a mini hydroelectric plant. All would be subject to various official permissions and regulations, none is universally applicable and none is yet likely to entirely replace an existing grid connection as (hydro possibly excepted), generation is dependent on the right kind of weather. Small-scale generation is happier at low voltages. A glance at any home's plug-in adapters shows that many domestic devices already convert 230V into lower voltages, but too many domestic appliances demand the full mains power, so small-scale generation has to have its voltage converted up. Storage is also a problem as current battery technology is expensive and bulky. At present there is no guarantee that the financial outlay, or even the environmental cost of an installation, will always be recouped in a reasonable time and so for those genuinely concerned with the environment there are less glamorous measures to consider first, such as to reduce usage.

Photovoltaic panels use straightforward, solid-state material properties to generate electricity from sunlight. Present installations tend to be expensive, large, static, roof-mounted and dependent on full sun, but these limitations might be expected to change. More mobile arrays would enable their use in gardens, and more discreet movable collectors,

Harnessing wind power is a natural option for the windy United Kingdom.

perhaps mountable behind windows, could also ease the uptake of the technology on protected historic buildings.

Domestic wind turbines rely for their efficiency on a steady wind, but wind is disrupted by buildings and trees and a rooftop is likely to be an area of local turbulence that causes the body of the turbine, rather than the blades, to keep turning to try to face the wind. If fixed to buildings, particularly old houses, there may be issues of vibration damage and noise as well as disfigurement. A larger turbine on a tower and on a hill is better, as medieval millwrights long ago worked out. In the future, smaller, cheaper, devices might be linked, say, around a large garden to iron out differences caused by turbulence, but this would only seem to be viable once costs, efficiency, storage and transmission have all been greatly improved.

Domestic Lighting and Power

Compact Fluorescent Lamps

All electric appliances will need to be used more efficiently, but lighting has become significantly more efficient. The conventional light bulb (engineers like to call it a 'lamp': tungsten filament or GLS – general lighting service) has been with us for over a century – but a 100Watt version turns most of that electric power into heat and only a small amount into light. A modern, low-energy lamp (the compact fluorescent lamp, CFL) may provide the same amount of useful light for only 20W of electrical power, so one-fifth of the consumption. British building regulations insist that some dedicated low-energy fittings exist in all new homes, while the EU is proposing to ban the GLS light bulb, so public attention has been focused on the newcomers, which are now available to fit most bulb-holders presently used for ordinary GLS lamps.

A compact fluorescent lamp is just that: a small version of the fluorescent tubes that have been around – and themselves developing – for many years. Old GLS bulbs do have the psychological advantage that they burn steadily at the yellowish colour humans have for many thousands of years associated with flame. Some CFLs still tend to the green tinge that has characterized fluorescent tubes, while others approximate to daylight or GLS light: buyers should establish which version of 'white' they are getting with any CFL lamp. CFLs try to match existing GLS shapes and sizes, but with varying success, so look at several manufacturers' products for the best fit. CFLs designed to replace GLS bulbs may not be suitable for existing dimmer switches or for control by automated switching such as photoelectric cells, though some CFLs have basic versions of these facilities built in.

Because a CFL relies on circuitry, it would seem more sustainable to have the lamp tube detachable from the circuitry for separate replacement (as with conventional fluorescent tubes). But those that offer this tend not to be as cheap as the all-in-one, disposable versions that fit into old bulb-holders (there is at least one CFL format that fits a GLS holder and has a detachable tube). Like the existing ranges of ordinary fluorescent tubes, CFL tubes and their circuits contain metals, such as potentially harmful mercury, which can call for special recycling. CFLs are certainly efficient in use and experience shows they can last a long time (but individual units can fail prematurely). Some CFLs do not light at full power instantly, particularly in cold conditions, which can be irritating – or soothing – depending on the circumstances.

Halogen and LED

Halogen lighting has become popular in homes, particularly for flood- and spot-lighting, they tend towards the daylight blue end of the white spectrum rather than the comforting yellow end, associated with flame and are available in mains and 12Volt versions. Noticeably brighter than GLS lamps, these are not as efficient as low-energy CFL lamps, but fashion has led them to be deployed even more inefficiently: Many modern kitchens use a ceiling full of halogen down-lighters to try to give general illumination, for which they are not well suited (see also chapter 6 for the damage down-lighters can do to old ceilings). Relatively new are mains LED (light-emitting diode) lamps, versions of which can fit the down-lighters intended for small mains, halogen spot-lamps. Though LEDs are presently not as powerful, and cost much more to buy, than halogen they do at least consume less energy for the same general effect, run at a lower temperature, creating less of a heat hazard and potentially have a long, useful life. There are bound to be more developments in this area and relative prices and performances may alter.

Existing and New Wiring Installations

If plastics and copper become more valuable, future rewirings of houses may need to reuse circuits that remain in good condition. This could save old houses from extra drilling and cutting about to take ever more cables: it is sensible to consider adding power sockets to sound existing circuits with spare capacity when more are needed, if that can be done safely and properly within all current regulations, rather than to rip out and start again. However, some older cables are not always up to modern technical requirements. If lighting circuits are being revised and old light switches are in the wrong positions, then it may be possible to keep the switch position but activate it from elsewhere by swapping for a simple remote control switch; this can save the unnecessary excavation of old walls for new cable runs. Since the end of 2004 it has been illegal for unqualified personnel to carry out many of the electrical installation jobs that some enthusiastic householders may have previously considered as ordinary DIY. Also new colours of cables have been introduced, which means that, in an old property, there will be a potentially confusing mixture of colour codes. New runs of cable in old houses can be made more vermin-proof by installing them in conduits, but this increases their diameter and so makes for more potential damage to the property. An alternative is to use 'MICC' cable, a thin, flexible copper tube containing granular insulation between the conductors, the outer tube being covered by a coloured plastic sheath (there are other colours apart from orange). If using conventional PVC-insulated wiring there is a 'low smoke and fume' grade, supposed to lessen those risks in the event of the cables' being involved in a building fire. It is advisable to reduce the risk of fire in the first place by making sure that cables are not needlessly buried in insulation to overheat, and that suitable control switches protect all circuits. Environmental concerns about PVC have generated PVC-free wiring

It is kinder to masonry to try to fix into mortar rather than bricks or stones; this applies to cable clips as much as accessories and this shows (here on modern brickwork) that fixing positions and drilling for cable can sometimes be juggled to avoid bricks, so long as the fixing is secure.

options, though perhaps not yet reaching ordinary domestic installations (*see also* Info pages: Safety and buildings – Electrical safety).

Off-peak
Some houses once installed with electric storage heaters are still metered to have cheaper electricity at night (daytime charges are higher), this takes advantage of the lower general demand at night, when power – particularly from major renewable sources – is still being fed into the grid. Consumers with this set-up can save money by ensuring that high power equipment, such as water heaters, dishwashers and washing machines, are timed to run off-peak. It can also help the supply industry to be more efficient and, one may hope, more sustainable by levelling out demand. Perhaps electricity suppliers will consider extending the availability of cheap off-peak electricity to promote this.

Security Lighting
Accused of light pollution and energy wasting, the powerful external floodlights (each typically with up to half the consumption of a single bar electric fire) triggered by infra-red detectors can also be a help to residents looking for keys. They are supposed to ward off intruders, but they can equally well provide useful light by which they can break in. Properly designed security and courtesy lighting is not necessarily a powerful poke in the eye but can be a matter of gently lighting the shadows so that there are fewer places for miscreants to hide in. Infra-red closed circuit television is sufficiently tiny and affordable to be considered as an alternative deterrent and can be monitored via the internet.

Electrical Safety
See Info pages: Safety and buildings.

Relevant Organizations
The National Inspection Council for Electrical Installation Contracting (NICEIC; www.niceic.com) has long been associated with electrical contracting and other organizations connected with building regulations compliance, and approved contractors can be found via the national building control websites.

Lightning Protection

A specialist survey establishes whether the risk warrants protection. Usually this relates to exposure. Some protection may be found to exist from the effects of surrounding, taller buildings and trees. Installations can be designed with care to minimize visual and physical intrusion, and, as with other services installations, this can require some ingenuity and determination.

WATER IN, WASTE OUT

Conservation and Use of Drinking Water

Drinking-quality water on tap is not just taken for granted, it even gets dismissed by consumers in favour of virtually indistinguishable bottled water, some of it trucked across Europe. Self-sufficiency is difficult: the village pump or well might now deliver water containing agricultural chemicals, while rainwater harvesting cannot readily deliver drinking-quality water, so tap water deserves respect. Supply companies are under pressure to reduce the leakage from old pipework and home owners can do the same by checking tank overflows and tap washers. There are measures to reduce the unnecessary use of drinking-quality water.

Water Management – Harvesting Rainwater and Recycling

The collecting of rainwater is not new, water butts have long been used for gardens and some of our ancestors used to have cisterns of rainwater for laundry. The use of harvested rainwater can help to conserve valuable tap water. W.c.s can be flushed with rainwater, and, as it is naturally soft water, it can be preferable for higher-grade uses such as washing clothes and cars. Plumbing would have to be reworked, but, as old houses often wear their plumbing attached as an afterthought rather than hidden away, it can be easier to adapt an old house. Such houses may have redundant attic tanks or space for new ones that could be part of a rainwater storage system. Many old houses are already partially plumbed for non-drinking uses to be served from a separate attic storage tank, so it is possible that minimal alteration would be necessary. There is

thought to be the potential for domestic roofs to deliver adequate water to serve these non-drinking uses, with a commensurate saving on water bills. The presence of leaves and creatures in conventional outdoor rainwater butts shows that there would be a need for filtering and light-fast tanks for any serious collection and reuse of rainwater inside the house, as well as the removal and treatment of bird droppings. These installations would require expert design and installation and the involvement of local authorities' building control departments as well as water supply companies to ensure that any new systems were legal, safe and did not contaminate drinking water. For listed buildings and in conservation areas, the local conservation officer should be consulted.

Water recycling reuses water rather than consigning it to the sewers straight away, for example, water from washing machines, dishwashers and baths ('grey' water) can be stored to flush w.c.s. This also requires some replumbing, and compliance with regulations but is arguably less satisfactory on a small scale because the poor quality of the raw material demands more aggressive filtering and treatment before its storage and reuse. Unless a grey water recycling or rain-harvesting system is simple enough to be fed by gravity, the environmental costs of providing and running electric pumps and filters can negate the environmental benefit of reuse. It is therefore not to be seen as an alternative to simply being careful with water use. It is simple enough to benefit the environment by collecting rainwater outdoors and to reuse that or unpolluted waste water for gardening.

Sanitaryware and Appliances

Showers are praised above baths in sustainability terms because they are supposed to use less water. That may have been true for the miserable trickle that has been the British shower for so long, but is less so now we are pampering ourselves with pumped showers. As with the use of fuels, sustainability is not necessarily about relative efficiency, it is about actual consumption. Showers are a cause for concern in old houses since they can push water into the fabric under pressure. And they invite impermeable tiles to be stuck all over walls that really need to be breathing.

If not providing reclaimed water for w.c. flushing, the amount of flush can be reduced. Old houses frequently retain high-level cisterns which take advantage of gravity to give the flush extra clearing power and these have proved more adaptable to having their volume reduced by special inserts (being careful not to snag the ball-valve arm). In practice, many old high-level cisterns can operate full-time with a reduced flush, while modern, low-level suites need a full-flush option. The w.c. also provides a small example of how 'sustainable' behaviours need to be thought through: flushing less has been officially promoted to save water, but less flushing can mean more limescale forming, which means more aggressive cleaning with all the chemicals and extra flushing that involves.

Limescale can usefully be softened by lemon juice (citric acid) which can help to free old taps for re-washering, and to chip away at the softened scale with a piece of wood or plastic causes less damage than metal tools. Taps may need to be soaked if they are very scaled-up and an old rubber glove, or similar rubberware, can be adapted to hold the lemon juice in close proximity (check first that citric acid will not also attack the metal finish).

Wastes, Drains and Sewers

Waste Pipes
Waste pipes are the pipes of about 30 to 50mm diameter (100mm for w.c.s) that join the appliances to the drains. Drains, typically 100 to 150mm diameter, connect the house to the public sewers (and may be carrying rainwater or foul water or both, depending on the sewer's purpose). Where waste pipes have to run within floors, layouts might be planned so that the pipes can run between joists rather than cut through them, and to join existing pipe runs where reasonable. In old houses, wastes will often have been sited on the outside of walls and might be elaborate constructions of cast-iron or bespoke leadwork with decorated brackets and joints. Some ingenious anti-syphonic systems survive and these need to be understood before any work is carried out. Try not to replace or augment interesting old pipework with soulless modern components; building control officers can be sympathetic to the retention of old

pipework, as long as it works and conservation officers may offer support. It is possible to recover heat from waste water (baths, dishwashers and washing machines) and this technology can be applied to grey water recycling.

Drains
Drains in old houses are quite likely to have been laid late in the life of the house, especially in country areas where mains drainage took a long time to arrive. Foul and surface water drains were constructed in similar ways within property boundaries, most usually 100mm (4in) in diameter. Victorian drains would be expected in towns and cities, post-war drains in country areas: until the mid- to the late twentieth-century domestic drains tended to be salt-glazed clay-ware with spigot joints and individually formed inspection chambers with brick linings and cement flaunching. Modern drains are usually plastic or made of plain clayware with plastic joints and preformed plastic inspection chambers and convenient rodding access points. Houses that have been altered or extended may have both, and it is not uncommon for old drains to be untraceable or appear to defy logic as they weave around obstacles and under buildings in a way that modern regulations would not tolerate in a new installation.

Joints in old drains can be a weakness, the jointing material can break down and leak or become rough and attract blockages. Drains can be fractured by ground movement, vehicle loading, digging or be infiltrated by roots from trees, shrubs and plants. Drains are laid to a nominal fall (traditionally this was 1 in 40 for a 100mm diameter pipe, 1 in 60 for 150mm), and any ground movement that causes the drain to level off or run too steeply may induce blockages as solid waste is left behind, either if the flow is too slow or if it is too shallow because the liquid has fled too quickly. Drains were not traditionally designed to accept much of the disposable waste that can now find its way into them. It is sound environmental practice and sound building maintenance not to try to force feed drains (and water-treatment plants) with anything that will not break down quickly. It is better to compost food rather than feed rats in drains, while waste-disposal units deny an opportunity to recycle food waste and packaging.

Grease and oil should be kept out of drains and they can clog septic tanks and reed beds.

As discussed in chapter 3, surface water has been traditionally either dealt with on site, by means of conducting it to a soakaway pit filled with absorbent rubble at a safe distance from any building, or piped into a separate public drain or sewer. Soakaways from pre-Building Regulations days may be inadequately sized and too close to buildings. In time, a basic pit soakaway can become silted up to the point where it no longer works well. Replacements or new surface water drainage on a site would be covered by the requirements of the modern Building Regulations or Building Standards (contact building control at the local authority). It seems probable that regulations would continue to assume that drainage should have the capacity to safely dispose of all likely rainwater, even if rainwater were harvested for household and garden use (*see above*). Depending on the local geology, rainwater might be better allowed to percolate into the soil and replenish the water table, saving pressure on the public drains, or the reverse may be the case in other areas that are prone to overloading with groundwater, risking flooding or land-slip.

Cess Pits, Septic Tanks and Reed Beds

Mains sewers brought flushing toilets to towns and most rural areas. There were, and remain, areas where it is uneconomical or impracticable to run sewers. These have been served by cesspools or cesspits (holding tanks emptied by tanker) or septic tanks (a series of chambers, originally brick, now plastic) that process waste to various degrees by using natural processes to break down and filter the waste – perhaps sufficiently well to discharge it into a water course or into sub-soil 'field' drains. These systems, and their modern green successors, the reed beds, are, however, upset by detergents, grease and household chemicals. Reed beds require a lot of space and use selected plants and filtering material to process human organic waste. By a curious turn of history, the earth closet – that was displaced years ago by the flushable water closet – looks set to make a comeback in the guise of the composting toilet that, like its forebears, ultimately produces a garden fertilizer. Urine is not a friend to some forms of composting toilet, but it is said to be a useful activator of garden compost, so there could be some interesting behavioural adjustments involved. Pressure on sewage treatment works and water supplies is likely to generate new versions of home treatment or pretreatment in the near future.

French Drain

A French drain, a simple variation of the agricultural field drain, is used to dry the soil immediately adjacent to a house and is not normally connected to any other drain or sewer; for details *see* chapter 8: Damp, etc. Its purpose is to generate ventilation rather than take away significant amounts of water. It is simple, cheap and, properly applied, can have refreshing and lasting benefits.

Sustainability, including Old House Insulation

THE ISSUES

The idea that modern civilization is rapidly consuming the planet's finite resources is not new. Many of the pressure groups devoted to environmental concerns were formed on the basis of concerns felt in the 1960s. There may remain some scientific debate over the causes of global warming but many of the world's governments have decided that an excess of carbon dioxide, one of the greenhouse gases that trap the sun's heat in the atmosphere, is responsible. This excess appears in the atmosphere as a result of burning fossil fuels, releasing carbon that has been held inside them for millions of years. Carbon dioxide is a naturally occurring gas that each of us exhales, also that trees and plants absorb to make carbon compounds while releasing oxygen into the air. The gas is odourless and colourless and is put into fizzy drinks. If the planet can really only cope with so much of it in the atmosphere at any one time, then our unlocking of more carbon from coal, oil and gas deposits could be upsetting the balance of nature. It is feared that this is causing ice caps to melt, sea levels to rise and the climate to change.

Some old houses have been around for a very long time – the oldest exceeding the expected thirty- to sixty-year life of a modern house ten- or twenty-fold.

There is common ground between those who want to phase out fossil fuels for these environmental reasons and those who fear that the sources of fossil fuels will become increasingly difficult to access. It is not only fossils fuels that are under pressure and subject to greater competition, the minerals consumed by industrial processes, as well as the most basic resources such as water, are also thought to be subject to serious shortages in the future. The common thread appears to be the over-exploitation, or unequal exploitation, of the planet's resources.

HOW SUSTAINABILITY IS MEASURED

A unified system for assessing the total environmental impact of various activities and the sustainability benefits of solutions would be very useful. But until the mechanisms behind the planet's problems are better understood, and agreed upon, sustainability has effectively been divided up among different groups to promote in different ways. The solutions that populations are being encouraged to adopt address not one single, well-understood problem but a network of problems. This has resulted in misunderstanding and confusion. While our civilization comes to terms with the necessity of sustainability, we can expect sustainable behaviours to be regularly redefined as actual environmental performances are thought through. Some emerging systems of measuring either the problem or solutions are as follows.

Carbon Emissions or 'Carbon Footprint'

Carbon dioxide is not the only greenhouse gas. Fossil fuels are not the only resource that is under threat. The use of carbon as a measure is therefore not addressing the whole problem of depletion or climate change. But the idea that so many tonnes of carbon dioxide result from burning so much fossil fuel does provide a rough measure of general consumption, since most of it involves energy. Individuals and organizations can now carry their environmental guilt around with them in the form of a virtual cloud of the gas (inaccurately depicted in advertisements as a black, smutty thing). The calculation methods can vary considerably and comparisons can be meaningless (should just the fuel used in driving a car 10 miles be considered, or should we add in a proportion of the emissions involved in making, maintaining and eventually disposing of the car, and the question of whether the journey was useful?). Terms such as 'carbon footprint' have entered the language and look set to stay.

Planet Equivalents

Another unit being used is the number of imaginary planet Earths required to sustain our individual or national behaviour. The highly industrialized countries are apparently behaving as if there were anything from two to half a dozen planets to go round (and, by implication, the non-industrial nations must be living well within their share of the world's resources). A person in Britain, even if he or she were living relatively frugally, apparently notches up at least around two planets' worth; it seems impossible to reduce this by being ever more self-sufficient as an individual because each of us has energy consumed on our behalf by the national infrastructure that supports us.

Economy

There are two meanings of economy: 'the economy' which, in industrialized societies, is the engine of commerce that appears to have become hooked on ever-continuing growth (an interesting idea in a finite world). And then there is 'economy', as in prudence. Economy, the prudential sort, can be an ally of environmental sustainability: monetary cost is arguably as good a unit of sustainability as 'carbon footprints' or 'planets per person' because the act of spending money, on ourselves and on our buildings, usually sets a series of events in motion that involve the consumption of energy and resources.

Energy-efficiency Ratings

This system has been around for some years: labels on domestic appliances show their relative performance in terms of energy efficiency, putting the appliance into a band. The system has been extended to cars and to complete houses. If such an assessment is restricted to the energy consumed in normal use it will not help in comparing the manufacturing, recycling or life-expectancy implications between products, so its value is limited. For example, energy-saving light bulbs do well in this sort of rating, but they are more complex than conventional light bulbs and can incorporate toxic metals that require special disposal – those factors may not be taken account of in a simple statement of energy consumption in normal use. This system also relies on sensible use by the purchaser: a light left needlessly switched on is wasting energy, however efficient it is.

Environmental Impact Rating

This is used as a modifier for energy-efficiency ratings. In terms of houses, a heating system may be energy efficient, but be using a fuel that increases atmospheric carbon dioxide. A similar house may have an inefficient system but be using a fuel with no adverse environmental impact. To address this, a house would have a parallel environmental impact rating which rates the output of carbon dioxide in a similar graphical way to energy-efficiency ratings. Again, this may show only a theoretical assessment of the building's potential and may not relate to its actual usage and emissions.

BUILDING CONSERVATION AS PART OF SUSTAINABLE LIVING

Building conservation is about minimum intervention and the minimum replacement of the existing fabric: minimum renewal, maximum life from the old. This fits very well with the requirements of sustainability, which are to consume less and to conserve more. So by adopting appropriate conservation techniques and favouring traditionally-based repairs and materials over unnecessarily industrialized ones, everyone with an old house can be kind to their house and kind to the planet at the same time;

- pre-industrial houses were built in a highly sustainable way
- all old houses have a long life to their environmental credit
- sustainability = conserve more and consume less = conservation.

OLD HOUSES TODAY

Sustainably Built, Long Lasting, Easily Repaired

In the days before mechanized mass transport, buildings – our 'old houses' – had to be built with reasonably local materials. Before fossil fuels were widely used, transport was limited to sustainable horse power over land or sail over water. Before steam and electricity, producers of building materials relied upon the power of man, horses, wind or rivers to chop, saw, mix, lift, drill and hammer. We know that local trees were cut for timber and local cornfields were a source of thatch; most schoolchildren have learnt that sticks, mud and amusing animal droppings were turned into walls. However, items that we now cannot think of without associating them with factories – bricks, mortars, glass, tiles, iron – were once the products of localized cottage industries. All this makes our oldest houses more eco-friendly than just about anything the present day can hope to come up with. Even the Victorians, who inhabited a world crossing from sustainability into industrial consumption, had an enviable balance of local industry plus an integrated public transport system.

The long life of old houses saves the need to continually expend more energy and materials building replacement homes. During most of that long life many old houses were equipped to be heated by burning wood, nowadays regarded as practically 'carbon neutral' and a way forward for us. Many old houses could revert to this method fairly simply and quickly. Old houses were sustainably built for sustainable use and have earned environmental credit by lasting a long time.

The Deficiency of Some Old Houses, the Expectations of Their Users

The one area in which old houses might not perform well, in a modern assessment of sustainability, is thermal insulation. This is partly because of raised expectations of comfort from their modern occupants, partly because those same occupants are not heating the house in the way that was intended: For example, a modern family that commutes to work is not going to be able to keep an open wood fire burning all day, every day.

After turning down the thermostat, this is the technology most suited to saving on heating bills – and if it is locally produced from renewable materials, repairable and recyclable, then it must be extra-sustainable.

There are well-insulated old houses: a cottage of thick earth walls under a thatched roof, while thick stone and brick walls can make for useful 'thermal mass' that can help to store heat. But many other, traditional forms of construction have tended to be considered cold, once the age-old habit of more or less permanent open fires was abandoned. This is partly due to draughts, which were once necessary to supply oxygen to those fires. In modern use many old houses have been draught-proofed and insulated, but this has not always kept pace with the occupants' desire for ever hotter rooms. Between fifty to 100 years ago, room temperature was considered to be respectable at around 13°C, now it is maintained almost 10° warmer in some homes. In past times insulation was applied efficiently up against the human body, whereas now the habit of heating every cubic metre of a house, so that summer clothes can be worn all year round, is grossly inefficient.

OLD HOUSES IN THE FUTURE

Technology to the Rescue?
Without returning to a pre-industrial culture, the type of sustainable living that built our old houses is not likely to be reinstated. Standards of living may be adjusted to reduce demand on resources, but science and technology will be expected to bridge the gap in some way. In the twenty-first century we are used to technology providing the answers to many of our problems, but sustainability is one problem that has, in part, been caused by an over-application of technology. In the future, unless there are some significant breakthroughs in energy generation, our relationship with technology is going to have to change and machines become better designed, longer-lasting and more appropriate to the task. We need to re-examine the logic of how we use energy: labour-saving devices have reduced daily exercise to the point where some people keep fit by taking time out of their lives to do unproductive exercise, and they may actually drive to the gym to do it.

Home Help
Various means for generating power, heat and hot water at home are discussed in chapter 7. Much of this technology is new and at an early stage of development, and some may struggle to repay not only the financial outlay but also the environmental costs (energy and materials) involved in its manufacture and installation. Some governments promote the technologies by subsidies. In a commercial world, product improvement seems to rely on the sales of early models to provide money and experience for the next generation. Pioneer users might not save much money, or much of the planet, but they could be contributing to making the next generations of devices more efficient, neater and, it is hoped in this context, more suitable for use in conjunction with old houses without compromising them.

Old Houses Are Part of the Solution, Not the Problem
Many old buildings are survivors from a time when few had ever seen a fossil fuel and when, for most people, there was no option but the type of low-impact living we now seek to re-invent, and so it makes total sense to learn from them (construction methods, repairability, longevity) rather than to sacrifice them in a panic of knee-jerk upgrades (sealing them up and removing ventilation) that might destroy them before we learn how to adapt them properly. There is useful experience that can be applied to reducing carbon dioxide in the modern world: re-adopting lime instead of cement, burning wood instead of oil. But we cannot retreat into the

past and some of our high-technology world will have to remain, perhaps treated as precious assets. The gap between the tried and tested methods of the distant past and some modern technology is quickly being filled by new ideas and promising, but as yet untried, sustainable products. Old houses have already lived through one round of eager technological progress in the last century, and suffered for it; we should not be too quick to force old buildings to wear untried new 'eco' clothes when they are intrinsically sustainable already. It should not be forgotten that, however much energy Britain may save, the engines of global warming are also being fuelled by much larger nations: there may be no turning back from a future in which Britain assumes the widely-predicted, Mediterranean-style climate in a generation or two. In which case, it is short-sighted just to adjust old buildings to cope with our present cold, damp winters when hot, dry summers might soon need to be addressed. We may pass through a similar climate to that of the early Middle Ages, when wine was widely cultivated here, a climate for which our oldest houses were designed.

Heritage is an important part of what we are and it would be useful to relearn from old houses, while remembering that it is not the houses but their occupants who have become unsustainable. Heritage organizations are seeking a degree of tolerance in applying new statutory, energy-efficiency measures that might adversely affect the important visual and historic roles of old buildings, as well as their technical performance. On a local level, a council's conservation officer would be a first contact towards ironing out problems where new regulations seemed to conflict with the appropriate care of an old building. Inappropriate modifications, however well intentioned, can sometimes worsen the performance of old buildings and the purpose of guidance such as building regulations is not to bring about the failure of existing buildings.

SOME INTERMEDIATE MEASURES FOR OLD HOUSES

Insulation

Part of the solution in dealing with cold, old houses may be to adjust our expectations of comfort. But, unless we actively want to return to a pre-industrial lifestyle, the other part of the solution must still be to increase their insulation, without depriving them of the ventilation and breathability which keep them in one piece and fight rot. Insulating old houses is not easy at the best of times and introducing insulation without considering the way in which the building operates and survives can create other problems. With so many untried new products suddenly on the market it is probable that the rush to better insulation may have some casualties, unless owners take the trouble to seek the right advice – that is, impartial advice from an independent conservation professional who can try to evaluate performance and suitability, tailoring them to a particular house. Some general principles and practicalities of insulation are discussed at the end of this section.

Old houses were built with small windows that do not waste as much heat as modern 'picture windows' and which can be adaptable to secondary glazing, *see* chapter 5. Houses with shutters or provision for curtains that can be thermally lined can achieve insulation values approaching that of double-glazing.

The Responsible Use of Energy and Resources

Energy use has two forms, direct consumption – at the point of use and 'embodied energy', the energy that has been expended in the past to create and maintain artefacts such as houses. The longer a house lasts, the more dividends that embodied energy can effectively pay. Making sure that the house is properly maintained protects that investment in energy. As for energy that is about to be used, occupants have the environmental responsibility and financial incentive to use that energy carefully. An old house, like any artefact, has limitations and cannot necessarily be pushed as hard as a modern version. Using heating appropriate to the spaces, the insulation and the design of the house is an adjustment the occupants have to make relative to living in a modern house. Using resources responsibly also includes looking at whole-life energy and material use in domestic contents, recycling, questioning fashions for wasteful consumption and composting waste where possible.

Heating and Ventilation
The past, present and future of heating fuels is looked at in chapter 7, along with heating controls and the orientation and management of passive solar gain. The 'stack' ventilation and summer cooling offered by traditional chimneys appears in chapter 1.

Water Management – Harvesting Rainwater and Recycling

Low-energy Lighting
See chapter 7.

THE SUSTAINABILITY BANDWAGON

Consumers Need All the Figures

Consumers are being steered towards buying new products that take less energy to run. From light bulbs and washing machines to cars and houses, this addresses energy conservation in the use of new products and buildings, but seems to ignore the energy and resources it takes to make those new products and the energy and materials embodied in old ones that will be thrown away. Consider a car that has lasted forty years in everyday use, relatively uncomplicated, it has been easy enough to repair with some standard parts and without special tools. It may offer 30 miles to a gallon of petrol. During that forty years many car owners would have changed their car up to a dozen times and now have a car that perhaps does 40 miles to the gallon. But we hear that a significant proportion of the environmental cost attached to the lifetime of a car occurs during its manufacture and shipping to the customer. So the owner of the forty-year-old car may have contributed considerably less to global warming and environmental damage than a neighbour on their twelfth car. Meanwhile, many of that neighbour's eleven old cars have not been displaced – they might still be running around. So owning a new, energy-efficient car might be seen as compounding the problem, not solving it.

Consumers seriously interested in the planet will want to know the actual, total environmental impact of their decisions – and that may mean keeping old products in use. This might not suit some manufacturers, but consumers serious about the planet want goods that are longer-lasting, easier to repair and to upgrade. Corporate thinking that celebrates the 'obsoleting' of old products is unlikely to remain commercially sustainable.

Government Intervention

Governments have the blunt instruments of taxation and legislation to encourage more sustainable behaviour. They might reasonably be expected to be wary of tripping up the economy by suggesting that their citizens buy fewer things, and they would also be unlikely to introduce stringent restrictions on behaviour that might be seriously unpopular with their voters. Society can expect to be educated about the problems so that changes in behaviour come from within. Meanwhile, official advice might appear to dance at the less controversial edges of the problem by talking about maybe not flushing w.c.s so often or turning off mobile telephone chargers.

However, government does have the power to act positively to free-up a lot of sustainable building practice: regulations that may be standing in the way of reviving well-tried and sustainable, traditional building methods should be re-examined. And 'tick-the-box' energy-efficiency assessments of new as well as old buildings might be replaced by holistic assessments of environmental performance, so that designers are encouraged to think up new solutions rather than be forced to recite old ones that comply with a standard model. Homeowners and occupants deserve the freedom to save energy in a way that is appropriate to them and their house.

Long life and repairability can make eco-heroes of unlikely candidates, if their life-long environmental impact is compared with the waste of the regular disposal and replacement of a string of artefacts of much shorter life.

Pressure Groups and Pioneers

If the struggle to achieve balance in environmental issues is seen as a tug of war contest, then the established industrial model has a lot of weight behind it, and a lot of inertia in terms of thinking and economic habit. Some environmentalists have taken a confrontational position and tried to raise the profile on their end of the rope by direct action or tactics that get publicity but risk alienating more people than they influence. The more canny environmentalists simply get among the prop forwards on the industrial end of the rope and say, 'Why are you doing this, do you know where it is going to lead?' and, after years of groundwork, it seems that their day has come. It is the nature of enthusiasts to push their view undiluted or else their message would be lost, but we are clearly not all suddenly going to move into houses made of recycled tyres and run them on 24 volts from a solar panel. Nevertheless, these pioneering ideas are helping to form our future. The Centre for Alternative Technology (www.cat.org.uk) is one organization that for several decades has been looking at practical applications for real buildings. In most cases, an old house has important differences (technical, visual and often in planning legislation) from more recent homes and so there is no 'one-size-fits-all' sustainable solution, but ideas can be adapted.

Fashion

Fashion has been responsible for much harmful and unnecessary replacement in old buildings. The more fashionable the alteration, a kitchen perhaps, the more likely it is to go out of fashion as soon as everyone else has one like it, so it 'just has' to be replaced. Some fashion is exploited commercially, but fashion also has its own life and already a fashion for not changing things is beginning to affect even kitchens. It has always been easy enough to copy a passing fashion and to shoe-horn it into an old house, but to create something that is as timeless and durable as the house, to ensure that it is as environmentally and ethically sourced as possible, to design for maximum effect and minimum energy use and to anticipate and provide for adding-in future innovations – all that calls for extra skills and imagination and should command higher praise.

Greenwash

A term for when environmentally-positive attributes are played up while the negatives are played down, 'greenwashing' can be deceitful but is probably in a similar league to other marketing hype. It is almost inevitable in a period of transition where no product can be perfectly ecologically sound, a manufacturer who has inherited an ageing product range cannot be expected to ditch it and sack their workforce overnight; or, a manufacturer of a new 'green' product who finds that Britain does not yet offer all the back-up required might be coy about how many miles the product has been shipped. Even the climate-change protesters seen on TV cannot free themselves entirely from the unsustainable trappings of modern life. This is a period of change and no one is likely to be unimpeachable, the important thing is that we are all seeking to travel in the same direction.

THE ENVIRONMENTAL CREDENTIALS OF TRADITIONAL BUILDING MATERIALS

All the building materials used for centuries were once, of necessity, mainly locally produced on a small scale. Now their modernized descendants are produced by high-volume factories and distributed by motorized transport and less by small-scale, local industry. In some cases local raw materials have been replaced by those from far away – meaning higher energy costs in transport. This in itself does not always necessarily make them environmentally unfriendly because economies of scale and mass-production might perhaps also be managed to have some environmental benefit. But the future nurturing of local production should help to improve sustainability, local colour and identity in building products. These traditional, or once traditional, products may not be perfectly sustainable in themselves but they can be better options than entirely modern products such as steel, cement and aluminium, centrally produced, often with a high energy consumption.

Lime

For thousands of years the basis of traditional mortar and render, lime is eminently suited to the needs of old buildings since it breathes and absorbs minor movement (*see* Info pages: Lime). It is manufactured at lower temperatures than its counterpart cement, and, although lime can be a localized and 'low-tech' product, it may often now share raw material quarrying, production and transport facilities with cement at large works. The raw material for lime is available in Britain.

As it sets, lime reabsorbs a large proportion of the carbon dioxide which its manufacture released; traditionally burnt lime would effectively offset more by using timber for heating, but even industrially-produced lime is reckoned more carbon-friendly than ordinary cement. Lime offers other environmental advantages in that it can be detached from other building materials such as bricks, enabling their reuse as individual units. This is not practicable with cement brickwork.

Stone

A natural product used in the past for walls and roof coverings without any mechanization but now involving highly mechanized quarrying, production, handling and transportation. Stone is of varying quality depending on its type, but if appropriately used it is very durable and, when used with lime mortars, readily reusable. Where stone can, or must, be used to blend with an existing historic construction it is likely to have to be the same as the local stone, but the progressive closures of small quarries mean that the nearest commercial quarry for a particular type of stone might even be in another country. Exotic stones have rarely played any part in smaller vernacular buildings (but perhaps, moving up the scale, marble in permanent features such as fireplaces and floor coverings). Owners and specifiers need to think hard before committing to transport stone long distances for transient, non-conservation uses.

Bricks and Tiles

These were once, like lime, available from localized production but now involve energy-intensive quarrying, production and transportation. A few smaller local brickworks have survived and those tend to be the ones producing the bricks of most use for the repairing of old houses; their products are likely to have the colours and textures of the traditional

The use of lime mortar allows the eventual reuse of bricks because it can be cleaned off.

products. But even these small brickworks cannot be expected to operate to medieval standards of sustainability in the modern world. Used and detailed correctly and laid in an appropriate lime mortar mix, traditional brickwork should last hundreds of years, be capable of localized repair, reuse and, ultimately, benign decomposition.

Unfired Clay and Earth Walls

Whether used in block form (clay lump) or mass construction, these materials were traditionally sourced from the site of the house, with any light fibrous reinforcement (straw, for example) being local. When the writer first discovered clay lump in a past fuel crisis it seemed an ideal low-energy product, but the twentieth century was too proud to consider old technology. Environmental concerns have now changed attitudes and modern sustainable building is turning to unfired earth, beefed-up with purpose-grown hemp and bound with lime. Like the historical precedents, this can be used in mass construction or blocks. The raw materials or finished blocks will most likely have to be transported by road in many cases and are unlikely to be dug by hand or mixed by farm animals as their predecessors were. But the blocks at least save energy in that they do not need to be fired at high temperatures and the raw materials are available; and, even if earth is not an entirely renewable resource, at least end-of-life recycling should not be an issue.

Timber

Timber locks up carbon absorbed from the atmosphere during its growth. Though not suited to all the extreme structural uses of steel, it has proved entirely adequate for traditional house building and for over 150 years timber engineering techniques have allowed extra structural versatility, more than is normally necessary in a house. Timber requires less energy than steel in manufacture and fabrication, it is relatively easy to rework, adapt and recycle and, historically, all that work was carried out without power tools. Timber, particularly tough hardwoods but even modern softwoods, has been shown to be remarkably durable if detailed and treated appropriately. To avoid accusations of deforestation and over-intensive production, timber used now should genuinely be from properly managed sources. Ways to vet this may change and details at any one time should be available by searching government information websites and those of independent conservation organizations. Endangered tropical hardwoods may not have featured in most vernacular buildings, but the more showy old houses may have used them in the past. Sourcing new supplies would now be unacceptable and a reason to explore 'faux' finishes (of which there are historical traditions too) or honest repairs that match as far as possible and stand as a record of our times.

Paint

In general, traditional painted finishes have advantages of breathability and benign weathering characteristics over conventional modern paints. Lime, distemper and linseed oil paint were largely produced from natural ingredients and by reasonably simple processes (see Info pages: Lime; also Paints. etc.). The disposal of unused paint is an environmental problem that can be lessened by greater care in use and ordering. Some traditional finishes, such as basic distemper and limewash, are eminently biodegradable, but, even so, they should not be disposed of carelessly. Local councils will have details of disposal centres.

Glass

Though the result of relatively low-technology manufacture in the past for house-building, and using an abundant basic raw material, modern glass uses large amounts of energy and is very centralized. Traditionally-produced glass or reproductions of it can be bought, often sourced from abroad, to match that in the country's old buildings. Glass has so many benefits and so few alternatives that it is a material whose financial and environmental costs and any other deficiencies will no doubt continue to be seen as a price worth paying. Ordinary plain window glass has been relatively adaptable to recycling (traditionally by cutting it down to ever smaller panes and incorporating it into sheds and greenhouses rather than by reprocessing). Some special toughened, laminated and coated glasses with enhanced performance require additional manufacturing processes and additives and may be less straightforward to recycle, yet their enhanced performance is valued and can be usefully targeted to certain areas.

Lead

Lead has a long and successful history in building, it can be worked cold, jointed at relatively low temperatures, its weight helps to anchor it and it is readily recycled. Though toxic, and being actively removed from drinking water supply routes, its use continues to be tolerated in roofing and some drainage because it is so versatile and not easily substitutable. There would obviously be problems in gathering drinking water from a lead roof, but any residual presence in waste water is presumably only one part of the burden of chemical and other pollution that regularly enters the system.

Iron

Wrought iron was once a product of the local blacksmith (many insist that only fully handmade, modern articles deserve to be called 'wrought') and hot metal would have been fashioned into nails, latches, hinges and other fixings for traditional housebuilding. In mass-produced products its place has been taken by steel and other materials. Like the other traditional building products examined here, the production of wrought iron now is inextricably bound up with other industrial processes providing the basic materials, so its environmental credentials are blurred by them. However, the methods of a true modern blacksmith would be recognizable to a

165

medieval smith. Old wrought iron can often be repaired by traditional methods, if not it can be recycled as more wrought iron.

Cast iron is associated with the mass-production and industrialization of the Victorians, but it was produced locally in country foundries from around the end of the eighteenth century, in association with agricultural machinery. Cast-iron production is now bound up with heavy industry and, even though it has proved extremely durable, its once familiar standard castings have now been superseded in manufacturers' catalogues by lighter steel or plastic. Cast iron was once regarded as impossible to repair, but local blacksmiths and metalworkers can often extend the life of pieces with ingenious repairs.

INSULATION FOR OLD HOUSES

Old houses behave in a different technical way from modern houses. Products intended for the insulation of modern houses can sometimes damage old ones and will in many cases require expert assessment before installation (that is, by an independent, conservation-accredited architect or surveyor, rather than salespeople alone). One problem is 'interstitial condensation', where warm, moist air penetrates from inside through the fabric until it reaches a point (perhaps within the thickness of the wall or within the insulation) that is cold enough for its water vapour to condense into liquid. This is similar to breathing out though a scarf on a winter's day, the scarf becomes wet and cold. Wet insulation is ineffective and can start decay in timber it touches. Unfortunately, it is not usually appropriate in an old house to adopt the measures that new houses use to fight this problem: insulation seems simple but it needs expert design. In the building industry the degree of insulation offered by building fabric or insulation is given a 'U-value' which, counterintuitively, becomes a smaller number as the insulation effect increases.

Loft First

Heat rises, so the most effective place to insulate a house is sometimes the easiest – the roof space. Loft insulation has been popular since the 1960s and in more recent years has been made mandatory at ever higher standards in new houses. Old houses may have been passed over, or left with lower levels of insulation that were never topped up. Since loft insulation is often considered a DIY project, some could

It is a good idea to reassess insulation from time to time in any house.

be laid in a way that might be dangerous, ineffective or liable to generate decay.

Danger can come through burying electric cables in the insulation as this can reduce the cable's capacity, and safety margins, through overheating. Danger can also arise when the loft 'floor', which is usually really only the top of a ceiling and not designed for foot traffic, is so swathed in insulation that it is no longer possible to see where it is safe to tread. Insulation can be ineffective if it is badly placed or allowed to become damp. Insulation can promote decay if it seals up the ventilation necessary to keep roof timbers aired and dry: damp attracts fungi and wood-boring insects. It is tempting to bung up the eaves with insulation to stop draughts, but in many cases those draughts have a protective effect on the roof structure (that does not need to be kept warm). It is difficult to contrive a way of laying loft insulation effectively without covering up the ceiling timbers it lays on, so the choice of insulation material should permit some ventilation at the boundary layers with the timber, by being breathable, and should not be directly stuck to it. Some insulation materials can cause skin and respiratory irritation.

Pipes and Tanks

Insulation can cause problems if, by being effective at keeping heat from the loft, it leads to any tanks and pipes up there freezing in winter. Tanks and pipes should be separately insulated; an old trick was to leave a gap in the insulation directly under the tank to keep it warm. Some older insulation may be dangerous asbestos, particularly on pipes and tanks (usually from the early years of the twentieth century, but possibly up to the 1990s, *see* Info pages: Safety and building).

Some Insulation Materials that May Be Found in Place

Glass fibre quilt was among the first popular loft-insulation materials, laid in the 1960s at a mere 50mm. The advised thickness has, roughly, increased by that amount for every decade since. The Building Regulations (Building Standards in Scotland) give the current insulation requirements for new buildings. Another mineral 'wool', made from volcanic rock, was also used early on for house insulation

A roof space becomes cold after ceilings are insulated and ventilation is provided, so pipes need extra insulation.

either in quilts, similar to glass fibre, or pumped into roof spaces as a fluffy, loose fill. Both these types may be irritant to skin and the respiratory system (but now also come bonded or wrapped to lessen exposure). The rock-based fibre products can provide additional fire-resistance benefits due their higher melting point that might be exploited by careful design and installation. This can be valuable for the non-structural division of large roof spaces to inhibit the spreading of fire; professional design is required.

Plastic foam boards and expanded plastic granules joined the fibre insulants and all these products were developed into a variety of useful forms, from rigid and semi-rigid boards, through quilts to loose fill. These highly industrialized products have each been criticized at some time on environmental or health grounds. Apart from the lung and skin irritation of the fibre materials, there have been concerns about their ingredients (formaldehyde was one) which may have the potential to seep out over time. Some plastic products, whether or not they have been effectively made 'fire-resisting' with chemical additives, have the potential to make fires worse by giving off toxic fumes or melting and raining down. 'Closed-cell' foams resist becoming waterlogged, so helping to retain their insulation in damp conditions; but airtightness limits 'breathability'.

Sprayed plastic foams that claim to insulate old roofs by sticking to the underside of exposed tiles and slates have appealed to many owners of old houses in

A typical mid-twentieth-century insulation installation, here using less than 75mm of loose mineral wool; electrical cables covered by insulation can overheat due to reduction in capacity.

the recent past as they promised to solve two problems at once: insulating while holding loose slates or tiles in place. These systems are criticized by conservationists because the roofing battens and roof timbers may be susceptible to decay if they encapsulated or are deprived of ventilation by close contact with the foam. They are also criticized because foam adhering to the undersides of the slates or tiles makes the roofing material more difficult, or impossible, to reuse economically in relaying the roof. In a traditionally-constructed, empty loft space there is much to be said for leaving the rafters well-ventilated while insulating over the first-floor ceiling so that energy is not used needlessly heating the loft. Draughts within the roof space would be welcome and should help to preserve the timber, while expensive heating stops at the ceiling below.

Newer Insulation Materials

Newer, tougher regulations designed for energy efficiency have brought a variety of insulating products to the fore. Sheep's wool, recycled clothing, recycled newspaper and processed plant material are among those that have a 'sustainable' feel. Some of these materials imply a vulnerability to fire, moths and vermin and they would have needed treatment to reduce those risks. Users planning to live with any

insulation material, new or old, need to find out exactly what treatments it has had and the substances that are in it, what they do, and how long they will remain effective. No product is likely to be perfect in all applications, and part of the problem in selecting a material has to be its track record in similar situations. Any insulation sprayed on to and adhering to timber in a way that reduces its ability to breathe is likely to be harmful to an old house.

Relatively new to the British market are thin insulating quilts that combine some of the conventional air-trapping qualities used in older insulations with the heat-reflecting qualities of metallic foils. At upwards of only a centimetre or so thick, these 'sandwiches' of foils and foams have claimed to equal the performance of much thicker, conventional, insulation quilts. If that is so, there are many narrow space applications in old houses. However, the installation requirements involve careful design to minimize physical contact that would otherwise lead to heat being conducted through the material. More worrying for applications in old houses, where breathability is so important, is that unbroken sheets of foils and plastics are not intrinsically breathable and so, without proper ventilation, such materials could have the effect of sealing in damp or encouraging condensation, each potentially leading to decay. Some commentators have expressed doubts about the degree of insulation that is practically possible with these thin, composite insulations and this, the breathability issue and conductive heat loss in practical use, need careful consideration.

Ventilation

Traditionally, there was plenty of air in a loft space because tiles and slates were not 'under-drawn' with roofing felt. The black underlay in use by the mid-twentieth century tended to seal up roofs unhelpfully, while insulation might fill any remaining gaps. A good cross flow of air is needed to keep timber roofs healthy, dry and free from condensation. When the moisture content in roof timbers rises above about 15 per cent, timber-boring beetles can take up residence in certain timber species, and, if the moisture content reaches 20 per cent, then fungal decay can become established. If an old house has been modified in the past or is being re-roofed now, it is worth considering the use of one of the more effective of the new generation of breathable underlays (remembering that some are better than others) and installing deliberate ventilation, such as through special discreet venting tiles or designing in other 'invisible' gaps, all of which can be screened against pests.

Insulation for Walls

Modern houses with masonry cavity walls are frequently insulated by filling the cavity. When built this way from new, a space can still be left to isolate the outer (potentially damp) leaf of brickwork from the insulation and the inner leaf, but when injecting foams or fibres into an existing brick cavity from outside, the insulation can end up by bridging the cavity. If that causes a problem, transmitting damp indoors, then it can be very difficult to remedy. Early examples of cavity walls might be tied together with ordinary iron ties that can rust quicker if surrounded by damp insulation.

Some old timber frame houses have thin, hollow walls. Injected cavity foams and other insulants are considered inappropriate for old buildings because of the risk of generating damp bridges and sealing up internal fabric that needs to breathe. It is also necessary to see exactly what is in there before acting: hollow walls in timber-frame have been effectively insulated when the walls were opened up for other repairs by using breathable designs (at the time, using rock-based, mineral-wool insulation), but these types of installation need to be carefully designed, installed and monitored to avoid damp problems. Such installations would have ensured that ventilation gaps and pathways were retained (for example, a ventilation gap or cavity of 50mm is often considered necessary). For information, in modern house-building, its thin-wall, timber-frame construction uses internal-facing 'vapour barriers' (basically plastic sheets) in association with insulation to control the environment within the wall, but, of course, these are generally avoided in conservation work because they work completely against the vital ability of an old wall to breathe. Putting vapour barriers in old houses could trap damp and advance decay. They would, in any case, be almost impossible to retrofit effectively, along with the other new-build style measures that would have to be part of their regime.

Roof timbers need ventilation to stay free of decay; avoid packing insulation too close and avoid sealing up useful air paths.

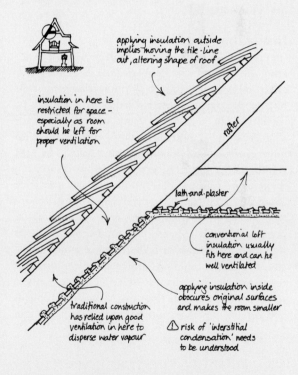

Some considerations when attempting to insulate an attic room: insulation risks blocking ventilation and encouraging dampness so new interventions in old houses should be professionally designed.

Generally, other methods of applying insulation to the walls of old houses also involve this issue of breathability. Will anything applied to the inside or outside tend to defeat breathing, seal up the wall, trap damp and generate decay? A parallel problem, aesthetically, is that any layers of insulation applied internally or externally would mask old features, alter the detail and the appearance of the wall and could make junctions with doors, windows, floors, roofs or ceilings ugly or technically awkward. A very thin film of expanded polystyrene used to be applied under wallpaper as an insulating lining and, while this may have been able to raise the surface temperature slightly, it has implications in terms of fire and breathability. Natural warm surface coatings like cork can also be at odds with breathability if the adhesives used create an impermeable skin over the wall. Insulation seems simple, but, in old houses, it needs careful and knowledgeable design to avoid creating new problems.

People may know not to block underfloor vents like these, but to insulate underfloor spaces designed to be vented might also lead to decay unless they are properly designed.

Insulation for Floors

In a uniformly heated house it can be worth considering the insulation of floors that are suspended over cellars or external passages. But otherwise some drift of heat through the internal fabric may actually be useful within a house. Many ground floors of Victorian and Edwardian houses were built with quite generous underfloor voids that have to be kept ventilated (by means of external air bricks) to keep them from rotting. This ventilation can easily be compromised by applying insulation, so installations would need to be carefully designed and capable of being monitored. Insulating solid ground floors implies excavating what is there and so is not generally a sensible building conservation option. But there may be circumstances where an owner wants to remove a later concrete floor that is causing problems and replace it with a more breathable floor that can

also offer a degree of insulation; lime concrete mixed with insulating aggregates, such as ceramic beads, has begun to be used in such situations, for example.

Insulating Doors and Windows

Old houses often have earlier features such as fixings for door curtains (an Edwardian favourite), window shutters and draught lobbies and these can be brought out of retirement or reinstated, together with ordinary window curtains that are thermally-lined (lining material incorporating reflective shredded foil is available, as well as conventional 'wadding'). Secondary glazing allows the original window frames and glass to remain, but it needs to be individually designed to be as invisible as possible and as elegant as possible. If secondary glazing is designed for conservation purposes to be ultimately 'reversible' (removable without a trace at some future point) then it might also be capable of being demounted in summer when the main windows need to be opened or maintained (*see* chapter 5: Doors and windows).

CHAPTER 8

Damp, Breathability and Ventilation

HISTORICAL PERSPECTIVE – HOW OLD HOUSES TRADITIONALLY COPED WITH DAMP

Water is necessary, it helps to hold us together and lubricates the world around us. Only when damp becomes excessive and permanent enough to cause decay do problems start in old houses. Nowadays housebuilders can call upon seamless, totally waterproof materials to keep damp at bay, but the original builders of old houses had little in the way of genuinely waterproof materials – none was both affordable and universally available. The challenge was to provide a good roof and walls out of the more accessible, local materials and ensure by design that they spent more time dry than wet.

How Old Houses Traditionally Coped with Damp: Roofs

Rain can be made to run off roofs by overlapping layers of straws, tiles or slates. In the case of straw, rain would slowly penetrate the thatch and so it would be necessary for it to dry out from time to time to maintain its performance. In the case of slates and tiles, the angle and the snugness with which they were laid and the overlap of each was critical to achieve a balance between the speed at which water was shed, the ability of the slate or tile to be held in place and the likelihood of rain being blown back under the overlap. Old roofs may not have been perfectly watertight in all conditions, but because there were always tiny air gaps between tiles, slates and the stems of thatch, any leaks could at least be dried out by ventilation.

Water vapour and air movement are essential parts of life, in an old house they just need to be kept in balance.

How Old Houses Traditionally Coped with Damp: Walls

Most traditional building materials are porous to some extent. Stone, brick, mud, lime render and timber all soak up some moisture on exposure to rain. After the rain they can dry out again if exposed to air and sunlight. The thickness of traditional walls, determined for structural reasons, was also usually sufficient to prevent their becoming totally water-logged before the next drying cycle, so that in a rainstorm the insides should stay dry.

It is not only rain that wets walls. Human occupancy creates water vapour from breathing, perspiration, cooking and washing, which condenses on the relatively cool surfaces of windows and walls, or even inside walls. Moisture can also be 'wicked' out of the ground through floors and walls in direct contact. For these reasons it would not have been appropriate to 'seal up' the walls of old houses with waterproof paint finishes, even if they had been available. Damp has many ways of getting into walls and the only way out was through the paint. So paint needed to be as porous as the walls – happily, it generally was (*see* Info pages: Paint, etc.).

A traditional solution to damp floors was to stand wooden furniture on glass cups.

How Old Houses Traditionally Coped with Damp: Floors

The earth was the original floor finish for many old houses, as built. Trodden to a firm base and perhaps dressed with renewable straw, ground moisture would have been drawn out by draughts on their way to the fireplace. Anything in constant contact would risk becoming damp. Later finishes such as brick, clay pavers or stone slabs would have been laid direct to the earth and, being porous, also permitted dampness to be 'wicked' out of the earth. Even timber floors suspended over the ground allowed damp air to be drawn out of the underfloor void by draughts blowing between the boards.

HOW MODERN HOUSES COPE WITH DAMP

Modern houses do not so much cope with damp as banish it. Damp from the ground, or from rain, is prohibited entry by firm, waterproof surfaces coated with waterproof paints and other compounds provided by twentieth-century industrial processes. Firm foundations in modern buildings mean that walls move less, so finishes that are waterproof (even if 'brittle') keep out damp better as they have not been cracked by movement. Even roofs have a second layer of waterproofing underneath the tiles. In more recent modern houses, any damp that is generated inside a house – by people breathing, cooking or washing – is quickly shown out via an extractor fan. Plastic vapour barriers do not give dampness much of a chance to get into walls and ceilings. The higher heat levels in modern houses and the fewer cold surfaces also mean that condensation is minimized. Modern houses do not tolerate damp.

MODERN METHODS UNSUCCESSFULLY APPLIED TO OLD HOUSES

The types of measure described above, that were so successful on modern houses, would, it was reasoned, improve old buildings too and they were eagerly applied. But that proved in many cases to be a serious mistake (*see below*). At the same time, changes in lifestyle meant that open fires and chimneys were abandoned, kitchens lost their connection with a permanent fire and its chimney, draughts were totally blocked, bathrooms were installed which, with kitchens, generated steam while heating became intermittent as whole families left the house during the day.

Modern Methods Unsuccessfully Applied to: Roofs

Under the tiles, slates, and sometimes even thatch, renovators inserted waterproof 'underlays' that, in modern construction, act as a second line of defence, say, in the event of a missing tile or wind-blown snow. But in traditional construction, which relied upon breathability, the effect was to totally eliminate beneficial ventilation entering between the tiles and slates. When combined with higher levels of loft insulation plus increased condensation within the home (from steamy kitchens and bathrooms), this lack of ventilation led to there being stagnant damp air in the roof space, which went to feed mould and decay on roof timbers (even modern construction was caught out by this and, as a result, roofing under-lays are now manufactured in varying degrees of breathability to help to overcome these problems; the most breathable of these may now be applicable to an old house).

Modern Methods Unsuccessfully Applied to: Walls

Traditional paints that often happened to be vapour-permeable were superseded in the twentieth century by newer, brighter, wipe-clean and much more water-proof paints and sheet finishes inside and out. These were fine on new buildings which had been built from the start to eliminate all damp from within the fabric that might otherwise need to get out. But old houses were forced to accept the new finishes too when the traditional ones went completely out of fashion. Not only do finishes, such as cement render and plastic masonry paints, lock in damp, but, for their success in keeping rain out, they rely on not becoming cracked – something that is difficult to avoid on an old building that moves (traditional lime surfaces, however, can tolerate a degree of move-ment). As if all that were not enough, old houses suddenly had new bathrooms and kitchens which

produced ample water vapour but no longer were there heated chimneys to draw it away. Consequently, damp became trapped within the walls and problems of decay were introduced. The twentieth-century solution was to zealously condemn all damp as 'rising damp' and install yet more barriers, which, unfortunately, compromised yet more traditional fabric and drove the 'problem' else-where in the house rather than solve it. (An inconsis-tency of twentieth-century repairs to old houses was, on the one hand, to apply damp barriers here and there, but, on the other, to use some gypsum plasters that might attract and hold damp.)

Modern Methods Unsuccessfully Applied to: Floors

Floors, too, were covered with impervious finishes from vinyls to rubber carpet underlay. Timber floors sealed up in this way could be susceptible to rot, especially if the process went along with the blocking of any external air vents designed to keep the floor ventilated. Often old, direct-to-earth floors might be dug up and replaced with impermeable concrete over a damp-proof, plastic sheet. This might seem to solve the floor problem – but it took no account of the way floors and walls interact, and so damp that used to evenly wick into the air across the whole floor might concentrate instead into the walls, generating another 'problem' for which the twentieth century was not slow to send someone round with a clipboard and moisture meter.

CAN OLD HOUSES BE MADE TO BEHAVE LIKE MODERN ONES?

In many old houses today damp is being kept out of sight by a series of waterproofing measures that conceal the problem rather than deal with it. The dampness needs to be drawn out into the external air, not trapped inside the fabric where it can cause decay. It has been estimated that the rate of decay of our timber-framed buildings has been vastly accelerated by the application of modern waterproof finishes, with the result that houses that have lasted for several centuries are now subject to rapid decay in a matter of decades.

Without almost totally rebuilding old houses, it

would not be practicable to install every damp-proofing technique that is part of a modern house's regime against damp. Not only are most of the old materials fundamentally different from modern ones, but the way they are put together – the architectural detailing and the way they look – is all geared to the performance of those old materials.

An added difficulty is that old houses had little, or nothing, in the way of foundations. They move a bit. This was probably never perceived to be a problem since, for example, a house built with green oak (unseasoned) was always going to twist. There were worse things in life. By luck or judgement, the old materials used for finishes and decorations could accommodate movement (*see* Info pages: Movement). Newer materials have been developed for comparatively rock-solid modern houses and so tend not to be designed to compensate for much movement when put on to old houses. and so these materials may crack. Water gets in via the cracks, but not out again through the modern, impermeable surface. The result is decay.

The answer then is 'no': old houses cannot be made to behave like modern houses. But yet people still try to beat them into submission. In fact, most old houses have been so altered with new finishes, extensions and alterations that they no longer can perform entirely like old houses either. It is necessary to recognize that many old houses are actually hybrids of modern and traditional construction. For this reason, extreme care, and experience, are necessary when assessing them for damp problems.

REINSTATING TRADITIONAL PRINCIPLES OF DAMP MANAGEMENT IN OLD HOUSES

This is not always possible, because the modern finishes that are thought to do most harm, such as cement renders and cement pointing or 'plastic' masonry paints, are quite aggressively attached and might not be removed without damage to the fabric. In some cases the status quo has to be managed as well as possible (in the future there may be better techniques to dislodge these tenacious materials).

The diagram on page 175 is the key to four simpli-fied examples of problems that might be found in old

Sealed-up by cement and plastic paint, dampness feeds decay.

houses today. On the left is a traditional damp-management regime, here on an earth-walled thatched house, an extreme example but one which applies to nearly all traditional constructions. On the right is shown what may have happened to that house in recent times to disturb the equilibrium.

Situation A: The Breathability of the External Wall Has Been Reduced

This can happen when an old wall is rendered in cement or painted with a 'waterproof' paint or when a brickwork wall is repointed in cement mortar. In many cases the hardness and impermeability of these new applied materials was incompatible with the soft, porous and moving structure beneath. If the new coatings developed tiny cracks, as a result of movement or loss of adhesion, then water could enter and begin the process of decay.

Sometimes it is possible to remove 'plastic' masonry paint; it is less easy to remove cement render (unless that has already lost its key to the wall) and it is often difficult to remove cement pointing to brick or stone work without damaging the bricks or stones (*see* chapter 4: External Walls and Info pages: Paints).

The traditional exterior renders, paints and mortars were often based on lime, which, though less 'waterproof' than modern alternatives, are usually more breathable and better suited to the way old houses can move very slightly. They are available nowadays to use (*see* Info pages: Lime).

To remove existing finishes can be a serious

intervention and suitably qualified, impartial, professional advice may be needed. In Britain, listed building consent may be necessary for listed buildings. Planning permission may be necessary for an unlisted building in a Conservation Area or National Park. Building Regulations/Building Standards approval may also be needed if changing certain features of the building. Ask the planning and building control departments in the local government authority. If it seems appropriate to leave cement render or plastic paint in place, then it is quite important to fill cracks – even hairline ones – as soon as possible to prevent water from getting trapped inside. One day there may be better removal techniques, but in the meantime it is best to keep water out where possible.

Situation B: Partially Trapped Ground Moisture

Sometimes internal floors have been relaid in concrete over a polyethylene sheet, asphalt or some similar damp-proof barrier. This can make an effective barrier so far as the floor is concerned and is a new, modern floor. But the ground dampness does not simply go away and may be deflected by the new floor into the internal and external walls instead. Once there, damp can overload the existing walls' capacity to cope with moisture.

Solutions depend upon individual circumstances and impartial, suitably qualified advice is likely to be necessary. Replacing the modern floor with one that accommodates underfloor ventilation might be one solution, but it would be extremely disruptive and so alternative approaches might look at increasing the ability of the walls to breathe and dispose of the added moisture. With a listed building, permission is needed for alterations to the interior.

Situation C: Sealing Up Roof Ventilation

The illustration shows original thatch having been replaced with tiles. This was a common change, often made long ago. Provided that the tiles allowed the passage of air between them, the ventilation was not inhibited. But at some time, as assumed by the illustration, the tiles may have been relaid by using a

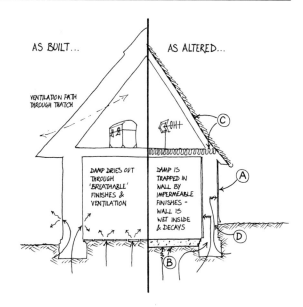

Some typical situations that are likely to be found.

roofing felt underlay beneath the tiles. By itself, or in combination with roof insulation pressed too hard into the eaves, this change can block much of the natural ventilation in the roof, leading to decay or mould growth. Fortunately, this can be relatively easy to deal with since there are a number of unobtrusive proprietary or custom-made vent designs that can be installed either in place of selected tiles or around the edges of the roof. Also, if re-roofing with underlay, there are now underlays which claim to be breathable, but advice should be sought as to the relative breathability of each type. When considering re-roofing, or even installation of some kinds of vent, permissions, as mentioned under Situation A above, may be needed, and this applies even if reverting to traditional roof-coverings from inappropriate modern ones.

Situation D: Bridging between Ground Moisture and Wall

External ground levels may be higher than internal floor levels in old houses due to pavements having been relaid over time or simply to accommodate a sloping site. This permits outside ground dampness to strike straight through a wall and affect the side facing the room. Where soil or leaves have built up against an external wall to above the floor level, dampness can be transmitted into the wall and into the house. It can usually be a simple matter to level the soil, taking care not to expose the foundations of an old house since these can be remarkably shallow.

Other variations of this problem are hard-surfaced paths which, even though they may be no higher than the internal floor level, allow rain to splash up the wall or which act to seal damp in the soil near the wall. Cutting back or removing paths can be a harder task, but there can be benefits in the reduction of damp if the paths immediately adjoining a house are made of gravel instead of concrete or asphalt.

interior of house

(if footings are really shallow, site french drain about one metre away instead of against wall)

fill trench at once with clean round gravel (20-40 mm size for this 'spade-size' trench)

garden

ensure that surface water runs away from house

nb. each old house will be different

a

b

c

slope trench base away from house

do not expose base of footings

⚠ beware cables and pipes also archæology

⌐ = air
→ = damp

how it works:
less damp should be available to enter the house if it has an opportunity first to make contact with ventilating air within the gravel

some possible refinements:
at a - edging to keep surface water and soil out
at b - a geotextile liner to keep soil from gravel
at c - a porous 'field drain' falling to a distant soakaway

A simple French drain installation to promote lower wall breathability.

Broken, leaking or blocked rainwater pipes and gutters can be continually wetting an area of wall. It is easy to miss these unless the gutters and downpipes are observed during heavy rain.

OTHER CONSERVATION REMEDIES FOR DAMP

Because conservationists prefer minimal intervention (the less that has to be done, the less is altered and destroyed forever), complex problems such as dampness may be tackled by applying a number of solutions in turn, working from the simplest and giving each a chance to work before moving on to the next.

A simple remedy can often be provided by carefully digging a 'French drain' adjacent to the walls. This introduces a gravel-filled trench in place of soil and dampness is encouraged to dry out into the air that should be then able to circulate below ground level among the gravel.

To help a French drain to work well, walls ought ideally to revert to breathable paint and lime render finishes, but this is not always so easy to achieve (*see* Info pages: Paints). Several summers should produce an effect if a French drain is going to work. However, if a wall has been damp for some time it can have absorbed salts that are not easily flushed out and these may still react with reduced levels of damp or with later redecorations to give the appearance of a persistent problem even though things may actually be a little drier.

TWENTIETH-CENTURY FIXES THAT MAY BE IN PLACE (BUT NOT BE WORKING)

The standard, late twentieth-century response to any suspicion of damp or disturbed decorations in old houses used to be to install a damp-proof course. Building societies used to insist on these in the belief that they were protecting their investments. Companies installing them would issue guarantees, but these could be contingent upon carrying out additional works, such as stripping internal plaster to about a metre above the affected area and replacing this with a hard and waterproof mix. In other words, if the new line of damp-proof course did not work for

A simple French drain being installed: this is a shallow trench because the actual foundations were shallow and should not be undermined.

some reason there was a second line of defence that kept the surface of the wall at least looking dry. However, this might simply trap damp in the walls and it introduced unsympathetic materials that can never breathe.

Remedial damp-proof courses included the following systems.

Physical Damp Barrier Cut into Place

This attempted to replicate the sometimes traditional practice of building on a bed of slates to discourage ground damp from rising. It involved cutting away a thin slice of wall, piece by piece and replacing it with overlapping lengths of new waterproof material. It was bound to be destructive if it was going to penetrate the full width of the wall in order to be thorough. It is difficult to install such a thing retrospectively and, once installed, it could cause even more destruction to remove it.

Injected Chemical Damp Course

The theory here is that chemicals can be fed into porous building materials to turn them into impervious ones. Quality control was difficult with the unknown internal make-up of many walls in old houses and inexperienced operatives might inject

into materials where the chemicals had no chance of doing their job properly (such as voids and air pockets). This method can be demonstrated to form a barrier to damp if everything is right, but, from a conservation point of view, this method introduces local areas of impermeability into a traditional system that always relied on total permeability, so it is an alien intrusion. It is also almost impossible to reverse unless some safe way of dissolving the chemicals is found.

Electro-osmosis

By applying a small electric current, or alternatively simply 'earthing' a wall, via a continuous conductor, it was claimed that water molecules would no longer be attracted up into the walls. While this system does sound more like 'snake oil' than any other (and was once abandoned commercially), there is said to be some scientific basis to it. It did not always work, for various reasons, but it has been seriously re-examined from time to time as it involves only limited intervention and would be attractive to conservationists if it could be properly verified. Evidence of this system existing previously would be bare copper wire or tape fixed horizontally at low level and attached to devices at the ends, which may be wired-in to some electrical gear. If in place, it might be worth getting a suitably qualified person to examine it, and also an electrician to establish whether it is still regarded as electrically safe.

Introduced Ceramic Vents

Several proprietary systems have existed for drilling ceramic tubes of one sort or another into walls at regular intervals with a view to encouraging dampness to dry out towards the exterior. In that these systems work with the traditional ideas of the transpiration of water vapour, they are probably much less harmful than, for example, an injected chemical damp course. Their drawback from a conservation point of view is that they involve physical intervention to install. They also try to concentrate breathability into a series of spots when it might be more satisfactory to strip out non-permeable, modern finishes to restore any original total vapour-permeability.

Sealed-up Walls

In desperation, many owners applied one of a variety of physical barriers to walls to hide damp. These ranged from brush-applied sealants, through sheets of aluminium foil or bitumen to quite heavy-duty profiled plastic boards. These all have the potential to trap rather than deal with damp. Sometimes a more sensible approach was taken by applying a lining to a wall, but leaving a well-ventilated air gap behind, so isolating the damp wall from any new finishes but still, possibly, allowing it to breathe. Perhaps some remedies and damp-proof courses were sold on the basis of a needle moving on the dial of a moisture meter, but meter readings need interpretation and they can be disrupted by things such as salts and applied finishes.

What To Do About the Above

Some of these old remedies may be working, some causing trouble, some doing nothing, but most are irreversible. They were all designed as 'patches' to solve a problem in something that was not so much broken as being used improperly (breathable walls had been 'suffocated'). Depending on how far the owner of the old house wished to go in restoring the original, breathable regime, these systems would need assessing to see whether they might interfere. As mentioned above, some installations went hand-in-glove with requirements to introduce other, non-permeable finishes or structural changes. For example, a chemical damp-proof course often came with instructions to strip internal plaster for a metre and to replaster in something then regarded as water-resistant; this would need expert analysis before attempting to reintroduce a more benign system of damp management.

Rot and Decay

HISTORICAL PERSPECTIVE

Before there were buildings there were insects and fungi dedicated to clearing up dead wood by using it as home and food. Once timber died or fell to the forest floor it was unable to defend itself against attack and eventually was consumed. In sustainability terms this was part of the original and natural carbon cycle: carbon absorbed into growing trees and released again by decay into the environment.

Houses are built by using wood that is dead. The big difference between a piece of dead wood in a house and one lying on the forest floor is that the one outside on the ground is going to be rained on, subject to morning dews and be suffocated by earth and leaf debris. Exposure to dark and dampness helps

to render the timber attractive to fungal spores and they in turn can encourage wood-boring insects to burrow deeper than the still soft outer sapwood that they tend to prefer. Wood-boring insects may be helped by dampness, but they are not entirely dependent upon it.

In theory, a piece of wood built into a house might be expected to be safe. Sadly, it takes only a minor and unnoticed building defect – a missing tile, a cracked lead valley, a broken rainwater pipe, a build up of soil against a wall – to allow water to become trapped in a building and thus replicate the conditions of the forest floor. The spores for the several types of wood rot can be floating around in the air virtually everywhere, and the wood-boring insects are generally equipped with wings, so it will not be long

Even woodland beetles prefer the softer sapwood near the outer edge of the trunk, while a few months in the damp encourages mould growth on a cut log.

179

before they find any suitably wet piece of wood ripe for their offspring to eat. Timber incorporated into buildings is, however, attacked by only a fraction of the many varieties of insect whose life cycles involve boring into wood.

MAKING THINGS WORSE

Nature's mechanisms for timber decay have been given a helping hand in that some modern materials used in the decoration and repair of old houses can trap dampness: cement renders over timber framing, plastic exterior wall paints and oil gloss paints on joinery, sealers on brickwork, even injected chemical damp-proof courses, can all prevent the migration and drying out of water trapped inside old, porous building fabric. Add to this the tendency of modern occupants to seal up useful ventilation and crank up the central heating thermostat, and all year round inside the walls of an old house it can be like a spring day on a dark, damp forest floor – just what the insects and fungi love. As a result, behind neatly-painted walls old timber lintels can be crumbling and timber frames softening and decaying.

CLIMATE CHANGE AND NEW PESTS

Timber decay is really only an extension indoors of the natural processes that might happen outdoors, and climate change may bring some new and exotic pests closer. The existing insect and fungal threats are not always found in the wild, for example the house longhorn beetle (*Hylotrupes bajulus* – large oval holes) has been in Britain for a long time, but seems to be restricted to a southern suburb of London by climate (it has been suggested that it originated overseas, imported unknowingly in wooden sea-chests). The wood boring weevil (*Euophryum confine* – small ragged holes) is apparently a relatively recent guest in the country's damp wood. If there is significant climate change here then the list of insect threats to houses may be expected to change or to grow, maybe to include termites, which are well established in France and have already been reported to have been found alive and well around south-eastern English ports and in the West Country, having presumably used a similar means of immigration to that ascribed to the house longhorn beetle – packing cases.

TWENTIETH-CENTURY OVERKILL

Having contributed to the problem by sealing up old houses, the twentieth-century solution was to try to comprehensively poison the insects and fungi for which such ideal conditions had been provided. There are enough old houses with a continuing problem from fungi and insects after chemical spraying (and also fumigation in the case of insects) to demonstrate that those solutions were not always effective. What they did do was to disperse into the environment chemicals that are, nowadays, considered too toxic for safe use alongside humans.

Limitations of Insecticides

Chemicals are difficult to apply into the heart of timber, which is where the insects may have burrowed. Deathwatch beetle larvae particularly, lurk deep in the wood for a very long time doing their damage, so killing the emerging adult beetle is only going to inhibit the next generation, and even that is difficult as the beetles may not be obliging enough to poison themselves by chewing treated wood on the way out – they use existing holes if possible. This makes them very difficult, some say impossible, to eradicate from a house.

Chemical treatment by insecticides does not discriminate between pests and natural predators – other beetles and spiders, which, unfortunately, could be eliminated more effectively by the insecticides if they happen to live on the surface of the timber. Insect infestations in roofs may be complicated by the presence of bats, which are protected, and that can limit the range and timing of any treatments; consult the local authority for access to a bat expert to find out how to check for the bats living in a particular area and how to work around them (*see* the Bat Conservation Trust).

Damaging Remedial Work for Damp, Fungi and Insect Problems

Perhaps to give their guarantees the best chance of success, some companies selling treatments for damp, and particularly dry rot, have insisted that finishes or timbers are removed from the treated area and for a distance around it and replaced by new timbers and finishes deemed to be, or hoped to be, damp-, fungus- and insect-proof. This was a view once shared by conservationists, but it is, of course, completely destructive of historic fabric and contrasts with the more relaxed attitude now seen in some high-profile conservation work, where the infestation is deprived of its fuelling damp and monitored until, it is hoped, it recedes and dies, leaving the valuable or interesting building materials intact even if they may require some repair or support. Having damp and insect problems properly identified in an old house by impartial experts (conservation organizations and conservation officers can be asked for those specialists sympathetic to conservation) lessens the chances of excessive and damaging work being done.

LOWER-KEY REMEDIES

Since the fungi that attack structural timber prefer the wood to be at a particular level of dampness (usually higher than 20 per cent) and wood-boring beetles are not averse to a habitat softened by damp and garnished with fungi, the most obvious route to getting rid of them all is to remove the dampness. Insects have varying tastes for moisture, but the household pests can tolerate down to a 15 per cent moisture content, which is within the upper limit of some timber as supplied for building.

Drying

Direct heat may not be appropriate to dry out the wood as this could damage the timber by making it shrink quickly. But, over time, improved ventilation, plus the immediate repairing of any leaks, should achieve an effective change. The removal of modern sealers, paints and renders may also be necessary to let the damp migrate out of walls and floors naturally. Specialist heat treatments have been developed to kill pests direct rather than to dry the fabric but these have to be carefully controlled and balanced with humidity monitoring to avoid sudden changes likely to damage the timber; at present, the processes may be too expensive and unwieldy for ordinary domestic applications.

The result of a long period of insect attack.

Natural Predators

Natural predators, such as spiders, can be encouraged for the flying insect timber pests, this means leaving strategic cobwebs in place during spring and summer. Deathwatch beetle populations may be accompanied by signs of another, smaller, beetle whose mission is reckoned to include seeking and destroying death-watch larvae. This beetle (*Korynetes caeruleus*) has a racy, metallic, blue-black finish in its flying stage.

Limited Insecticide Treatment

Chemical treatment may still be appropriate in conservation, but it tends to be applied locally (literally only to the worst signs of live infestation) and employ the least hazardous and most environmentally innocuous products currently available. Such treatments are realistically aimed at the reduction of pest populations rather than complete eradication.

Treatments Being Developed

Since many of the chemical treatments have been progressively limited by legislation or are now difficult to sell to wary customers, new treatments are being developed to target the weaknesses of the insects and fungi. Their need for moisture is one weakness, their reaction to heat or cold is another and insects might also be trapped and killed (by tailoring existing commercial and horticultural insect-trapping devices such as light and pheromone traps) as they fly about looking for a mate. There will be more ideas over time and, until they are fully

181

It is important not to panic, things may not always be as bad as they look and sometimes a simple repair can dry the fabric sufficiently to kill off the fungi before they do serious structural damage.

developed and tested, the customer might, rather than go straight to one or two treatment companies, consult an independent expert. They should be able to identify whether or not there is a problem and its scale, and to advise whether there is an effective remedy across the whole spectrum of new and established treatments. As with the treatment of damp, it can be useful to start small and see what works rather than launch an all-out assault with an expensive, deadly weapon that may also have unfortunate side effects on human health or the building itself.

PHYSICAL REPAIRS TO AFFECTED FABRIC

In time, fungi and insects can severely weaken timber and it may be necessary to repair or replace the affected areas, sensitively, before they fail (*see* chapter 4: External walls – Timber frame). Perhaps the biggest worry facing a house owner is whether rot or insects have caused decay that has weakened the house structurally. Superficially, this can be difficult to detect – even by experts – and it is one of the factors that the unscrupulous have used to frighten people into excessive remedial works in the past. On the other hand, the severity of some insect attacks is concealed by an apparently sound surface. An independent expert can sometimes indicate whether the

species of timber is naturally resistant to attack, or whether the more vulnerable sapwood present is limited enough to leave sufficient harder heartwood in place for structural purposes. Many old houses, simply because they are old, have suffered the worst of any insect damage many years ago.

There is always some risk in living in an old house since so many potentially dangerous things, other than insects and fungi, are unknowable about its construction, history and condition – until the workings of the building are exposed. Unfortunately, the act of exposing one problem can reveal or set off others until the nervous owner may feel that only completely rebuilding the house will set their mind at rest, a disproportionate response. The owner has to take responsibility for balancing the risks against the practicality of eliminating them. The risk-averse might prefer a modern house, but even then there could be chemical vapours off-gassing from modern building materials and furnishings to worry about.

IDENTIFICATION

This is a specialist area suited to an independent expert. Treatment companies, even some experts, tend to be wedded to particular treatment regimes, so the owner of an old house needs to probe intelligently. Below are mentioned the two most likely insect pests and the difference between wet and dry rot is discussed. To recognize dry rot could form a whole book in itself and a single picture here could be misleading. In the case of insect attack it is worth establishing, especially when one is new to a house, whether the evidence seen is left over from an old infestation and only partially active or whether it is current and thriving due to poor maintenance in the past.

Wood-boring Insects

There are a variety of insects that burrow into and weaken timber, some follow on in the wake of fungal decay. The two most commonly cited in building defects are the deathwatch beetle and the furniture beetle (but *see also* house longhorn beetle and wood boring weevil above), sometimes called 'woodworm' because their eggs hatch into larvae that do burrow into the wood.

Deathwatch Beetle

An insect with a matt brown body and wing cases, about 6 to 9mm from head to tail (*Xestobium rufovillosum*). It makes a rapid tapping noise in spring, usually heard coming from within the timber structure. It exits to mate, flying about well into the summer, landing on cardboard and newspapers where it can make quite loud noises – which might help its chances of mating but increases its chances of extermination by humans. Its approximately 3mm-diameter exit-holes can be found in timber and finishes. The deathwatch seem to prefer hardwoods, which, unfortunately, include the oak in old houses. But old houses have been around for long enough to have hosted beetles for many years so the presence of exit-holes alone does not always prove an active infestation. Scotland is reckoned to have been largely exempt from deathwatch beetle, but that may change along with the climate.

A very rough assessment of its numbers in a house year-by-year can be made by counting the carcasses found in a particular area and by continually blocking exit holes with something fragile such as tissue or wax and seeing which ones are reopened.

Furniture Beetle

Piles of fine dust, from spring into summer, appear around the (up to 2mm-diameter) exit-holes in timber. The furniture beetle (*Anobium punctatum*) is

A deathwatch beetle exhausted by mating (rule is in centimetres).

An old, plywood wireless set has entertained some furniture beetles.

supposed to prefer the softer sapwood in all timber, but experience shows that it is not that fussy and seems to enjoy plywood too.

Fungi

There are many varieties of fungus that live off building timber. Conventionally, they have been divided into 'dry rot' and the rest – the 'wet rots'. They literally suck the goodness out of timber.

Dry Rot

Often misdiagnosed and its name used inappropriately, dry rot has an insidious reputation which can frighten people into drastic action. Its popular reputation suggests that, once it has a foothold, it can rampage through a house without needing water, like some unstoppable video-game space monster. But it is vulnerable because, like any organism, it does need water and a conducive environment to survive and grow, and so the trick is to ensure that *all* its water supplies are well and truly stopped. It can send out fine, tendril-like probes across barren territory in search of more water. This tends to alarm people as each strand, they feel, will become a new outbreak, spreading beneath plaster and through walls. That may be true, potentially, but the air generally contains spores with a similar potential – an outbreak is dependent on suitable timber being suitably damp. A moisture content above 20 to 22 per cent is often quoted (less damp than for some other fungi, hence

ABOVE: *An old outbreak of rot that has dried and hardened.*

LEFT: *Typical of many fungal attacks, including dry rot, is timber drained of its 'body' and shrivelled, as here, or cracked into cubes; here sealing the timber and walls with gloss and plastic seems to have helped to retain damp and nurture the rot.*

the name) and, as a comparison, specially dried timber for building use comes at moisture contents specified within the range of 8 to 20 per cent, which rises if it is left in damp conditions. Fungi also like warmth, with central heating providing them with a comfortable 20°C or more.

Dry rot (*Serpula lacrymans*) does not always look the same, it depends in part on where it is growing and at what stage is being viewed, and, while an expert might tell at a glance or at least with a microscope, its visible forms can be broadly similar to other types of rot. A reddish-brown fruiting body with white edges (and a passing resemblance to a dusty pizza thrown at the wall) is the most spectacular stage of dry rot, but other manifestations are white fluffy strands and greyish root-like strands. Affected timber can crack into square blocks or morph and disintegrate. The conservative treatments for the fungus would be similar to other fungi: remove the water supply and also remove the rot if at all possible.

Wet Rot
Wet rots include a host of different looking fungi with different habitats, from white and furry, through mushroom-like growths to big, colourful

'fruiting bodies', depending on the type and growing medium. They are all indicative of there being too much damp, and, if caught at the right stage, they are all potentially treatable by removing that damp permanently. Cellar fungus (*Coniophora puteana*) is one that is common in buildings and its dark strands might have helped to persuade people their homes were hosts to dry rot.

The identification of fungi is a specialist task and, as mentioned above, usually best left to an independent specialist who can advise on appropriate remedies. Treatment companies' promotional material tends to focus on the negative and dramatic aspects, things can quickly get emotional and destructive works put in hand. A proportionate response is called for. If appropriate a 'natural' treatment is to remove the organism's water supply, isolating the timber from any damp surroundings while increasing ventilation. Where fungi have damaged the structural integrity of timber then, as with insect infestations, there is no option usually but to carry out a repair, at which time it would be sensible to ensure that the rest of the timber is isolated from direct sources of dampness, but still able to be ventilated on all sides.

CHAPTER 9

The Professionals

HORSES FOR COURSES

This book has set out to explain how old houses are intrinsically different from new ones and how old houses may be damaged, visually and physically, by the inappropriate use of modern decoration and repair methods and materials. Since this is still not fully understood across the whole spectrum of the building industry, it follows that professional architects, surveyors, engineers, builders and decorators need to be carefully selected for work on old property. Before modern building technology ousted centuries of trial-and-error experience, craftsmen knowledgeable in traditional building could have been found in every town and village. Craftsmen and women in traditional building now fill a specialist niche, but the effort to find them should be worthwhile and every link in the chain of building skills can be made up of people sympathetic to old buildings.

Before selecting professionals and builders the owner might usefully contact the local authority's conservation officer for general advice. Whether builder or architect, there is a distinct difference between someone who has 'done work to' historic buildings and someone who understands how old buildings work. It is generally better to work *with* an old building on its own level of technology rather than try to beat it into submission with new technology, because modern interventions may never be

*Sooner or later an old house
will need professional attention.*

fully compatible with what has gone before. In addition to competence and experience in their field, anyone engaged to work on an old house will inevitably be around their client for some time; the two should be on the same wavelength, whoever is engaged is going to have to be trusted, not just with the property but with ensuring that it gives the owner pleasure for years to come.

Client
In the case of simple DIY, the 'team' may go no further than this. This book is not a step-by-step guide to DIY, but the reader should by now be aware that even simple DIY jobs such as repainting and gardening can have a pronounced effect, for good or ill, on an old house. And even simple jobs can benefit from professional experience and buying advice specific to a building should bring confidence and save misguided, expensive and damaging work. Now that some car dealerships charge more per hour for their mechanics than do many architects, engineers

Despite all the signs, this building's days were not over and it was able to be repaired and returned to use.

and surveyors for professional advice, it makes spending money on a house look cheap, and a house is generally a much sounder long-term investment than a car.

The client is responsible for starting the whole process of any building repair or construction. As it is their own money being spent, they have a duty to themselves to select a team wisely, give them clear instructions in good time and also enable the team to meet obligations further down the line by paying them on time. One of the causes of projects overrunning and overspending is the making of changes, last-minute ones are the worst. Sometimes these are

unavoidable and unpredictable, but professional involvement would offer the chance of filtering out the regular pitfalls – and help the client to understand properly what to expect visually – so there should be less room for unpleasant surprises. Each of the professions below might usefully be prefixed with the word 'conservation' as this looks to be the way that specialists in the field are likely to be described in the future.

Architect

The need for an architect for a new building, extension or alteration is generally understood as the processes are a complex mix of art, science and dealing with legislation. It may seem an expensive luxury to involve an architect in routine repairs to an old house, but architects who specialize in conservation can guide their clients through planning issues (often involved in repairs to a listed building, for example – *see* Info pages: Red tape for more about regulations, grants and tax) and their technical experience should help clients to avoid expensive and potentially damaging, inappropriate work. Whether building new or repairing an old building an architect is called upon to analyse what is visually 'right' and, with an old house, this skill needs to be exercised with great sensitivity.

Architects engaged in conservation can also be well placed to carry out historical research and prepare documents such as Statements of Significance and Conservation Plans (sometimes required for houses in the higher grades of statutory listing). During the time when traditional building crafts were scarce, building professionals had to take on a quite detailed knowledge of practical conservation skills and traditional building methods, and this legacy of knowledge can be a valuable resource.

Size and Type of Firm and Finding an Architect

Larger firms may have a broad spread of resources and skills. Those at the top of the organization, directors or partners, are 'charged out' at higher prices per hour than the junior staff member, who may carry out much of the work. Smaller firms can find it easier to offer a single point of contact, more likely to be the partner or director who may also be carrying out the work. Firms of architects may trade as partnerships or companies. The term 'architect' has long been protected by British law (some international qualifications are accepted) and an architect is required to be registered with the Architects' Registration Board (ARB). Registered architects can become Chartered Architects by joining the RIBA and, if their practices subscribe to Chartered Practice status, the RIBA promotes them. Architects' practices may be found by personal recommendation, advertisements, entries in directories and their own websites. For architects specializing in conservation the AABC register online www.aabc-register.co.uk (Architect Accredited in Building Conservation) lists individuals by region who have met its experience criteria and this is now a recognized starting place for the selection of an architect to advise on an old building.

Fees

Professional advisers normally charge either a percentage of the construction cost (there were once standard architects' fee scales for various types of project) or a 'lump sum' based on their assessment of the work necessary. In either case, the fee might be paid in instalments according to the length of the project. For one-off visits to look at particular issues, the firm may quote an 'hourly rate' which may cover not just the visit to site but also time preparing a written summary afterwards. Expenses make a difference, and firms and clients should agree which costs are to be charged as extra and which are included.

Appointment

A written appointment setting out their duties and terms for payment is compulsory for architects. These are becoming easier to read and understand, but some jargon is inevitable; it is important to query anything unclear at the outset and an appointment document can be a good test of the communication and rapport that would be beneficial when it comes to a building contract.

Impartiality, the Dual Role of a Contract Administrator

Although the architect, or other lead professional, is acting for the client, they are required to administer the terms of a building contract impartially between the contracting parties, client and builder. The architect also has legal and professional responsibilities beyond the contract. Engaging an architect is a curious mix of commissioning a free-thinking artist to turn abstract ideas and wishes into physical form and hiring an administrator who has to run on rigidly-defined rails of responsibility.

Building Surveyor

Many of the generalities above can also apply to building surveyors, especially when in the role of lead professional. The Royal Institution of Chartered Surveyors maintains a conservation accreditation scheme for its members (www.rics.org.uk). Like the RIBA, the RICS also issues guidance on the engagement of its members. A twentieth-century view of the distinction between architects and surveyors was perhaps that architects tended towards the aesthetic plus technical design of new building works and building surveyors towards practical management roles, which included the maintenance of existing buildings. But now, in conservation work especially, the traditional responsibilities of surveyor and architect frequently overlap.

Pre-purchase Surveys

The choice of an appropriately skilled professional begins when looking to buy an old house. There is an important difference between a survey to assess valuation (say, for a building society) and one to assess its condition and repair liability. Prospective purchasers of an old house seeking a full survey would be wise to consider a building surveyor accredited in building conservation since old buildings work differently from modern ones, and employing appropriate expertise may avoid damage from invasive investigation. Building societies have in the past made their mortgage loans conditional upon recommended 'remedial' works – some of which, with hindsight, ignored the ways in which old houses were intended to work. For example, remedial damp-proof courses are not always necessary just because the house was not built with one, and a paper guarantee is little compensation for misguided interference (*see* chapter 8: Damp. etc.).

New at the time of writing are Home Information Packs (Purchaser's Information Packs are proposed for Scotland). Ideally, these would recognize that old houses operate differently from modern constructions and, in consequence, acknowledge that their occupants may use them differently. Part of the purpose of the packs is to present data on energy performance, so inspectors and prospective owners should be aware that energy performance results modelled from questionnaires should be examined in the light of actual fuel consumption and fuel type (*see also* Info pages: Sustainability).

Structural Engineer

Traditionally engaged at the request of the lead professional to tackle structural issues, there is no reason why a client should not approach an engineer direct to target a specific problem. With old buildings, engineering problems tend to be either dramatic – things about to collapse – or to concern the structural design of alterations. As with all other members of the building team, it is important that the engineer is already familiar with the strengths as well as the limitations of traditional buildings, otherwise there could be a greater tendency for repairs and interventions to be heavy-handed and unsympathetic. Like surveyors and architects, the boundaries of responsibilities and knowledge have become less clear-cut recently and engineers have developed specialities in a variety of conservation repairs. Engineers who are comfortable with old buildings and the performance of old materials can produce some innovative and clever solutions. The engineers' professional bodies, the Institution of Civil Engineers (ICE) and the Institution of Structural Engineers (IStructE), have established CARE, the Conservation Accreditation Register for Engineers.

Party Wall Surveyor

Recent legislation (The Party Wall, etc. Act 1996; www.planningportal.gov.uk for downloadable information) makes provision for agreement between neighbours on details of work affecting boundaries. This does not just apply to dividing walls between dwellings, but extends to plot boundaries and any features within certain distances of them that might be affected. An independent party-wall surveyor can be provided by those carrying out the work but selected by those on 'the other side of the wall'.

However, a relatively informal agreement is also possible. As the legislation is new to most of the country, and unfamiliar to many, it makes sense to be alert for neighbouring building works.

For Larger Projects

CDM Coordinator (formerly Planning Supervisor)
Legislation aimed at improving building-site safety, the 'CDM' regulations (*see* Info pages: Safety and building) was introduced in 1994, revised in 2007 and is likely to be extended in the future. The early measures exempted certain domestic works (usually by virtue of their size and duration) from the full administrative burden, but not necessarily from compliance. The regulations require designers, owners and builders to consider the full range of potential present and future dangers that their operations and the finished building would involve. A profession, planning supervisor, was created out of the regulations; sometimes architects and surveyors had this as a dual qualification. The 2007 revisions have changed this role to that of 'CDMC', with more continued input into a project's design and implementation. It is important for clients to understand that they have direct responsibilities under the new regulations, one of which is the appointment of competent persons to undertake the several roles. The 2007 regulations emphasize the developing of the design alongside the contractor, which runs counter to the established practice in many small domestic works of issuing a complete design to the builder.

Quantity Surveyor
This is someone who keeps an eye on the money and is involved with cost forecasting. In larger projects, where specialized cost control is worth paying for, then this professional can be of value. A QS's familiarity with conservation issues such as the supply of traditional materials, the weather-sensitivity of some traditional processes and the terms of any grant-aided work can be an asset in financial planning.

M&E Services Engineer
Trained to design the installations for electricity, telecommunications, gas and water supplies and for waste and drainage, this profession is founded firmly

in the industrial age so it is perhaps asking a lot for it also to be conservation-oriented. A high degree of sensitivity is required when designing and installing all basic mechanical and electrical services, as well as installations to conserve or generate power, in historic buildings, after all, punching holes in floors and walls goes against the conservation ethos. Since the impact of M&E installations may not be obvious in listed building applications, an M&E engineer prepared to think through the nuts and bolts of an installation with other members of the team would be valuable in helping to respect the appearance and future of an old building.

Clerk of Works
Now all but extinct, this on-site post used to be filled by a knowledgeable, senior tradesman or perhaps a retired professional who was engaged by the client as their independent representative on-site. Nowadays, in the largest modern building projects, the contractor is sometimes also the client and there are, anyway, a multitude of other lines of responsibility, guarantees and self-certification, so this post has faded away. But, on a smaller-scale domestic project, it is still a useful idea: who is it that checks that things look sensible from day to day and who looks after the client's interests on site when the client themself or their architect is not around?

Building Contractors
Builders range from one-man outfits to larger firms, usually styled 'building contractors'. Traditionally, building firms kept a permanent staff of tradesmen and would regularly apprentice younger incomers to the several trades. Now they may have a core of full-time employees and take on self-employed trades-people and labourers from time to time, as the workload requires. At the time of writing, there is a tendency for conservation skills to be offered through small- to medium-sized firms of building contractors, some independent or old-established, others affiliated to larger firms.

Even for small jobs a building contractor can offer a useful organization and back-up, though this usually comes at a higher price than employing a single tradesman. All the on-site skills are important but the builder's representative on a site (once the

Sweep away the cobwebs but keep the window; repairing old houses calls for people with an affection for old buildings and a willingness to gently revive rather than replace.

'site foreman') has to provide the workforce with the means and motivation to carry out the work while correctly interpreting the instructions coming from the client or the architect.

It is common for householders to appoint builders direct to carry out repairs and redecorations, but, while many builders genuinely try to serve their customers' needs well, they are not usually constituted to take on responsibilities for the analysis and design of repairs. Builders might feel obliged by long tradition to roll their eyes when the architect turns up on site, but contractors do appreciate clear direction, organized payments and someone to handle planning and regulations queries. Good builders want to get on with a job and get it finished, but, like anyone else, they become demotivated if there are obstacles and indecision, which can cause their complicated logistical process to break down.

Tradespeople, 'One-man' Builders and Decorators
A tradesman or tradeswoman is someone with recognized qualifications and experience in a particular trade. Some trades are highly organized and regulated; for example, it is now illegal to have most types of work done to gas, electrical and some other installations by someone without the relevant type of qualification from the appropriate regulatory body. There are also grades of qualifications within a trade that require extra training for certain tasks. Other trades

may have training schemes and nationally recognized qualifications, but no legal restriction on who may do their job. Anyone with a van can still offer general building or decorating services, so customers rely on their wits and on personal recommendation. It is probably fair to say that conservation skills are less likely to be found in a 'one-man' general builder, but the necessary skills and attitudes are bound to filter through to this part of the industry as more people are trained in conservation work. Some intensely traditional conservation skills and specialized crafts are provided almost exclusively by sole-traders.

Smaller builders and individual craftspeople are just as grateful as anyone else in the building industry for prompt and correct payment. Where there is no professional adviser the client may not fully understand what a builder has had to do to complete a job. To minimize disputes builders need to try to explain their work clearly to their customers in advance and offer written quotations. If customers are unhappy with the bill, they may want to ask for more information, a detailed breakdown of costs, for example.

Builders' Merchants and Suppliers

Throughout the country there are old-established, local builders' suppliers and chains of national builders' merchants who normally deliver materials to site and may hire out special equipment. Some conservation materials, such as lime putty, are now much more easily found, others may need tracking down – preferably via professional advisers, or perhaps through the magazines of conservation organizations and the internet (bear in mind that neither necessarily vet their advertisers for suitability or quality, though a few do carry out some screening). Traditional materials tend to be more sensitive to wet and cold than their modern counterparts, so carriers may not automatically give them the care they deserve. Appropriate storage should be available on site as soon as materials arrive.

FINDING PEOPLE

Some trades are highly conservation-specific and may seem hard to find. Entering the word 'blacksmiths', for example, into a search engine could bring up links to individual firms in Australia, maybe trade organi-

zations and a rock band or two, but not the blacksmith down the road who does not have a website. For more specific enquiries about traditional building trades the Society for the Protection of Ancient Buildings is a charity dedicated to conservation and may be able to help in locating skills.

While searching, try to establish whether any trade or professional organizations exist for the skills wanted. Organizations whose main objectives include training, customer service and high standards would be preferable to those that really only lend an impressive-sounding name or some advertising in return for an annual fee.

GETTING THINGS UNDER WAY

Tenders and Prices

Where architects and surveyors have prepared a written specification or drawings plus a draft building contract it has been usual for building contractors to be selected on the basis of a competitive tender. Depending on the complexity of the works, three or four weeks is a common period for pricing purposes. Alternatively, building contractors can be appointed through the negotiation of price, without competition. Builders' prices tend to be quoted without adding on the necessary VAT. Remember to check and add it on if necessary (*see* Info pages: Red tape – Tax).

In less formal pricing there is a distinction between the words 'estimate' and 'quote', the former being vaguer and implying change. A builder can only reasonably be expected to give a firm quotation if there is good information about what is likely to be involved. Clients owe it to themselves and the builder to give clear instructions and to have understood the implications of what they are asking the builder to do. It can be difficult to visualize and predict a building operation, which is where architects earn their fees.

Building Contracts – the Documents

For a long time building contracts were special in contract law in that they allowed for variation of price if there were variations in the work. Building contracts have always been complex and the terms potentially contentious. There are 'standard forms', based upon long experience of what is seen to be reasonable in various circumstances. If it does come to a dispute, the client can be at a disadvantage if they have no professional adviser; some standard building contract forms are potentially confusing, but to enter into a building project without a proper written contract is irresponsible. There are simplified standard contract forms for householders to engage contractors direct.

Some of the things usefully appended to contracts are: a firm breakdown of the costs of the elements of the work (useful if work is omitted) plus some formula for calculating the cost of extra work. All aspects of the work should be agreed, including in what state the builders will find and leave the area of work and who disposes of waste. The timescale should be stated in the contract and any critical dates identified. Insurance responsibilities should be clarified (see Info pages: Red tape). This is only a sample, the more misunderstanding that is avoided, the happier the experience is likely to be. If there is a problem each party should explain, or ask questions, before launching into conflict.

Programming the Work

Traditional materials benefit old houses, technically and visually and their use involves giving up one or two modern short cuts, such as drying them very quickly or their use in cold weather. To get the full benefit from using traditional materials, the work often needs to be programmed to allow for limitations such as frost-sensitivity, which usually means a start in the spring and finish before autumn. If the works require official consents (for Planning or due to Listed Building, Conservation Area or National Park status, for example, or Building Regulations/Standards) or liaison with other parties such as neighbours (as in Party Wall Awards) or 'statutory undertakings' (utility companies) then there will be a lead-in time of perhaps many months as documentation is prepared and submitted for approval. Any such permissions, along with the obtaining of contractors' prices, need to be dealt with before the previous winter is over to allow a prompt spring start.

The Experience

It can appear to some householders that builders do not stay where you put them, they roam about switching off stop-taps or needing power outlets or propping things up. Building work can generate unbelievable dust and mess, and suddenly people who used to try to make even the cat wipe its paws can be faced with a room full of dusty people with power tools. Builders can be asked to help to clear the decks and protect vulnerable surfaces, but householders should also help themselves by removing delicate possessions. Old houses can be vulnerable to the hammering and thumping of building and it is sensible to ask, well in advance at the design stage, about options such as using nail-guns, or even screws, instead of hammer and nails in certain work to reduce the likelihood of dislodging lath and plaster ceilings and walls. By the way, builders really do appreciate being offered tea. And so do architects.

PLANNING FOR MAINTENANCE

Many historic buildings are served by a regular inspection regime such as a quinquennial survey, which results in a list of repair and maintenance items graded according to their urgency. Conservation architects and surveyors would normally be happy to provide this service for old houses. Historic properties are also the subject of Conservation Plans, which identify strengths and weaknesses, desirable features and threats, for example, so that these may inform future decisions about the property.

There can be several advantages for the owner of an old house in commissioning reports of this type for their property: A major benefit is an overview of actual and potential repair liabilities for the immediate future which can help in planning the budget. The same knowledge will enable work to be programmed in a sensible order: For example, repointing a chimney stack might be a simple extension to the facilities that would be in place when re-roofing happens, but it might be expensive to arrange scaffolding separately for the chimney and possibly disrupt an old and fragile, or a newly relaid, roof, so the two jobs could be assessed to see whether they could be programmed together. Or perhaps the owner may want to know if it is worth stripping external, non-breathable paint at some time in the future, because this may help them to make decisions in the meantime about the types of

Pleasing compositions of old buildings can seem to have come about almost accidentally; it is not always easy to produce this sort of casual harmony deliberately, but sadly it is all too easy to destroy.

internal decoration that might be considered. Reports of this kind can be valuable to new owners taking on an old house, especially if it is their first one, as it can help to address priorities and emergency works. A conservation professional's experience may be able to help to avoid the wasting of money on panic repairs or on building work that seems reasonable but which could actually turn out to be ineffective or even damaging.

EXTENSIONS AND ADAPTATIONS

Many of the principles that go with conservative maintenance and repair can also be applied to new extensions and adaptations. If an extension is absolutely necessary, then the existing building ought to be respected and destruction of original fabric avoided. An extension to an old house is more likely to respect the existing building if it is designed to ensure that the new work is reversible (it can be removed without leaving a 'scar') and also so that it does not interfere visually with the main views of the house. Houses that are part of an attractive composition, whether a formal and designed one like a terrace or an accidental one like a grouping around a village green, have a responsibility not to 'break the spell' by introducing a jarring new feature.

The sensitive design of a new extension or carefully thought-out adaptations can increase the value of a house. However, botched or insensitive alterations can have a detrimental effect on the quality and attractiveness to others of an old house and this can, in turn, affect its value. Professional help is highly advisable (*see above*). Because work on old houses demands sympathy with the existing building, there is usually less opportunity for architects to stretch their imagination too far into the unusual – but client and the architect need to agree at the outset what the ground rules are for design and not forget to bring in the local planning authorities at an early stage. Projects can have a long lead-in period and council staff can change, so record and confirm critical statements of policy or acceptability as agreed with planning officers and heritage organizations.

Red Tape: Planning Permissions, Building Regulations, Grants, Tax and Insurance

THE PLANNING SYSTEM

Listed Buildings

In Britain the 1947 Town and Country Planning Act and its successors have ensured that, not only new building works and demolition are controlled (by planning permission), but that there is a list of existing buildings that are of special architectural and historic interest (works to which are controlled by Listed Building Consent). These 'listed' buildings have been subdivided into grades according to their perceived importance. Broadly, the older and more original a building was, the more chance it had of being listed; but other factors, such as historical associations or uniqueness, have also been influential and now quite recent buildings can be listed if they are interesting enough. The several grades (currently I, II* and II in England and Wales, A, B and C(s) in Scotland and A, B+ and B (1 and 2) in Northern Ireland) might perhaps be more clearly named, but in each case government and local government websites give the detailed criteria for each category and the practical implications of each level of listing. In addition to these national lists, local authorities can also

Statutory listing applies internally as well as externally, so a listed house like this would need very careful work to preserve its past character while also making it habitable for the future.

list buildings independently – 'local lists'. A separate category of Scheduled Ancient Monument exists with its own approval procedures, however these tend to be structures other than dwellings. (There are moves to streamline and simplify the planning process for heritage buildings and these may be announced after this book goes to print.)

Where Listing Applies

There is a common misconception that listing applies only externally or to features that are named in the summary attached to the list (*see* the local planning authority website for how to view this on-line for any one building), but actually statutory listing can be assumed to apply to everything, that is inside and out and regardless of age. The listing can even impact on a neighbouring property if that is deemed to be a 'curtilage' building, sometimes interpreted as being within the 'natural' boundaries, as opposed to the current legal or ownership boundaries of the principal listed building. An example of that might be an outbuilding to a listed country house, such as a stable block that has since been sold into separate ownership. Outbuildings may be subservient aesthetically, but can display and preserve interesting and rare vernacular features. Features within the curtilage that were in place when the 1947 planning laws took effect (1 July 1948) are also deemed to be listed; however, this does not necessarily exclude later features. Old maps can be a useful source of information.

What Listing Does

Listing acts as a notification that applications to alter a building (including any sort of demolition) will be specially scrutinized by the planning authority. It does not necessarily mean that all change is automatically forbidden, as the system sets out to preserve the character of the buildings, though naturally this tends to favour preserving fabric. Owners should feel encouraged that their investment is going to benefit from informed guidance that is designed to preserve its character and therefore should help it to keep its value. There was a time when people thought that listing was an imposition, but that was before it was realized that a well-preserved, listed building can be an asset. Anyone living in a listed building with

surviving original features such as fireplaces, cornices, panelled doors, sash windows and polished floorboards, may owe all that to planning legislation. How much less would the house be worth now if it had, instead, teak-effect electric fires, asbestos-reinforced, texture-finished ceilings, plywood doors, PVC window frames and chipboard floors?

As listing has legal force and is underwritten by government, it comes with stiff penalties for breaking the rules: government and local planning authority websites may explain fines, prison terms and examples of enforcement procedures. Prospective purchasers of listed buildings should check to see that every past alteration has been properly approved or they may find themselves suddenly responsible for putting right past illegal alterations.

Is Listed Building Consent Necessary for Repairs?

Where the repair is going to affect the appearance or the historic fabric then the conservation officer should be consulted, but it is in all cases best to talk with them as they might be able to offer some valuable guidance. Strictly, even proposals as simple as changing the colour of paint can be the subject of a listed building application. Generally, the rules are assumed not to be such as to impede ordinary like-for-like repairs. However, if, for example, removing modern cement render from an old house in order to replace it with traditional, breathable lime render, or replacing a window, even if 'like-for-like', then an application would almost certainly be necessary (*see also* Tax below). As stated above, it is a common misconception that internal work is exempt, that is not so – everything is listed and change requires permission; even the removal of inappropriate, late twentieth-century additions need approval. There has been no charge for applying for listed building consent alone (but if a parallel planning application is necessary that would attract the usual fee).

Conservation Areas

These recognize that certain groups of buildings, open spaces, trees or aspects of the built environment are making a positive contribution and should be enhanced and preserved to the extent that changes are monitored and controlled. Trees within a Conservation Area are automatically protected

Village and town centres with interesting collections of buildings are selected for Conservation Area status.

against unauthorized pruning or felling. Residents need to approach the local authority for permission before making certain changes to their buildings. Some of the 'permitted developments' for which regular planning permission is not necessary outside a Conservation Area may need formal permission inside one. The precise list can be tailored to each area and the local authorities have details of the boundaries and requirements of each of their Conservation Areas, as well as being able to guide

residents on the processes for seeking permissions. Replacement windows and doors and boundary walls and fences are examples of features that are commonly covered – and may affect modern buildings as well as old ones. There has been no charge for applying for Conservation Area consent.

Other Special Areas
National Parks and Areas of Outstanding Natural Beauty have individual rules governing buildings

and are intended to preserve the quality of those areas. The park authority (or local authority for AONBs) provides details and also processes planning applications. Communities within district councils have been encouraged to produce design guidelines generated by the community, an example would be a Village Design Statement. As these local design statements become more complete across the country, they are likely to acquire status with district and county councils. At present they can be a useful checklist for parish councils, where the meeting may be essentially voluntary and without professional support. Applicants should enquire about the existence of such a document and try to ensure that their proposals are sympathetic to the community's aims.

Conservation Officers

Local authorities in Britain usually have a person attached to their planning department to deal with Listed Buildings and Conservation Areas. Though strictly their remit might not include old buildings that are not protected in some official way, the more enlightened councils might feel that the appropriate care of their entire built heritage is worth providing for. A conservation officer should have an appreciation of the type of historical design it is their duty to protect and would often be the person in a local authority who initiates local design initiatives. They can be an invaluable source of information and assistance to the owner of an old house and his or her professional team. They can equally be, when proposals regarded as inappropriate have been developed in isolation and without proper advice, the person at the end of the long chain of authority who has to say 'no'.

A conservation officer and the local planning team may offer guidance, but it is not their job to design an applicant's project for them. A design can comply with the letter of the law and still look unappealing: the owner can look beyond just 'ticking the boxes' of a local development plan by using dedicated and expert design advice with a view to making the building as attractive and rewarding as possible.

The Application

The applicant for listed building consent should seek advice on conservation issues at the outset of his or her proposals. The planning guidelines may be set out by the conservation officer, but the conservation input for the design or repair would come from a professional such as a conservation-accredited architect, which then becomes part of the total solution along with design, comfort, budget, safety, accessibility, sustainability, energy-efficiency, etcetera. If no specialist conservation input is sought then time and money can be wasted if the scheme has to be amended or abandoned later. This is all the more relevant to buildings in the higher grades of listing (for example, in England grades I and II* and for Wales potentially any) since applications are also put before the statutory heritage agency (English Heritage, Cadw, Historic Scotland) and the relevant amenity societies that are statutory consultees.

The planning and listed building application process is, at the time of writing, about to be streamlined (so there may be some changes) and on-line applications, already possible, will no doubt be encouraged. Traditionally, forms, drawings and any ancillary documents such as design and access statements (an explanation of how the proposals satisfy various criteria) have been submitted by post in sufficient numbers to be circulated to all the relevant local councils. A planning application has for a long time been a separate, though often nearly identical, set of documents to a listed building application (this may change). The applications are each addressing two separate sets of rules. The prevailing application procedures should be posted on local authority websites or available, along with any printed forms and guidance notes, from their offices.

Rules exist about how much time should elapse before a decision is given (and how to appeal against a refusal), but the current practical interpretation of these should be enquired about from the planning office. There are normal planning procedures requiring the advertising of proposals and inviting comments – which may include objections – from local people, which are taken into consideration. It has been the case that some applications may be decided at a public meeting, others – for example, if they are reasonably straightforward and uncontested – might be approved by the planning office. The applicant may appeal against a refusal (and there has been talk of one day allowing objectors an equivalent right to appeal against consent). Complex cases may come before a planning inspector.

Listed building consent (like planning permission) can be granted with conditions attached, so that detailed compliance can be deferred until the project is at a fuller stage of development. The permission when granted is valid for a specified number of years and would usually have to be renewed with a repeat full application if work has not been substantially begun during that time (check with local authority for the current expiry period and interpretation of 'substantially').

BUILDING REGULATIONS

Also known, in Scotland, as the Building Standards, these are a set of government-sponsored regulations that have traditionally been administered by local authorities. Once towns and cities had individual building codes but the Building Regulations introduced a nationwide system of guidelines for soundness of construction, health, safety, amenity, equality of access and, increasingly now, energy conservation. Now that methods of building are much more diverse and there is a need to harmonize with other countries, the regulations rely more on satisfying performance requirements than laying down exactly how and with what a building should be designed and built. Some of the compliance is also now devolved to persons who qualify as competent to assess certain installations. Nevertheless, for the majority of owners of old houses the local authority's building control officer is still the most likely point of interface with 'The Regs'.

The regulations are regularly updated and cover, for example, thermal insulation, drainage, fire precautions and structural stability. They are available to download through government websites (www.planningportal.gov.uk offers the Approved Documents for England and Wales and www.sbsa.gov.uk for Scotland offers technical and procedural handbooks; for Northern Ireland, see www.dfpni.gov.uk) and there have always been very useful books explaining them in straightforward language, though, with ever more frequent and more complicated updates to the regulations. these guides can now date quite quickly. While building control officers may be helpful, it is not their job to design

the building, extension or repair for householders: a suitably qualified professional such as an architect or surveyor will usually be needed to interpret the regulations and carry out any negotiations with the local authority and to organize a formal application (forms and drawings) or other routes to compliance (such as a 'building notice' where applicable) as necessary.

Current regulations can, at face value, appear to impose 'modern house' standards of performance on old houses that are undergoing repair or alteration. If carrying out such works would threaten the character or fabric of an old house then it should be possible to seek some reasonable relaxation of the regulations or negotiate alternative methods of compliance since the regulations were not conceived to fight historic buildings nor to undermine something that was already working satisfactorily.

OTHER LEGISLATION

A professional adviser would be aware that there is a multitude of legislation potentially affecting their area of work. It is not possible to give a complete gazetteer here but the following may have to be considered.

Health and Safety
The Health and Safety Executive website (www.hse.gov.uk) explains the Construction Design and Management Regulations 2007, though domestic clients may need help in interpreting the requirements that may affect their projects. *See also* Info pages: Safety and building.

Party Wall Act
A download is available from the government planning website (www.planningportal.gov.uk) *See also* chapter 9: The Professionals – Party wall surveyor.

GRANTS

Grants are available from time to time and the local authority would be a useful point of enquiry for those relevant to old buildings; they may be associated with an incentive for general regeneration or improvement perhaps. Grants (or tax incentives) may occasionally also be available for insulation and for the installation of devices linked to energy saving (*see*, for example, www.energysavingtrust.org.uk), but may not necessarily be geared to the special requirements for preserving older buildings. Grants can be quite generous, but it is in the nature of things that they may need a degree of persistence to pursue. Any public money is likely to come with administrative requirements intended, understandably, to ensure its proper use. Sometimes in the past the well-intentioned conditions attached to grants could inflate the cost of having the work carried out – to the extent that the benefit of the grant might have been cancelled out.

TAX

Value added tax is levied at standard rate on most building works, but, up to the time of writing, and on dwellings, certain specific types of work among those for which listed building consent has had to be obtained might be zero-rated (this does not apply to professional fees). Enacting this zero-rating is ultimately a matter between the building contractor and their local tax office and is subject to various rules and their interpretation, which can be discussed with the VAT office. Clients, their architects and surveyors, can help by being clear about their intentions in the drawings submitted for listed building consent and by discussing the matter with the contractor and the tax office at the earliest opportunity. Listed building consent is necessary where *alterations* are being carried out: there have been requests to governments to encourage the correct *repairs* to old buildings by extending tax concessions accordingly. From time to time, tax refund incentives may be introduced to encourage certain other kinds of building work; for example, domestic conversion work or work on vacant property. It is worth checking for the current position with the local tax office and HM Revenue and Customs website (www.hmrc.gov.uk), from which explanatory leaflets may be downloaded. Tax is complex and building professionals may generally not feel they are able to give detailed advice, but there are now specialist, independent tax advisors for building-related VAT matters.

Remember that the building industry tends not to include VAT in its prices because many of its transactions are business-to-business, but VAT is still payable for work by those registered so check whether tax is included in any quotations. Builders and others with an annual turnover below the VAT threshold are not required to collect VAT, unless they have registered to do so (firms charging VAT should show a VAT number on invoices); that is a legitimate exception and is different from the situation of those who are seeking to avoid tax liabilities by working for undeclared cash payments.

INSURANCE

There can be a difference between what an insurer thinks of as adequate reinstatement of an old building that has suffered damage and what the building deserves, and what the owner and the conservation officer want to see. In the not too distant past old buildings would routinely be repaired with modern methods, believing them to be better: a damaged lath and plaster ceiling replaced with plasterboard, for example. Now that traditional skills and materials are available again, reinstatement can be properly like-for-like. If the house is listed, the insurers should want to know this. Not all traditional repairs are significantly more expensive than modern ones, but old buildings can sometimes incorporate high levels of workmanship – in decorative detail especially – that can be costly to reinstate. Thorough drawn and photographic or video records of a house, securely stored away from the property, would enable any reinstatement after a disaster to be reasonably accurate. Faced with flooding claims that can be linked to climate change, some insurers are talking about adjusting premiums according to the sustainability measures in place, as well as to reflect direct risk; it is hoped they would also recognize just how sustainable old houses already are without needing gadgets to be fixed to them (*see* Info pages: Sustainability – Old houses are part of the solution).

If a house is undergoing building work it is wise to inform the insurers, doing so may be a condition of the policy because building operations could alter the risk. Formal building contracts usually incorporate options for apportioning or sharing insurance responsibilities between owner and contractor during building works, the format chosen should be agreed between all parties.

Maintenance Checklist

EXTERIOR

Blocked Rainwater Routes

Spring and autumn high winds help to strip trees of dead leaves and these can quickly block gutters, downpipes or gullies. Water running down walls can promote decay and lead to expensive repairs in the future. Get gutters and rainwater goods checked out, cleared and repaired before problems occur. Check for problems that have started: Brave the next rainstorm to look for the following from the ground (*see also* chapter 3: Rainwater disposal).

Is water cascading over the edge of gutters? If it is, they are likely to be blocked at or before the outlet to the downpipe (or possibly falling the wrong way). Get the gutter cleared (or realigned). Leafguards: cages that slot into the opening to the downpipe trap leaves before they get into the downpipe, but sometimes they just make things worse by damming the gutter; if fitting them anew treat them as an experiment and watch progress.

Old houses can be resilient, but they respond to proper care.

Are the gutters leaking or dripping at a joint? A persistent drip can eventually wear away mortar, paint or render where it hits and cause damp problems in walls.

Is nothing coming out of the end of the downpipes even in heavy rain? There is probably a blockage either high up at the gutter outlet or somewhere in the pipe, perhaps at a bend. (The water that should be in the pipe will probably already be obvious spilling over the walls.) It is better to fix the problem with the gutters and pipes now rather than let it develop into a major building repair as well.

Is water coming out of the back of the pipe? Badly painted, iron downpipes can rust through and leak. A leak may be only a joint that needs remaking, but if the pipe is broken or rusted through then it is usually preferable to replace the pipe in the same material.

Do the gullies (at ground level) fill and overflow when it rains? Clear any leaves above the grid. If it is still full of water then there is most likely either something blocking the trap (sometimes the trap is a U-bend) underneath the grid or some problem with any underground pipes that take the water away. Make sure that the pipes run freely so that water runs away rather than rising up the walls.

Roof Leaks

High winds may have dislodged tiles or lifted leadwork, so get these checked if anything looks amiss from the ground (it may help to use binoculars). Tiny holes or cracks in leadwork can admit quite a lot of water and are difficult to see even close up. Sometimes, if this is possible, a trip into the roof space can help to pinpoint a leak.

Flat Roofs

Do not forget these, all outlets should be clear so that if they get piled up with snow it can melt away safely.

Underfloor Vents

Leaves may have mounded up over ventilating grilles to underfloor spaces. Clear leaves and soil away from these grilles to maintain ventilation and to protect the underside of timber floors.

GENERAL INSPECTION

Check over the house to see whether there are any places where water might be able to get in.

Tiny Cracks in Paintwork around Timber Windows

These, and particularly on cills, can contribute significantly to water getting into the fabric of an old house. Rubbing some linseed oil glazing putty into small cracks in painted traditional woodwork can help to keep things together until the weather is right for repainting.

Check Rendered Walls for Cracks

For those lucky enough to have an old house complete with lime mortar or lime-rendered finishes, then spring is the best time to have permanent repairs in those materials carried out; any repairs made in the autumn may be damaged by frost and need to be done again in the spring. But even that can be far preferable to introducing impermeable modern materials. If the house has been cement-rendered or painted in plastic paint, it is important to keep these free from cracks as these materials do not allow dampness to dry out of old constructions as adequately as it can through lime render and finishes.

Outside Taps

In winter turn these off (preferably at their internal isolating valve) and wrap them and any exposed pipes in insulation for the winter to help to prevent damage from freezing.

Climbing Plants

Make sure that any plants that grow over the walls of the house are not obstructing gutters, downpipes or gullies at ground level. Those plants that have lost their leaves for winter can be more easily trimmed away from windows and roofs before next year's growth.

Plants at the Base of Walls

Ensure that any plants are kept clear of the walls and that earth has not been mounded up against house walls as this may cause damp to transfer into the walls.

Trees, Fences and Walls

It is a good idea to carefully check for signs of weakness or damage. Trees in certain areas may be protected and require permission before any pruning work is carried out; some species should be trimmed only at certain times of year. Local authorities may be able to advise.

INTERIOR

Water Leaks

Leaks from pipework inside a house can cause serious problems if allowed to go undetected so check the following.

Heating Check around pipes, especially under junctions, taps and bends where leaks are most likely to occur. Ensure that radiators are not trapping pockets of air (by having them 'bled'). Remember also that sweeping chimneys – for open fires – and servicing boilers makes for safety and efficiency.

Plumbing Check internal plumbing fittings to make sure that these are leak-free. Look under w.c. soil pipes at the junction with the pan in case an undetected leak has occurred. If not already done, consider insulating those pipes that run in unheated areas such as lofts, outbuildings and cellars (be aware that old insulation to pipes and boilers, for example, might contain asbestos and if in doubt do not disturb it and seek advice from the local authority (*see* Info pages: Safety and building).

Insulation

Most old houses can be difficult to insulate in a way that also protects the fabric from inadvertent damage, so, for example, insulating walls can often present difficulties. However, roof spaces are often able to be insulated with a suitable quilt product laid above the ceilings (*see also* Info pages: Sustainability – Old house insulation).

Roof Insulation For the long-term benefit of the house it can be preferable to choose insulation that is totally removable (not 'glued' to the structure) and which does not encase or seal up the fabric. Old

houses need to breathe so do not use products which prevent this. Some products may produce irritant fibres or fumes which people may wish to avoid in their homes. Products that are non-combustible and will not produce toxic fumes in the event of a fire are a sensible choice for roof spaces in old houses. Be careful not to block up those all-important ventilation paths at the eaves or at the back of the tiles since ventilation can help to stop roof timbers from decaying. Do not trap electric cables (or the tops of light fittings) inside where they could overheat. If laying insulation as DIY wear protective clothing, mask and goggles as appropriate to the product.

Water Tanks Make sure that water tanks in unheated roof spaces are insulated too (leaving out the insulation just beneath them is an old trick to ensure that they get some heat from the rooms below).

Draughts No one likes to sit in a draught, but remember that air movement is vital to old houses as it can help to keep them dry and free from decay. It may often be difficult to banish draughts completely from an old house anyway, there are so many nooks and crannies, so adopt some of our forebears' ideas by making use of heavy curtains and keeping doors shut.

LADDERS

A great number of DIY accidents involve ladders. If unsure about them or without a head for heights then get professional help and stay on the ground. Carry out work only within personal capability and where safe. If using ladders make sure that they are at a safe angle, securely tied and anchored, before climbing them. Use footwear which grips the rungs well. Do not carry heavy loads up ladders and do not over-reach (*see* www.hse.gov.uk for download: 'The safe use of ladders and stepladders – an employer's guide' and *see also* Info pages: Safety and building).

[This maintenance checklist has been reproduced from www.oldhouse.info]

Postscript

If climate change and the depletion of resources are the most serious issues threatening our civilization, then it makes no sense to destroy the originally sustainable houses our ancestors built, so that we are forced to squander new resources replacing them. Old houses are also one of the prime monuments to the lives of the people who have populated Britain: to scrap or mutilate them in the face of an ill-understood crisis would be, as the old saying has it, throwing out the baby with the bathwater. On an individual level, owners of old houses have invested heavily in their properties, it is to their benefit to understand how they might be looked after in a world that is coming to terms with revised values and sustainability. It is hoped that this book will help owners to avoid the types of mistake made with old houses in the recent past, when society was in a hurry to modernize, and to take a balanced view on preparing for the future. The owners need to know what sustainability could really turn out to mean to them and try to avoid new adaptations to their properties turning into new threats, while staying alert to new and unexpected challenges that may emerge from climate change.

A council house built in the 1920s but demolished before the end of the century; it was built from unfired earth blocks and would now be considered a beacon of sustainable construction.

Further Information

INTRODUCTION

The purpose of this book has been to introduce the basics of conservation-thinking on problems affecting the maintenance and repair of old houses. Readers interested in furthering their knowledge about specific issues are urged to look first to non-commercial expert sources: English Heritage, Historic Scotland, Cadw (for Wales) and the Northern Ireland Environment and Heritage Service, these bodies have a remit to inform their public, while the conservation officers employed by local planning authorities should be able to offer local perspectives. Many local authorities publish general guidance for works to their listed buildings or those within their conservation areas. This information is often available via post, telephone or internet.

Some local authorities run practical courses in maintaining old buildings. Owners of old houses or those simply interested in old buildings might consider joining the Society for the Protection of Ancient Buildings (London and branches) to access information, courses and to benefit from the experiences of other owners and professionals. Professionals with an interest in building conservation can apply to join the Association for Studies in the Conservation of Historic Buildings (London). The National Trust charities and the national heritage 'quangos' mentioned above maintain old properties, sometimes whole villages, most of which are open to the public. These can be viewed for inspiration and might reasonably be expected to be examples of good practice in maintenance.

SOME RELEVANT UNITED KINGDOM ORGANIZATIONS

Amenity Societies, Interest Groups and Statutory Consultees

These are sometimes charities which may have an academic, educational or practical slant (or all three) on their area of interest, those starred could act in a statutory capacity to comment on planning and listed building applications.

Ancient Monuments Society* – www.ancientmonumnetssociety.org.uk
Architectural Heritage Society of Scotland* – www.ahss.org.uk
Association for Studies in the Conservation of Historic Buildings (ASCHB) – www.aschb.org.uk
Civic Trust – www.civictrust.org.uk
Council for British Archaeology* – www.britarch.ac.uk
Council for Scottish Archaeology* – www.scottisharchaeology.org.uk
Garden History Society* – www.gardenhistorysociety.org
Garden History Society in Scotland* – www.gardenhistorysociety.org
Georgian Group* – www.georgiangroup.org.uk
Scottish Civic Trust* – www.scottishcivictrust.org.uk
Society for the Protection of Ancient Buildings* (SPAB) – www.spab.org.uk
Twentieth Century Society* – www.c20society.org.uk
Victorian Society* – www.victorian-society.org.uk

(Renowned architects may also have their own dedicated society.)

Architects

Architects Accredited in Building Conservation
 (AABC) – www.aabc-register.co.uk
Architects Registration Board (ARB) – www.arb.org.uk
Royal Institute of British Architects (RIBA) –
 www.architecture.com
Royal Incorporation of Architects in Scotland
 (RIAS) – www.rias.org.uk
Royal Society of Architects in Wales (RSAW) –
 www.architecture.com
Royal Society of Ulster Architects (RSUA) –
 www.rsua.org.uk

Conservation Officers

Institute of Historic Building Conservation (IHBC)
 – www.ihbc.org.uk

National Trust Charities

The National Trust (England, Wales, Northern
 Ireland) – www.nationaltrust.org.uk
The National Trust for Scotland – www.nts.org.uk

Planning and Building Control

England and Wales – www.planningportal.gov.uk
Northern Ireland – www.ehsni.gov.uk and
www.dfpni.gov.uk
Scotland – www.sbsa.gov.uk

See also local authorities' websites and www.national-
parks.gov.uk

Statutory Heritage Agencies

Cadw (Wales) – www.cadw.wales.gov.uk
English Heritage – www.english-heritage.org.uk
Environment and Heritage Service (Northern
 Ireland) – www.ehsni.gov.uk
Historic Scotland – www.historic-scotland.gov.uk

See also local authorities' websites and www.national-
parks.gov.uk

Statutory Nature Conservation Agencies

Cyngor Cefn Gwlad Cymru (The Countryside
 Council for Wales) – www.ccw.gov.uk
Environment and Heritage Service (Northern
 Ireland) – www.ehsni.gov.uk
Natural England – www.naturalengland.org.uk

Scottish Natural Heritage – www.snh.org.uk

Structural Engineers

Conservation Accreditation Register for Engineers
 (CARE) – www.ice.org.uk/knowledge/
 specialist_buildings
Institution of Civil Engineers (ICE) –
 www.ice.org.uk
Institution of Structural Engineers (IStructE) –
 www.istructe.org.uk

Surveyors

Royal Institution of Chartered Surveyors (RICS) –
 www.rics.org.uk

BOOKS

Conservation common sense has yet to banish all the ingrained attitudes of the twentieth-century building industry towards old buildings. Some publications are still 'off-message' about self-evident issues such as breathability in old buildings. Because building is full of misapplied rules of thumb and common misconceptions, these can still find their way into print. Readers need to keep this in mind and, when it comes to a real project, back up their reading with some professional advice. For general building information, public libraries may offer free access to British Standard/EN publications relevant to building, which may help to explain conventional modern practices, though these do not cover all traditional crafts.

MAGAZINES, EXHIBITIONS AND BROADCAST MEDIA

Magazines, exhibitions, radio and television have taken an ever keener interest in old buildings, moving gradually from lifestyle into conservation. Environmental organizations might be found at exhibitions, promoting sustainability next to stands dripping with 'greenwash', but each learning from the other. The major television channels have the power to end much of the misguided, if well-intentioned, refurbishments by owners of old houses and also promote the sustainability of old buildings. Juggling education with entertainment is not easy, and, unfortunately, the message may sometimes get diluted for the sake of a good gloss. Magazines and exhibitions survive by letting space for commercial promotion and the consumer should not expect that products on sale have been vetted on their behalf for suitability. But magazines may also be providing informed editorial for readers, and exhibitions may have expert 'clinics' for visitors. Independent, non-commercial and charity organizations may also be represented at exhibitions. When information gathering, the first thing heard may not be the only story, so check out the credentials and try to seek information from as many trusted sources as possible. An old house is a one-off and so, ultimately, specific, professional input at the property is the optimum way to target information.

THE INTERNET

The internet is a vast information resource, some of it genuine but some might be spectacularly erratic. Websites can, like virtually all publications and remote consultations, provide only generic information, which cannot possibly be expected to apply to every situation. As with other media, a site's advertising policy, sponsorships and editorial independence can be relevant to the quality and impartiality of the content. It is up to the surfer to decide if they trust the site, but surfing opens up the field to the enquirer even if the choice is to keep some information at arm's length. As the internet is worldwide, the information may not always be applicable to British conditions. Names of search targets should be sufficient in most cases to obtain a result from a search engine, but if these result in 'deep-links' into an unknown site always click back to the home page to double check that the site is authoritative and that it refers to the relevant geographical or legislative area.

UPDATES

The techniques of traditional building are fixed in history, but publications, suppliers and organizations will be subject to changes. Readers are invited to visit the website www.oldhouse.info where it is hoped to provide quick reference details and links relevant to the content of this book.

Index

In the main, only principal references are given;
+ indicates start of a chapter or longer sub-section
including that subject.